Fight Directing for the Theatre

Fight Directing for the Theatre

J. Allen Suddeth

Heinemann
Portsmouth, NH

Heinemann
A division of Reed Elsevier Inc.
361 Hanover Street, Portsmouth, NH 03801-3912
Offices and agents throughout the world

Library of Congress Cataloging-in-Publication Data
Suddeth, J. Allen.
    Fight directing for the theatre / J. Allen Suddeth.
        p.   cm.
    Includes bibliographical references and index.
    ISBN 0-435-08674-X
    1. Stage fighting.   2. Theater—Production and direction.
I. Title.
PN2071.F5S8   1996
792'.028—dc20   95-45317
                                                                                        CIP

Editor: Lisa A. Barnett
Production: J. B. Tranchemontagne
Design: Mary Cronin
Cartoons: Greg Poretta
Manufacturing: Louise Richardson

Printed in the United States of America on acid-free paper
99 98 97 96 RRD 9 8 7 6 5 4 3 2 1

Dedicated to my wife Grace,
daughter Nicole, and son Patrick

Contents

Contents

Foreword

In the fall of 1970, I was a freshman in college, inspired by the theater arts and attending Ohio University. One afternoon, while exploring the theater building, I heard a commotion behind the door of one of the acting studios. Carefully, I eased the door open and—behold!—there was a room full of students who were sword fighting! I had never considered such a thing, and I stood, rapt, in the doorway. I was on the point of leaving, and this book would never have begun but for the teacher's generosity and offer of "Come in and watch awhile." Well, that pretty well did it: I was hooked and haven't put down the stage combat flag since.

Many years passed before someone said to me, "When will you write your book?" At the time, nothing could have been further from my thoughts. I was busy acting, teaching, and staging fights in New York and around the country. But as the years went on, I couldn't get that simple question out of my head. It has become obvious to me, after repeating myself hundreds of times, that the wealth of common knowledge that I take for granted is not available to those who are coming up through the ranks. It is also true that in the last twenty years, there has been renewed interest in stage combat that has generated a common vocabulary, healthy debate, scores of university-level classes, combat workshops, books and dissertations, as well as technical advances in the safety of theatrical weapons. Therefore, I began to write down the most common problems that spring up in theatrical fight directing, as well as some common-sense solutions.

Fight directors must be concerned with the safety of the performers who must go out night after night and perform fights. These brave actors and actresses, who don the mantle of Richard III, Cyrano, Cassio, D'Artagnan, Tybalt, St. Joan, and Macbeth, must always keep some part of themselves in reserve so as not to *really* cut their acting partners in half and yet must have just enough panache, élan, and Za! in the fight to make it believable. To the average non-theater civilian this may seem easy. To those who have gone through it, my plumed hat is off to you!

As show business becomes more complicated, young performers (and seasoned veterans!) are asked to have at their fingertips athletic and acrobatic skills unheard of just ten years ago, and the opportunity for injury multiplies. If by reading this book just one injury is avoided, then the book will have been worth writing.

There is, however, no justification for producers' failing to hire a competent fight director to safeguard performers. Amateurs and drama students are particularly vulnerable to injury by overenthusiastic fight directors. There are still, sadly, too many stories of productions where the performers are left to their own devices and injuries occur or where undertrained and self-interested fight directors endanger the cast.

However, no book on fight directing could possibly cover every eventuality, detail all the techniques, or anticipate every safety problem that will come up! Mistakes and injuries are usually a combination of problems overlooked: a shoe that slips, a weapon that breaks, a helmet that obscures the vision at a crucial moment. This book will help solve some of these problems: how to cultivate an awareness of safety issues about stage combat, how to approach the job of fight directing and how to research a fight, what performers need to know about acting and rehearsing the fight, where to buy weapons and how to make them last for a few years, techniques for blood effects, and finally how to safely approach the issue of firearms on the stage.

For fight directing is a *process*, much like acting or directing. The study of this book will help fight directors with that process, for the book is a step-by-step guide to fight directing. It is not a substitute for years of study, however, and a serious student of fight directing *must* spend thousands of hours in the classroom studying with hands on weapons and with many different master teachers. This book will not teach you how to engage in a sword fight, box, or perform a forward roll. However, no matter what your level of skill, any fight scene you attempt to perform or stage will be helped by some portion of this book. Here is how to use it. If you wish to stage and direct fights, by all means study this book carefully from cover to cover. Become familiar with the practical and theoretical principles it advances. However, hands on experience is the best teacher, and you must apply this information to real-life situations many times before it becomes second nature. If, on the other hand, you are a student, actor, university or drama teacher, or a theater director who is only using this book to research an upcoming project, pick and choose the sections you read more selectively. There is a lot of information within these pages, but if, for instance, you are concentrating on firearm safety, don't neglect to read the section on how to rehearse a fight. Each chapter contains material that supports information in the others. Finally, through this book I hope the reader will understand that even though stage combat appears to be a narrow field of study, there is not only a philosophy involved, but a method.

Stage combat is not just "something the actors do," it is the job of the entire production staff from the producer to the interns. All of the details of a fight scene must be worked out collaboratively by each department of the production team: directorial, lighting, scenic design, costumes, props, stage management, and finally the fight director.

Study this book with care. Within these pages are thousands of useful tips, especially if you've never worked on a "fight show," which will serve as guidelines for your production.

Many years of working as a professional fight director and teacher have confirmed in my mind that fight directing is a multidisciplinary skill. It combines elements of collaboration, execution, communication, choreography, as well as the historian, safety expert, problem solver, first-aid specialist, acting coach, performer, teacher, and director.

For those who work in the theater, keep this book where rehearsals take place, props are built, and costumes designed and worn. This book will teach nothing if it is left to gather dust on a shelf and is only referred to after an accident has taken place.

Refer to this book before tackling a play with fights, especially if you've never done one before—or even if you've done a hundred. Perhaps it will fire your imagination, perhaps it will prevent an accident!

To all of those who read and apply this information, you are on the right road. I applaud you! I encourage you! I wish you the best success for your production! And as my esteemed teacher, Patrick Crean, unceasingly says, **"SAFETY FIRST!"**

J. Allen Suddeth

Acknowledgments

Thank you to those who have gone before and to all the teachers, actors, directors, and choreographers who have helped me along the way: Patrick Crean, for noble inspiration; Robert Hobbs, for the gift of the theater; The Society of American Fight Directors—David Boushey, J. R. Beardsley, Drew Fracher, Erik Fredricksen, Dale Girard, David Leong, J. R. Martinez, Richard Raether, Christopher Villa, and David Woolley; Fights R Us; The Actors Combat Training School; The fight masters past and present; The Ken Zen Institute and Rev. Sushin Kan; The Westbeth Theatre center, Bill Hoffman and Arnold Engleman; my students; my assistants over the years—Robert Walsh, Gary Morabito, Gary Phillips, Steve Vaughan, Richard Raether, Jane Ridley, Robin McFarquhar, Brian Byrnes, Rick Sordelet, Ken Smith, Richard Lane, Michael Donahue, Dale Girard, Geoff Alm, Colleen Kelly, Ricki Ravitts, Martino Pistone, and Jack Young; sword makers Kolombatovich, Graves, Meek, Casteel, Poor, and Shaw; my first teachers, Eric Uhler, Larry Carr, and William Burnett; Theater for a New Audience, Jeff Horowitz; The North Carolina Shakespeare Festival, Louis Rackoff; The Jean Cocteau Repertory Theater, Eve Adamson; and The Celebration Barn Theater, Carol Brett.

Special thanks go to Erica Bilder, A. C. Weary, Kim Zimmer, Richard Raether, David S. Leong, Cynthia Grimes, Lisa Barnett, and Susan Shulman.

Special thanks also to Greg Poretta, a talented cartoonist who worked untold overtime hours, creating original and detailed drawings, and to Matt Servitto who brought us together. Thanks to all the photographers whose work is represented in this book: Gerry Goodstein, Jim Manley, Bill Savage, Lewis Shaw, A. C. Weary, and Zane Williams. All unattributed photos by the author.

I wish to thank The Metropolitan Museum of Art, The New York Public Library Rare Books Collection, The Newark Public Library Special Collections, and The Hart Picture Archives for permission to publish illustrations from their collections.

And thanks to all the people who read the manuscript and gave invaluable comments: Brian Byrnes, Armand Schultz, Ricki Ravitts, Steve Vaughan, and Lewis Shaw.

Introduction

Why Do People Fight?

If conflict is the essence of theater, then physical confrontation is a natural outgrowth of that conflict. Certain characters can no longer resolve their differences with words—and swords, fists, or furniture throwing is their only solution.

Playwrights fully understand the nature of conflict, and where to let it boil over into physicality. Shakespeare's plays are wonderful examples of where to place the fights within the text to help drive the plot of a play.

Take, for example, *Romeo and Juliet*. The fights in this play are positioned in act 1, scene 1; act 3, scene 1; and act 5, scene 3. The first fight sets up the conflict between the families, as played out by their servants and young sons. It also serves to open the play with energy and a bit of spectacle.

The second fight turns the plot from a pure romantic comedy into a tragedy. When Mercutio and Tybalt are killed and Romeo is banished, Shakespeare has used the device of a stage fight to completely change the direction of the play and the main characters. Romeo and Juliet now have major obstacles to their love affair and secret marriage. Blood has been spilled on both sides of the family, raising the stakes for everyone involved.

Finally, Shakespeare uses the fight between Romeo and Paris, in act 5, as a final obstacle to Romeo's carrying out his desire to die with Juliet. The conflict between Juliet's suitors, Romeo and Paris, comes to a head in the churchyard when Paris faces Romeo, who—maddened by grief and bent on suicide and allowing nothing to interfere with his plans—kills Paris.

It is clear when studying Shakespeare's works that he used the dramatic device of the fight many times. The timing of the fight scenes in his plays are quite obviously deliberate. They begin plays, they move plots in a new direction, or they climax plots. Here are some examples:

Act 1	Act 2 / Act 3	Act 4 / Act 5
	Hamlet	Hamlet
		Richard III
	Richard II	
	Julius Caesar	Julius Caesar
As You Like It		
	Othello	Othello
	King Lear	King Lear
	Macbeth	Macbeth
Coriolanus		Coriolanus
		Cymbeline
	Twelfth Night	
		Henry IV, Part 1
Henry VI, Part 1	Henry VI, Part 1	Henry VI, Part 1
		Henry VI, Part 2
	Henry V	
Romeo and Juliet	Romeo and Juliet	Romeo and Juliet

However, beyond the question of placement within text, the question of why people, or characters, fight is central to the performer, director, and fight director. If we look at a sampling of characters who fight, male and female, modern and historic, we will immediately see that the emotions we are dealing with are strong, consuming, and volatile.

Rage, revenge, jealousy, and lust are not emotions to be trifled with! Macduff is driven to avenge the murder of his wife and children. Romeo is enraged by the death of his friend Mercutio and lashes out at Tybalt. Othello strangles Desdemona out of his misguided and passionate jealousy. These characters fight when human emotion simply boils over and reason is left behind.

While it is always wrong to substitute complicated fight choreography for good acting and staging, the cathartic quality of violence is central to the character's, and the audience's, experience of the text. Production concepts that remove fights from the play seriously shortchange this very human activity.

Whereas characters in period dramas often fight for "higher" motives such as honor, religion, or the good of the state, modern plays in the late twentieth century offer examples of personal, random violence. Plays such as *Extremities*,

Search and Destroy, and *Marisol* expose senseless violence for what it is: ugly and depersonalizing. In these cases, characters fight not only against each other but against problems and situations that they often cannot themselves see. They struggle and are as much victims of society's problems as of their personal demons.

Our world is filled with images of violence, some justified and some senseless. The job of fight directors and performers is to reflect that violence on the stage—neither romanticizing it nor belittling it—as part of the human condition.

Stage Combat Safety

1

Before launching into the how-to's of fight directing, it's vital to have an overview of the safety issues pertinent to staged combat. Without some perspective on safety during the conceptual, rehearsal, and performance process, the fight director and performers will be courting disaster! Advance preparation is the key. You aren't a fight director until you are an expert at fight choreography and working with actors, until you understand how to arm and prop a fight safely, and until you have a working knowledge of firearm safety.

The most important thing about any kind of fight, be it on the stage or screen, is *Safety First*. Nothing is more important than protecting the performers from injury. An actor has one body to last a lifetime, and in show business an actor's body is the actor's profession. This means that a serious accident is not only deplorable, painful, and costly but can permanently jeopardize a performer's career.

The concept of stage-combat safety is all encompassing. Fight directors must keep an eagle eye on safety issues and must be responsive to each performer's movement skills, must embrace the space in which the actors are performing, and must involve the things they are using. In other words, fight directors must consider the performers, the fight, the set, and the props/costumes.

The performers themselves are the most random safety element, since performances are subject to change; therefore, the fight choreography must be intrinsically safe from first rehearsal to closing night. The stage set and "trappings," such as costumes, swords, lights, and props, once correctly conceived, must remain safe through the run of the show.

No book could possibly cover every safety problem. Safety is a process, an attitude. It begins with the conception of the fights, is carried on through preproduction and rehearsal, and is followed through in performance once the final elements are layered on. It demands a sharp eye and constant attention to detail. Too rigid an attitude, or concept, can be as dangerous as one that is too loose. A simple punch that is safe for one performer may be very unwise for another. If the fight director is unbending, then he or she is not listening to the physical needs of the performers. It can be said that an unloaded pistol is "safe" and can't hurt anyone; but I have seen an actor's head split open after being accidentally hit with it. I have also seen "unloaded" pistols go off in an actor's hand. Is the pistol safe? Who is to say? More important, who's responsible? Responsibility for accidents is usually laid at the feet of the fight director.

This chapter deals with anticipating safety problems before they arise. Fight directors should read it over before rehearsals start and note how these issues relate to their productions. In some cases, I have given advice that might dissuade a fight director from attempting a particular effect. In other cases, I recommend that only trained professionals arrange certain sequences. In these cases, I believe, it's better not to attempt anything beyond one's reach and to be safer than sorrier.

Safety First

Advance planning is *vital* to the success of a safe fight. Preparation to perform a fight takes many forms, from leading performers through a warm-up to weapons selection and purchase. Many of the preparatory assignments fall on the fight director. He or she, in consultation with the director/producer of the production, decides on such things as costumes, period or style of fighting, audience safety, lighting, stage surface, special effects, rehearsal period, casting of principals and fighting extras, weapons purchase, and many other variables that will affect the ultimate safety of the production. Most problems in these areas can be solved by making decisions ahead of time.

What follows are *some* of the questions to answer if one is mounting a production with fights. Remember that each production has its own eccentricities, and each fight its unique pitfalls.

The Performers

Every producer, director, and fight director must have a *realistic* appreciation of the physical condition of the performers (Figure 1-1). Physiological

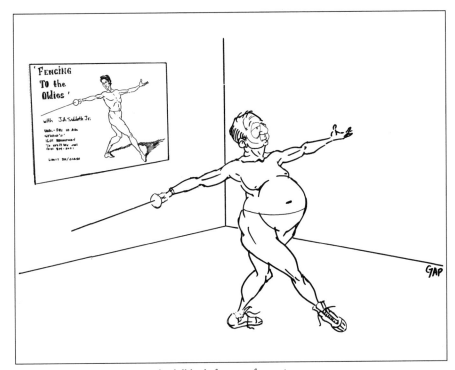

Figure 1-1. *Never overestimate the skill level of your performers!*

3

factors such as age, height, weight, strength, breath, balance, center, and the status of old injuries must be weighed with training, intelligence, and such psychological factors as real aggression and macho attitude, on the one hand, or passivity and stage fright, on the other.

Stage-fight choreography is not necessarily safe because it is created by a trained, safe choreographer. It must be suited physically to the performer's capabilities. Otherwise, it may be unsafe from the beginning, and accidents may happen.

Questions of strength—such as whether a certain performer is capable of physically sustaining a sword fight, carrying another performer, or falling on the floor—must be answered before opening night. Can this person be supplied with a lighter weapon? Can the fight be cut short? Can the fight be adapted so that there is an interruption by other characters, thereby shortening the time that this performer is required to exert himself? Just because a scriptwriter indicates that "Roger hits the old man over the head with a shovel" doesn't mean that some poor character actor is clobbered for eight shows per week!

Today, many performers have some stage-combat training. It is good business to exploit these people and let them show off their skills. They can be safe fighters. However, it is wise to remember that many "trained" performers may have only been presented with the rudiments of stage combat. Many years may have passed since they received such training—or, more importantly, practiced it! When casting or rehearsing a fight scene of any type, a fight director should probe the limitations of the trained performer and not assume too much. It is better to be surprised by a great deal of skill than to presume too much and perhaps risk an injury.

Because performers are usually eager to get involved in a "fight scene," they bring a lot of energy and enthusiasm to rehearsals and performances. Care must be taken to train them not only in the "moves" of the fight but also in "how" to rehearse. Most actors will dive into the fight too quickly and with too much energy too early in the rehearsal process. They want the satisfaction of "product," or perhaps they are a macho type and merely revel in the thrill of sweat pouring and muscles pounding. They see the end result and ignore the process.

Slow and steady is the key to fight-choreography rehearsals. A fight director should continue to keep the pace slow by mutual agreement until quite close to the opening night. The performers will continue to learn details about the fight in slow motion every time they do it—details that are lost to them when they fly through the choreography.

Once the elements of the set, costumes, lights, and props/weapons are settled, the performers must work with the fight director to make the choreography fit like a glove. A tremendous bit of choreography that is always "iffy" in rehearsals should be cut, and both the performer and the fight director must be able to let that section go. The fight director should create alternate choreography! One that is as exciting, but safer. The fight director should know when to say LESS!

Costumes

Costumes not only play a vital part in the overall creation of a play but can have a profound effect on safety as well. Clothes that don't fit, shoes that slip, and hats or helmets that cover the face are the most obvious problems to a fighter. The following questions, when answered early in the process, will save time and stitches on both the actor's clothes and skin.

- ➤ How can the costumes enhance the fight movement?
- ➤ Will clothes be restrictive to the performers' movement?
- ➤ Will the shoes be well made, and will they have nonslip soles and heels?
- ➤ Will gloves, belts, hangers, baldricks, or scabbards for swords be provided by the costume shop or by the prop department?
- ➤ Is padding necessary, and can it be hidden in the costume?
- ➤ Will lace at the sleeve get in the way of sword hilts?
- ➤ Are major stress points (arm, groin, knee) reinforced so as not to tear?
- ➤ Will armor pieces be used? Will they be metal, cloth, or plastic? (Metal armor must be preordered months ahead of time for proper fit and must be sized to the actor to prevent pinching. Armor is very restrictive and must be rehearsed in for several weeks. "Homemade" armor pieces are difficult to build and run the risk of injuring the performers.)

➤ Will the performer's vision be impaired by helmets, cowels, turbans, masks, hats, wigs, or other headgear?

➤ Will capes, coats, or other outerwear impede movement?

➤ When will the costume pieces be available for rehearsing fights?

➤ Are rehearsal clothes available?

➤ Who is responsible for blood effects—the costume shop, makeup artist, or the prop department?

➤ What provision will be made for bloody clothes to be cleaned?

➤ Are breakaway, or tearaway, costumes to be constructed? How will they be serviced?

Historical Period, or Style, of Fighting

The fight director and the director/producer must agree on the period of the play and the style of the fights. Usually, it's obvious. But sometimes a director may choose to alter the period of the play for interpretive purposes. *Hamlet* might be set in modern day Heidelburg, or *King Lear* in the Appalachian Mountains. This type of choice will dramatically affect the style of fighting chosen to complement the play.

Once the style of the play is chosen, and the fighting style and weapons agreed on, the next step for the director and fight director is research. Now is the time to go to the library and find primary source material, accounts of people of the times, illustrations or photographs, weapons of the era, and styles of movement. If the director calls for a modern-day saber-fencing match, the fight director should find out everything possible about saber fencing. I say to the fight director, *Do all you can to stack the safety deck in your favor.*

The common trap in choosing a very specific fighting style is not having properly trained actors who can learn the fights in the rehearsal time allowed. It is all very well to conceive of a hard-driving boxing match, Schlager duel, Bowie-knife fight, or barroom brawl; but if the performers can't do it, CUT IT! Safety in fighting often boils down to being able to cut, alter, or shorten well-thought-out choreography to fit the capabilities of the actors involved. No one gains from a fight that is unsafe because it is too long, too complicated, or too "historically accurate"! Better by far for everyone to cut back and *do less!*

I often see productions where an actor has been forced to move in a false pseudohistorical manner. Forcing performers into a mold of the fight director's invention is usually difficult for them, sometimes funny to look at, and potentially dangerous. I remember a production in which a large man of over 250 pounds had been forced to wield a broadsword with one hand and perform modern "fencing" footwork and who ended up mincing across the stage to the great amusement of the audience. The character's (not to mention the performer's!) dignity must be preserved for the audience to take the action seriously. Fighting movement must have as much inherent truth onstage as the entire performance and must organically and seamlessly fit the moment for the audience to believe it. While research and study can suggest wonderful historical clues, line drawings do not make a fight. The production team must make the fight come alive!

Audience Safety

One area often overlooked in the preproduction stage is the safety of the audience. Where will the first row of the audience be in relation to the fights? How close will the fighters be? Will any weapon disarms, throwing of props and furniture, swinging swords, or special effects like smoke and explosions or gunshots threaten the audience? *This cannot be allowed to happen!*

Care must be taken ahead of time that the fight choreography does not actually threaten the audience in any way (Figure 1-2). Simple mistakes can quickly become audience danger, such as a cape sweeping over the front row or a disarmed sword sliding downstage! These are safety violations of the first order and must be prevented by advance planning.

All fights, stunts (like rope swings or high falls), and special effects must be rehearsed well in advance with someone in the house to oversee any safety problems. We hear too often of innocent theatergoers being injured by flying blades and hurtling bodies. I have witnessed sword fighting, performed on a raised platform over theatergoers' heads, where the blades missed them by scant millimeters! These paying customers were not only in danger of being injured but were rightly incensed and angered by the choreography that put them in danger. I have seen props flying into the audience. I have seen a rope swing rehearsal where the rope broke, the actor fell into the house, and—

Figure 1-2. *Never threaten your audience's safety!*

while he was luckily not injured—the seats he landed on were broken into pieces!

Remove these kinds of safety problems by *planning ahead* and *never* take anything for granted!

Stage Lighting

Lighting can be a help or a hindrance to a performer. Common sense dictates that underlighting a fight or having bright front- or sidelights in the performer's eyes to the point of near blindness can be a major safety problem.

Discussions with the director and lighting designer in preproduction can usually solve most of these problems. The only thing left to do is to see the actual lighting in technical rehearsals. Have the fighters perform the fights at one-quarter speed to see if they can see. Check that "shin busters" (floor level instruments) aren't in the way of fast exits (Figure 1-3). Take care of low-hanging overhead instruments, they can catch a blade and even electrocute a performer!

I have often had to perform difficult sword fights with strong light directly in my face. I tended to lose track of my partner's blade and had trouble seeing the attacks. I got used to this during rehearsals, but it is disconcerting and uncomfortable at first. Modern, thin rapier, or épée-bladed weapons are quite hard to see in even the best light. Strong, high sidelights are always preferable to strong front- or low sidelights. Strobe lighting is almost impossible!

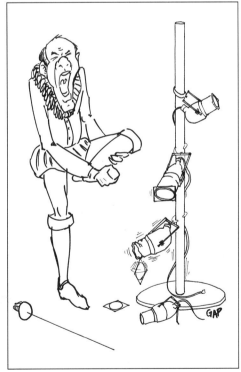

Figure 1-3. *Check that "shin busters" (low-hanging lights) are not in the way of fast exits.*

Rehearsal Lighting

A well-lit rehearsal hall is very important. The performers must be able to see each other and the weapons. Bright, even lighting is vital! If extra lighting must be arranged, it should be organized in preproduction meetings.

Common safety problems are low ceilings, or low-hanging lights, either incandescent or fluorescent. Both of these can shatter magnificently, sending sharp glass over a wide area. Performers have been injured and even permanently blinded by breaking lamps, especially long fluorescent tubes. If the lights cannot be raised or moved, they must be protected by a heavy wire mesh, or other safety devices.

If the regular rehearsal room will not do, another room must be arranged, or rented, for the fights to be rehearsed safely.

Stage Surface

Linoleum is a killer. So is cement. So is an outdoor wooden stage wet from a summer shower. Wood splinters unerringly find their way into muscle. Extremely raked stages eat actors for lunch. Screws and nails in the set always work free.

Needless to say, each set designer will have a different approach to stage surfaces. Wood flooring is usually safe, but a last-second paint job can turn it slick. Carpets are soft to fall on, but slide and slither with a life of their own if not nailed down. Old-style oil-based fog machines can turn an otherwise safe surface into a skating rink.

These are only some of the problems I have encountered. Obviously a regular program to keep the stage swept and mopped before performances will help, once the production is under way, but surface preparation must be decided on early in the design process and carried through. No single solution is right for every play. Sometimes simply adding sand to the paint will solve a footing problem. Sometimes it's the fault of the shoes! The fight director must oversee surface problems from preproduction, through opening, and beyond.

Another problem on the stage is liquid. Water is a killer. A wet spot onstage can make performers slip and injure themselves or others. Prior to a fight scene, ALWAYS arrange to mop up any spills, food, soap, drinks, breakaway glass, sweat, or anything slippery. If intentional spills, such as a glass of water or wine in the face, or even blood effects, occur during the action of a fight, they must be accounted for in the choreography and avoided by the performers. These spills should be cleaned up during the action or the next blackout.

I have seen an actor fall and separate his shoulder in a chase during act 3 of *What the Butler Saw*, by slipping on something as forgettable as flower petals strewn carelessly on the floor in the previous scene!

To avoid problems, one should arrange for nonslip shoes, a nonslip surface, and a regime of cleanliness involving mopping and sweeping, even to the point of including a rosin box offstage if necessary (rosin is available at dance supply stores).

Special Effects

What are "special effects"? They are any pyrotechnics, gunshots, rope swings, flying rigs, hoists, air bags, high falls, fire, large breakaways, hydraulics, ratchets, hanging by the neck, squibs, or anything else involving machinery, explosives, electricity, or a high degree of risk. These things should not be attempted without supervision by *trained, qualified personnel*. Because of the safety problems involved with special effects, and because of local fire and safety laws, insurance problems, and the possibility of liability, even simple effects like smokepots must be supervised by qualified individuals.

Don't make the mistake that so many have of thinking that movie stunts and special effects are easy. They are made to look easy, by years of experience, months of planning, and *lots* of money.

Don't play with fire! You will get burned!

Explosions

Explosions are often achieved by using a flashpot, a device that combines electricity and black powder (or flash powder). Legally, only someone with a powderman's license or an electrician should build this device. Flashpots should be placed far away from flammables like people, curtains, clothing, and furniture, with a metal plate placed underneath them. Fire extinguishers, of a type that can extinguish electrical and cloth or wood fires, must always be placed nearby. Flashpots should be manufactured by a professional.

Occasionally, explosions are simulated with a burst of fog, or smoke, with sound and lighting effects added to them. This can be very effective and requires no true explosion or any true combustion.

Occasionally, compressed-air machines are used to create a "bang" and throw "dust" and "debris" around. Care must be taken when using these devices since they can hurl objects at high velocity. Consult an expert and never place performers in the pathway of these machines. Baby powder, fuller's earth, pieces of foam rubber or Styrofoam®, and leaves are reasonably safe to place near the air blast to be "blown" onto the stage. A less expensive solution to the air compressor is to have stagehands throw "debris" by snapping a sheet filled with safe material from offstage combined with a smoke burst.

Squibs

These are electrical devices designed to trigger a small explosion that simulates a bloody gunshot wound on an actor, or "hit," on the set. These devices are very dangerous if not built by an expert, since they involve electricity and gunpowder, or electric matches in close proximity to the skin of the performer. Do not attempt to use these devices without a trained professional involved in the design and setup.

Flying

Fly rigging or flying a performer with a harness is another very dangerous undertaking. Whole companies devote themselves to this art form, such as "Flying by Foy." If flying is necessary, contact an experienced person or company.

High Falls

High falls are another potential high-risk stunt. For certain performers, falling a yard or a meter into a truckload of feathers is risky. A performer's physical state, height/weight ratio, and age, as well as the height of the fall and what the person falls into, will determine the safety of the fall. High falls should not be taken lightly. Witness the fact that head injuries are common on the cheerleading circuit these days, even when these falls are carefully rehearsed, and involve strong, young catchers.

If a high fall is necessary, consult an expert to design it and to hire or train the individuals who will perform it. Different techniques are required when falling into water, foam pits, air bags, or other performer's arms (Figure 1-4).

Figure 1-4. *A high-fall training session. Here, specialist Linwood Harcum falls twenty-seven feet into a special foam pit.*

Hanging by the Neck

In film and television, a "hanging stunt" is a highly paid, high-risk stunt (Figure 1-5). Onstage, this stunt is even more dangerous, since it must be done within the "flow" of the play, and it must work every time. Obviously, the person being hanged must wear a safety harness of some kind, one that will

13

Figure 1-5. *The author rigged in a hanging harness for a television stunt on* ABC's One Life to Live.

spread the weight around the body. Some of these harnesses cross under the crotch, and others place the weight under the feet. The rope itself must NEVER be tied off, for if the safety wire breaks the rope must be allowed to fall with the performer—otherwise, it will actually hang him! The hanging device must be rigged with airplane wire and a clip, or carabiner, strong enough to withstand the sudden jerk of weight without breaking; and it must involve a safety wire as well, in case the primary wire breaks. This kind of stunt should not be attempted by those unfamiliar with the rigging of it. A slip, or accidental breakage of the line(s), could snap the neck of the performer—killing him!

Falling Debris

A few plays call for debris to fall on the performers from above. The best method of dropping things is usually a "tip box" positioned strategically in the flys. A tip box is a flat platform where the "debris" is placed and can be dropped on cue from offstage. It is usually hung with wire and has two stationary points and two "slip" points. On cue the slip points allow the box to tip its contents out onto a prearranged spot.

Appropriate debris might include fuller's earth, potting soil, baby powder, shredded newspapers, confetti, foam-rubber shapes (rocks, wood), Styrofoam®, or any other lightweight material. Larger items, such as "beams," should never be dropped and allowed to fall free and bounce but rather should always be secured at one end. This way, the end that does fall will fall within inches (centimeters) of its "mark."

Performers who must appear to be hit by falling debris should be careful to remain upstage of the tip box and should be careful not to look up since they may get material in their eyes.

Fire Gags

Fire burns, or "gags," are the most dangerous of all stunts. Performers who make money doing this kind of stunt are highly trained individuals. No one should attempt this kind of stunt onstage if not fully conversant with the safety materials used and the precautions necessary!

Tip!

Staging explosions, flying performers, high falls, hanging performers by the neck, and fire gags should not be attempted by schools or theaters without properly trained personnel and facilities.

Gloves

Hand protection would have been common sense to a period combatant wielding a sword. Unfortunately, theater budgets frequently omit purchasing gloves for performer's hands. Gloves are vital first line safety equipment and should not be ignored!

During the stress of performance and rehearsal, a performer's nervousness and physical exertion cause the hands to sweat. Sweaty palms are slippery. Many a sword has slipped, or been accidentally wrenched, from the sweaty grip of a performer. Leather gloves help to absorb the sweat and create a "tacky" grip on the handle of the sword, particularly on smooth metal grips.

While a well-choreographed sword fight should never injure the performers (!), it does happen that the errant point or edge comes in contact with an actor's hand or wrist. A leather glove will protect against these accidental cuts and abrasions. When the choreography demands that a performer grasp his own or a partner's sword, as in a move to disarm, the hand must be gloved not only to protect the performer but to preserve the illusion that the weapon is sharp! *Always use gloves in sword fights!*

Casting Performers Who Must Fight

Hiring a trained performer for a fighting role is a very important safety step that a director can take. In the theater, this is often overlooked. It is understood in films that casting a well-trained fighter (or stuntman/woman) opposite a "star" makes for a better production and a more exciting, and safer, fight.

Directors, and casting directors, will always look for good acting skills first when casting principal roles and may forget that they must also carry a fight scene or two! Many performers are now adding stage combat to their "special skills" to increase their chances of success when auditioning for a role. Overall production safety is raised considerably when primary and supporting roles, or extras, are cast from trained talent.

I cannot stress too strongly the need for trained stage fighters in roles such as Tybalt (17 speeches, 3 fights), De Valvert, Young Seward and other roles in which lines are minimal and fight skills are called for in the text. This is not to discount the importance of training in the leading roles. Where rehearsal time is short, trained performers not only increase the safety margin but can add immeasurably to the excitement of the audience's experience.

It is also very important for performers to know that they may be cast in a play, a film, or commercial and that after arriving on set may be asked to perform fights they were unaware of. They may be asked to perform fights, or even stunts, that they feel unqualified or downright scared to do. Always remember, actors have the right to say No! Their union will always back them up. The Screen Actor's Guild (SAG), the American Federation of Radio and Television Artists (AFTRA), and Actor's Equity Association (AEA) all have rules governing the safety of their members. Nonunion performers must have the guts to stand up for themselves.

Rehearsal Time

Question: What is the safety problem with *every* production of *Hamlet?* The answer? Not enough rehearsal time for the actor who plays Hamlet! You can always get rehearsal time with Laertes, but Hamlet is too busy! This illustrates a common problem with "fight" productions, and it basically boils down to money. Rehearsal time costs money. Time in the hospital also costs money. It's a difficult tradeoff for producers.

My colleague Drew Fracher uses this maxim: "For every five seconds of fight, a minimum of one hour of rehearsal." Therefore, a ninety-second fight should have a *minimum* of eighteen hours of rehearsal. This does not mean nine hours per day for the last two days before opening. The process should be spread out, ideally beginning near the first week of rehearsal, with the finished choreography available to rehearse many times within the context of run-throughs. This allows the performers to pace themselves within the play. It is physically difficult to perform five acts of Shakespeare and then do a long broadsword fight in full armor on three different levels on the set. It is even harder if the fight is underrehearsed, has never been done to full speed, or has never been done all the way through without stopping. Time MUST be taken and planned for by the production staff.

It goes without saying that a qualified fight director should be hired before the first week of rehearsal (before *that*, if possible).

Safety Last

Every show that has a fight scene, be it an extensive sword duel, a small "pushy-shovey," or a major battle can benefit from applying safety principles from some of the sections above. Lighting, costuming, rehearsal time, and stage-floor preparation are universal to all theater pieces. Before reading on to gain more specific knowledge, be sure your production measures up to these common safety benchmarks.

Remember:

SAFETY FIRST, SAFETY LAST, SAFETY ALWAYS!

Staging the Fight

The moment of truth in a Macbeth–Macduff fight. Photo by Zane Williams. Arthur Pearson, left; Mykael O'Sruitheain, right. American Players Theater.

2

Imaging a Fight

Alright. Imagine that you've been asked to stage a fight for a play, and you want to know where to start. My advice is that you stop yourself from jumping into the choreography armed to the teeth and that you imagine what the fight will look like from the beginning, right through to the end. Here are some questions that you must ask yourself:

➢ What are the characters trying to accomplish?
➢ What is the story being told?

➤   Why has the playwright chosen to use combat at this point?

➤   How can I serve the story *and* the performer's interpretation of character?

➤   What do the historical period and style of the show suggest?

➤   How does the fight fit into the scenic design of the play?

➤   How experienced are my performers?

Presuming that SAFETY lies at the bottom of all your choreographic decisions, the answers to the above questions should suggest a direction for your fight, and that direction is tied directly to the text and characters in the play. Fight choreography created without a sensitivity to place, time, and character is just random movement. Take your ideas from the text and from the performers' capabilities. Listen to the way they speak, and watch them move about the set. Does height, age, or weight ratio suggest any kind of specific movement? How would each character hold himself or herself, and how would they react in a moment of physical confrontation?

Fight choreography must be based in reality. That is to say, the techniques that you expect the performers to learn must not only fit their bodies, and be natural for them, but must also be based in "real" fighting techniques, whether contemporary or period. A common mistake is to choreograph for yourself and expect performers to be able to copy your personal style. What is easy for one person may be impossible for another. Have a realistic approach to the physical capabilities of your performers and the amount of rehearsal time that you will have. It is not enough that you can do the choreography, the performers have to. Maximize their talent.

The fight choreography must also reflect the concept of the play. Is it a hard-boiled realistic drama such as *Short Eyes* or *Extremities*? In this case the fights should be short and violent, and the pain should be "felt" realistically. Is it a broad comedy piece such as *The Servant of Two Masters* or *Le Bourgeois Gentilhomme*? Then the fight should be funny, the reactions broad, and the movement enlarged or minimalized. Is the play a musical such as *West Side Story* or *Man of La Mancha*? Then the musical score and the dance style must be taken into account. If this advice is not taken, the fight may not "fit" into the overall production and may look "tacked on."

Any fight scene must be organic to the rest of the production. It must also reflect human society as a whole. Most playwrights don't write combat scenes for the blood and guts effects, but to further the plot and comment on the human condition. How does violence affect the characters in the fight? How does it affect the onlookers or the parents or children of the characters fighting? What is the aftermath of a fight? Terror, pathos, shock, devastation, loss of a loved one—all of these emotions come into play within and around a confrontation scene that erupts into physical violence.

When trying to imagine your fight on the stage, try to keep in mind *all* the characters that will be on the stage at the time. Do not forget those noncombatants, the onlookers who will be filling stage space. Not only can they be used to frame the fight, but, if forgotten, they might get in the way of the fighters and may be injured. Keep in mind all the scenic and prop elements, too. I have often lost precious time redesigning a fight when a sofa, wall, or tree suddenly made an appearance where I had thought I had a bare stage. As far as the props go, don't ever be caught not knowing *exactly* what props are going to be used for your fight scene. Don't count on props or set furniture to be safe for fighting unless you have checked them yourself beforehand. Keep in mind the costume pieces, too, since a surprise helmet, or high heels, can radically change the way the performer can move. Do your homework on these elements of the production long before the first fight rehearsal.

Once the story is clear, and the logistics of set, costumes, props, lights, and special effects are available to you, sit down and imagine what the fight would look like under the best of conditions. Let your imagination run free. Look for dramatic high points and a few surprises for the audience. Use the whole set. Let the idea of the fight flow freely in your mind before committing it to paper. Start from the beginning of the combat and run your characters through to the end, then pick out the high points that worked the best, keep them, then start over while adding more and more details. This way, you are free to stop and start, make mistakes, and keep going, without endangering the performers.

When you are satisfied with your imaginary fight, begin to put it on its feet or on paper. This should give you a solid start when you get to the rehearsal hall, where the performers will be waiting to start learning their choreography.

Fight-Choreography Research

All fight directors have different ways to approach their fights. These approaches will differ depending on the size and scope of the combat, as well as on familiarity with the material. Certainly, being familiar with the script is vital. If you don't know what's supposed to happen, then your choreography can't reflect it! Read the play! Read the whole play! This will help you to get involved in the period and to understand the characters and is vital to your research.

Once the circumstances of *"Who* fights," *"Why* they fight," *"Where* they fight," and *"What* they fight with" are answered, many fight directors will research the historical period. Answering the *"When* they fight" question can help suggest movement choices for the fight.

There are many books full of illustrations of people who are fighting. Every library has a collection of books on weapons, military equipment, war, fencing, and boxing. Each period in history and each ethnic group has a very specific style of fighting. Research can hold out choices for interesting weapons, costumes, and movement patterns. It is fascinating to read of the different approaches to Renaissance swordplay even within a few hundred miles' distance. Italy, Spain, France, and England all had quite specific and differing philosophies, which are reflected clearly in the illustrations from that period.

Films are another great research tool. A list of the great films that include combat scenes would be too long. Suffice it to say that videotapes are easily rented that can give you a visual sense of how characters dressed, spoke, and fought. Many famous plays have also been made into films, most especially Shakespeare's tragedies. Other genres to explore would be Westerns, science fiction, Japanese (especially Kurosawa films), martial arts films, "sudsers" (pirate swashbucklers), and the various treatments of classics such as *The Three Musketeers,* Zorro, and the oft-told *The Prisoner of Zenda.*

However, do not limit your research to martial subjects. I try to read books on the painting, architecture, social manners, and customs of an historical period. Listen to music composed from the period. And by all means, if the subject of the play is a well-known historical one, research related material dealing with it.

For instance, if you are choreographing *Henry V,* search for books on medieval warfare, accounts of the Battle of Agincourt, books on archery and armor.

Read *Henry IV, Part 1*, and *Henry IV, Part 2* to have a clearer understanding of Henry, Falstaff, Bardolph, Pistol, and Nym.

As a fight director, you must have a working knowledge of how people fight. Contemporary fights may be researched in newspapers, magazines, videos of films, television reports, and your own personal experience. Researching historical fights, battles (see section on battles), and duels will not only give you clues to the social fabric of the time but will also give you a healthy respect for the formal set of rules that governed combat.

It is important that you familiarize yourself with these rules, for if you are to succeed in staging an historical sword fight, you must understand the nature of these encounters as well as the playwright does. To this end, let's briefly look at two styles of dueling: (1) the trial by combat of medieval times and (2) the private duel of a later age (the Renaissance through the Restoration periods in Europe).

The Trial by Combat

A trial by combat was an arranged fight between two or more antagonists and was known from the Middle Ages to the Renaissance. This was substantially different from a street fight, or a brawl, in that it was fought "in cold blood" as opposed to the hot-blooded encounter that might be fought in a public tavern or along a deserted road.

In earliest times, all the way back to the thirteenth century, the trial by combat was arranged between knights (common folk were not allowed to duel) to settle matters of honor or to decide on legal issues that the courts or kings would not settle. These events were public occasions of great ceremony and were often fought to the death. It was thought that "Might makes right" and that God would descend and favor the party with the valid claim, thereby punishing the wrongful party. The trial by combat was a very serious matter for both parties, since the loser not only could forfeit his life but could be stripped of his title and lands and his family either killed or turned out into the road with nothing.

A trial by combat must not be confused with the popular jousting tournaments of the time (Figure 2-1). These displays of manly prowess were not duels at all but athletic displays of horsemanship and martial skills. If an unfortunate combatant was wounded or killed, he did not forfeit any of his lands or

Figure 2-1. *Tournaments provided a focus for the martial training of knights and squires and were considered a holiday for the common people.*

titles. Tournaments provided a focus for the martial training of knights and squires and were a holiday for the populace, from the nobility down to the common people. Fighting in the "lists"—a place where status might be gained other than on a battlefield—was an honorable accomplishment for the noble youth of Europe.

A trial by combat fought in a "champ clos" (literally, "closed field," since the dueling area was inclosed by barriers) was carefully prearranged. Details as to date, time of day—and, most especially, the weapons to be used—had to be agreed upon by both parties. This set a precedent for duels in the sixteenth and seventeenth centuries.

A typical trial by combat might begin with a ceremonial parade of the combatants and their retainers. The field would have been prepared ahead of time and standing on opposite sides would be colorful pavilions where the combatants would rest and arm themselves. Flags and music would accompany the arrival of each party, and a herald would read out to the crowd the reason for the combat. The reviewing stands would often include the nobility, and even royalty. The grounds would be alive with common folk present to witness two rich, well-armed knights in the serious business of trying to kill each other. The throngs would include food sellers, trinket vendors, and roving musicians and mountebanks to keep the public entertained. Soldiers lined the field to prevent anyone from entering into the lists or helping either party.

Before the fight could commence, the herald would summon both parties before the king and nobles and make them swear that their cause was just and true and that they would accept the "decision" of the combat. True to the times, each also had to swear that witchcraft or other black arts were not being used to unfair advantage against the opponent. After the squires armed their men, the deadly business began.

The combatants might fight on horseback, on foot, or both. If on horseback, the principals might be armed with swords and sharpened lances. A set number of lances, as well as a set number of passes, would be agreed upon. An unseated combatant would have to fight from the ground. The combatants would of course be wearing similar armor (also agreed upon) and would have at their disposal several ground weapons. A short list of medieval ground weapons might include the following:

two-handed sword	mace
one-handed sword	ball and chain
large dagger	shield
axe	fighting pike
halberd	poleaxe

These weapons would have to be provided to each combatant, making participation in a trial by combat an expensive affair, when the cost of pavilions, horses, food, armor, costumes for scores of retainers, and gifts to the Church to pray for intercession were factored in.

Famous trials by combat in this period are rich in detail, not only about the weapons and the actual fights but about the surrounding panoply. The reader may find further details in "The Ancient Method and Usage of Duels before the King," reprinted from an old manuscript of Elias Ashmole, Esq., quoted in "Miscellanea Aulica" (1702), and found in Chapter 8 of *The Sword and the Centuries* by Alfred Hutton. This book details not only many trials by combat but private duels throughout Europe. Another source of material is Robert Baldick's book *The Duel*. The reading of these first-person accounts is invaluable to the serious student of fight choreography.

One of the most famous trials by combat is the encounter between the Sieur de Jarnac and Chastaigneraie. This duel took place in France in 1547 between two of the king's favorites. It turned into a rout, however, because of a dishonorable blow to the back of the knee that was given by Jarnac and that felled Chastaigneraie. Jarnac then repeated the stroke on the other knee and sealed Chastaigneraie's fate. Since then, the "Jarnac stroke" has come to mean an underhanded, or dishonorable, attack.

Shakespeare gives us an example of a trial by combat in the play *King Richard II*. Here, in act 1, scene 3, the characters Mowbray and Bolingbroke enter the lists to resolve their differences before the king. Although the actual combat is prevented at the last minute by King Richard, you can get a sense of the panoply and formality of the occasion.

The Private Duel

The custom of dueling someone to settle private differences was common in the Renaissance and Restoration periods in Europe. Civilian and military weapons were commonly worn in the towns, cities, and courts of Europe. A gentleman's honor, courage, and even politics could be challenged at any time by another person (of equal social rank), and a private duel arranged. Duels were, of course, frowned upon by the court and clergy, and the cost of being caught was often prison and even hanging.

Many rules governed the "art" of dueling. These were called *code duellos*, were printed in many languages, and became must reading for the youth of the day. These rules pertained to correct procedures for dueling and detailed when one might duel, how to arrange a duel, and how to reconcile the duelists. It was important that the "principals" of the duel—that is, the actual combatants—were removed from the details of arranging the fight and prevented from meeting face to face before the event. These arrangements fell to their "seconds," usually friends or relatives, to try to settle the dispute. If it became clear that reconciliation was unobtainable, the seconds were in charge of the duel itself.

What were the reasons for dueling? Aside from a certain amount of macho strutting and bragging rights, duels were fought for many reasons: lying, cheating at cards, treason, insults to one's person or honor, and political and social gain. The first cause of a duel—and an unpardonable insult—was a physical blow. If D'Artagnan strikes Aramis, then Aramis must defend his honor by dueling. The second cause of a duel would be a lie, a verbal provocation of some kind, or an insult. Shakespeare called this reason a "word," and in *Romeo and Juliet* (3.1) Mercutio urges Tybalt to raise the stakes by adding a physical blow to an insult:

> MERCUTIO [to Tybalt]:
> And but one word with one of us? Couple it with something, make it a word and a blow.

In the Renaissance, insulting someone by calling them "boy," "villain," "hind," or other less savory names was reason enough to fight. Lying about someone—or worse, lying about or defaming a female—was tantamount to throwing down a gauntlet in medieval times. Indeed, the science of the insult is reflected in Shakespeare's Touchstone (*As You Like It*, 5.4) who nominates them in ascending order of seriousness:

> TOUCHSTONE:
> . . . the Retort courteous . . . the Quip modest . . . the Reply churlish . . . the Reproof valiant . . . the Countercheck quarrelsome . . . the Lie with circumstance and the Lie direct. All these you may avoid but the lie direct; and you may avoid that too with an If. . . . Your If is the only peace-maker: much virtue in If.

A direct lie in those days was a direct invitation to cross swords.

Dueling had clear steps that both combatants and seconds were supposed to follow in setting up the actual encounter. Without question these rules were much abused and broken, but they remained guidelines to follow. Let's look at them nevertheless, since they can give us insight into the mind of the duelists of another age and can help us visualize an onstage duel.

Step 1: The Insult

Clearly a blow, a word, or an insult to oneself or someone close in blood or affection. A challenge could be made immediately. The offended party would leave the details to his seconds. It was also the job of the seconds of the principals to prevent "hot-blooded" encounters and make peace. Steely politeness was vital to the proceedings.

> BENVOLIO [to Tybalt and Mercutio]:
>   We talk here in the public haunt of men:
>   Either withdraw unto some private place,
>   Or reason coldly of your grievances,
>   Or else depart; here all eyes gaze on us.
>   (*Romeo and Juliet*, 3.1)

Step 2: The Setup

The seconds were required to be of "rank" equal to the offended party and of rank equal to the challenger's seconds. There was usually a head second (someone knowledgeable about the affairs of dueling), and a younger second. A formal written challenge, called a "billet" or "cartel," would often be written, such as:

> Dear Sir,
>
> It is clear from your actions that you disrespect my wife. I cannot brook this type of behavior toward my family or my name. You show yourself to be, sir, a dog of the lowest order. Kindly allow me the honor to dispute with you at greater length with my sword, Friday morning at dawn, behind the Boar's Head Inn.

This letter would be delivered by the seconds of the challenger to the seconds of the challenged party.

> BENVOLIO:
> Tybalt, the kinsman of old Capulet,
> Hath sent a letter to his father's house.
> MERCUTIO:
> A challenge, on my life.
>   (*Romeo and Juliet*, 2.4)

DR. CAIUS:
You jack'nape; give-a this letter to Sir Hugh; by gar, it is a shallenge: I will cut his troat in de park; and I will teach a scurvy jack-a-nape priest to meddle or make.

(Merry Wives of Windsor, 1.4)

Step 3: The Attempt at Reconciliation

Seconds were required to attempt to reconcile the parties before the duel took place. These negotiations might take place immediately or might be protracted over several days.

Step 4: The Ground Rules

The challenged party was given choice of weapons, ground, and time of the duel. Usually, a place and time was chosen to avoid being seen by onlookers or by soldiers who might stop the duel and arrest the combatants. Weapons were chosen and examined ahead of time by the seconds to ensure that they were of equal weight, strength, and length.

HAMLET:
This likes me well. These foils have all a length?
(Hamlet, 5.2)

In the case of firearms, they were tested to make sure that both parties had an equal chance.

Step 5: The Duel

Upon arriving at the duelling ground, the seconds met and tried for one last reconciliation. Often, the duel would end here, the combatants thinking better of risking their lives.

SIR ANDREW:
Plague on't, an I thought he had been valiant, and so cunning in fence, I'd have seen him damned ere I'd have challenged him. Let him let the matter slip, and I'll give him my horse, grey Capilet.

(Twelfth Night, 3.4)

If denied, the duel went forward. Doctors, as well as clergy, might be in attendance. A judge might be chosen to oversee the proceedings. Swords were checked again and perhaps sterilized. If firearms were used, they were loaded by the seconds in full view of each other. The combatants were readied for the duel, often stripping off coats and only wearing light shirts and gloves. The terms of the duel were often read aloud by the judge, and the combatants took positions for the fight. At a signal from the judge, or head second, the duel began.

Step 6: The Fight

Accounts of real duels vary tremendously in their detail. It is clear, however, that the rules of the fencing salon were rarely in evidence. While some *code duellos* state that "first blood" should stop the duel and that the combatants should then be asked to reconcile, in reality most duels continued until one or both combatants were "well blooded" and could no longer defend themselves. Duels were often stopped when blood was drawn. Wounds might be bound with cloth, doused with spirits, and the fight allowed to continue. Devastating wounds to arms, legs, and vital organs were common. Blood loss and shock probably took most victims; unsanitary conditions and inadequate medical care accounted for the rest. Puncture wounds were the hardest injury to cure and accounted for great loss of life. Severed tendons in the arm, hand, and leg were common, as were deep lacerations to the face and neck area that could maim and disfigure a combatant for life, if he survived at all. Imagination cannot adequately recreate the details of a real sword duel. Two individuals bent on destroying each other with sharp swords, with adrenaline pumping, heart pounding, and feet slipping on wet grass, is a frightening image that cannot fully be recreated on stage.

Shakespeare's plays are replete with details and images of private duels. They range in style from the most serious to the farcical. The comedic duels in plays such as *Twelfth Night, or What You Will* and *The Winter's Tale* mock the serious side of dueling and are full of braggadocio. Indeed, many real duels must have been fought by combatants who would have appeared farcical to an unbiased eye. Wizened, or overweight, trembling duelists, wigs and stockings akimbo, must have been as common a sight as athletic figures graceful as modern Olympians (Figure 2-2).

Figure 2-2. *Many historical duels must have been fought by combatants who would have appeared farcical to an unbiased eye.*

This brief look at historical dueling is but the tip of the research iceberg. Before you begin to stage a duel, or any type of fight, spend time at the library studying fighting styles with which you are unfamiliar. It is a lifetime study for a fight director to become conversant with all styles of violence from all periods in history and from all cultures. However, even a few hours of work will inspire visual images and detail that will feed your choreography and help you tell the story of the play.

Researching Period Illustrations

To give you a start, here are some historical illustrations from some of the most famous sources. Before attempting to re-create any of these techniques, however, I must warn you that they were developed specifically to inflict injury on one's opponent. Only careful modification can adapt these techniques safely to the stage.

The first three images are from Talhoffer's *Das Fechtbuch* (1467). Figure 2-3 clearly shows how physical a broadsword fight could become. Not content simply to bludgeon each other's armor it is clear that tripping is within the scope of the two-handed broadsword fighter.

In Figure 2-4 the four figures demonstrate equally dynamic techniques. On the left, the near combatant has released his sword and is avoiding a downward blow while preparing to trip his opponent. Notice the position of his right leg behind that of his opponent, as well as the position of the arm behind the thigh, ready to lift and shove. The men on the right side of the illustration are demonstrating the classic hilt and pommel attack to the head. Notice the unusual reverse grip on the sword of the man on the left. In battle, gauntlets or chain-mail gloves would prevent injury to the hand when grabbing the blade.

Figure 2-5 depicts a situation often found on the street or battlefield and indeed perhaps on the stage. Here, one fighter is being attacked by two, and he is simultaneously trying to attack one while defending against the other. Notice the unusually small bucklers. I translate from the original text that accompanies this drawing:

> It's a forced position to be in when two are against one. I want to hit one. The other hits with the hand turned in quarte, and wants to turn around and hit the one behind him. That one also wants to hit. Here he parries with poignard and buckler.

Notice the hairstyles of these fighters, and notice their clothes and their shoes. They are certainly in practice clothes and not armor. These illustrations were drawn by the book's author, Talhoffer, and are unusually clear and fine. Later books, such as that by Sainct Didier, used woodcuts to illustrate their books, so the figures are more stilted and less refined.

An illustration (Figure 2-6) from Sainct Didier's book *Traict Contenant les Secrets du Premier Livre sur l'Espée Seule* (1573) shows the teacher (Le Lieutenent) and the student (Le Prevost) in a stiff pose after a disarm. The dress has certainly changed, and the weapons have slightly evolved. The method of grabbing the point with the naked hand must surely be a last resort or be intended to illustrate the hand position clearly. To be able to put this illustration to use, a great deal of imagination must come into play to decipher what might have come before. The same holds true for the next woodcut, though it has more life and clearly shows a struggle.

Figures 2-3, 2-4, 2-5.
From Talhoffer's Das Fechtbuch
(1467).

Figures 2-6, 2-7. From *Sainct Didier's* Traict (1573).

In Figure 2-7, both combatants are grappling over control of each other's hilts, with the object of disabling or disarming the sword. Note the point in the face of Le Prevost: an excellent technique in 1573, but hardly recommended for the stage.

The Renaissance brought a wealth of fencing books and manuals written by the masters of the day. Achille Marozzo was an important Italian Renaissance master. An illustration (Figure 2-8) from his book *Opera Nova* (1550) shows a classic en guarde position of two fighters positioned on a "magic circle," centered on the Renaissance concept of symmetry in all things. This type of geometric illustration might be what Mercutio refers to as Tybalt's style of fighting "by the book of arithmetic" in *Romeo and Juliet*, as an example of someone learning rapier technique from an Italian master who not only gave classes in London but published his techniques in books such as this.

Salvator Fabris was a well-traveled master of arms, and his book *Sienz e pratica d'arme* (1606) clearly shows (Figure 2-9) that the weapon of choice was then a thin-bladed rapier. Compare Figure 2-9 to Figure 2-8 and again notice the symmetry of the fighters.

This was an age in which the dagger accompanied the rapier as often as not. However, more important, notice the flow of the artwork and the attention to the dynamics and tension in the illustrations on the following pages. We can almost feel these fighters moving through space, gauging each other, waiting for an opening. Note the extension of the body and the line of the weapons. These figures are balanced, graceful, and centered: qualities that many performers never achieve.

The cape was an article of clothing that many civilian gentlemen wore and that could, if necessary, become an instrument of offense or defense if one were attacked suddenly. The dramatic illustration in Figure 2-10 of a rapier thrust through the chest has come either after struggling over possession of the cape or after throwing the cape into the air to distract or blind the man on the left. Either way, capes onstage in Renaissance rapier fights are quite in keeping with the period; and if the "kill" in this illustration is adapted to an upstage, masked thrust between the chest and left arm, it just might do!

The thrust, trip, and shove in Figure 2-11 is almost timeless in its simplicity, and you would easily find similar illustrations in modern books on martial arts, police procedure, or Greco-Roman wrestling.

Figure 2-8. From *Achille Marozzo's* Opera Nova (1550).

Figure 2-9. From *Salvator Fabris's* Sienz e pratica d'arme (1606).

36

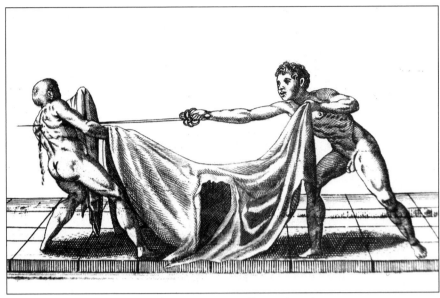

Figure 2-10. From *Salvator Fabris's* Sienz e pratica d'arme (1606).

Figure 2-11. From *Salvator Fabris's* Sienz e pratica d'arme (1606).

37

Finally, Figure 2-12 shows it all. These techniques were deadly serious to the men who invented them and to their students. The consequences of losing a rapier and dagger duel are clear as crystal in this drawing.

Though it could never be re-created on the stage, the value of this drawing is that it shows the potential for sudden death for either combatant during a sword fight. Actors must understand that when playing a dramatic scene that involves a fight, sure and sudden death could await at any moment. The characters of the play would understand that. Performers often get lost in the technique of the fight rather than its horrifying potential ending.

By the late Restoration period, masters such as Domenico Angelo (Malevolti) had achieved great renown in England. The weapons had changed significantly—to smallswords. Men's clothes had also evolved, as is seen in Figure 2-13, an illustration from Angelo's book *The School of Fencing* (1763). Notice the tricorn hat, breeches, stockings, and shoes that the fighters wore. Again, though illustrations like this one may appear formal, somewhat stiff, and even effeminate, duels with smallswords were not for fops or dandies!

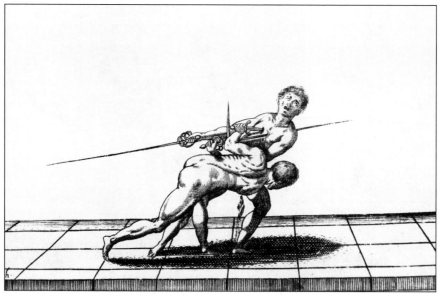

Figure 2-12. *From Salvator Fabris's* Sienz e pratica d'arme (1606).

Figure 2-13. *Domenico Angelo Malevolti, known as Angelo, founded a three-generation reign of fencing masters in London about 1760.*

Figure 2-14 shows a disarming technique by seizure and leverage, while presenting the point behind the back—a very theatrical pose, one that might end a phrase or be a button of a fight.

Figure 2-15 shows a mismatched weapons encounter. The figure on the left holds a smallsword and cape held defensively in front of him, while the figure at right holds a lantern. In the darkened streets of eighteenth-century London or Paris, a lantern could not only light your way home but might also be used to blind an opponent. I've used this technique with great effect on stage, replacing oil lanterns with electric ones.

Figure 2-14. *Disarming after the parade on the outside of the sword (parade is the old English for parry).*

Figure 2-15. *The guard of the sword and the cloak, opposed by the sword and lanthorn.*

The next three illustrations demonstrate how physical a smallsword fight might become. Figure 2-16 shows a parry of a thrust to the chest by using the left hand to deflect the blade to the side. I recommend using a glove when trying this parry.

The next two illustrations show a disarming technique and a threat with the opponent's sword after disarming. Notice in Figure 2-17 that the disarming relies on leverage to the opponent's hand by passing the left arm under the right wrist and applying pressure, while parrying in prime and passing forward onto the left leg.

Figure 2-18 helps explode the myth that smallsword fighters were always completely balanced, graceful, and had flawless technique. What could the next moment of the fight be like? The possibilities suggested by this illustration include stabbing at the chest, forcing the opponent to the ground, or running him through with both weapons. Another option might be that the disarmed man would reach down and grab the fallen scabbard to use it against the swords. We know that sword and scabbard were often used instead of sword and dagger, so we've solved the problem both historically and choreographically. The use of the scabbard would certainly surprise an audience and might be enough to turn the tide of the fight in favor of the disarmed man. Finally, Figure 2-19 shows a little-used technique of smallsword and dagger (poinard), reflecting methods from an earlier rapier-dagger style. For theater, perhaps the daggers might come into play toward the middle or end of a sequence, raising the stakes of the fight as it escalates.

Images such as these cannot help but influence sword-fight choreography. Use your research to feed your imagination, and you will always create more visual stage pictures. Remember, though, that the illustrations in this book and in the originals were meant to depict the art of injuring and killing your opponent. Onstage the fight director must adapt these techniques to ensure the safety of the performers. To attempt to stage a full body slam while holding a broadsword, to attack the head and face with the point of a sword, or to trip someone while simultaneously delivering a pommel attack to the neck, is irresponsible and dangerous.

Use your picture and illustration research as a departure point to discover interesting and individual positions, weapons details, and visual contrasts. This is not only true for plays with historical sword fights but is also true for combat situations from all periods of history and all cultures. There is a wealth of

Figure 2-16. *The parade against the binding of the sword from the inside to thrust in the flank, called flanconade, by reversing the edge of the sword, called cavez.*

Figure 2-17. *Disarming on the carte, or second thrust, after having parried with the prime parade.*

Figure 2-18. *Second position of the disarming after having parried with the carte thrust.*

Figure 2-19. *The return in tierce after having parried with the poignard.*

43

photographic research starting from the beginning of this century. Each war and civil broil has been documented by famous photographers, such as Mathew Brady (American Civil War), and unknown camera buffs and eye witnesses.

When approaching a new project, never assume that you know all there is to know about it. Challenge yourself! Dig deeply into your local library's research books and you will be amazed at the difference in your choreography!

Now, inspired by your research and confident of the director's production concept, armed with some knowledge of dueling, it's time to write your fight story—one that will ultimately come to life on the stage!

The Fight Story and How to Use the Text

The fight director must decide how elements of character aggression, fight techniques, and historical style blend into a fight scene. What story (within the playwright's story) will you tell? Shakespeare's famous stage direction "They fight" leaves too much to chance. I suggest that you write a fight story that will detail your ideas of what you wish the fight story to be. It must serve the play and be approved by the director and principal performers (who may want a hand in writing it!). It will give you a springboard into the fight and a skeleton upon which to hang your choreography.

The fight story should involve the characters' movement within the set and should detail some acting beats clearly, such as:

> Roger picks up a metal fireplace poker and begins to move downstage left to Isabelle's chair. On the line "You'll never know how much I love you!" he swings the poker back, ready to crash it down on her. Just as he says his line, though, Bill enters from the doorway up right, hears the line, and yells, "Look out!" on Roger's backswing. Isabelle looks up in time to see the poker rising, and she dives out of the chair onto the rug (knocking over a low table with breakaway vase of flowers) as the poker descends onto the chair, missing her. Roger then spins around and charges at Bill, who pulls a pistol from his pocket and aims it at Roger. Roger stops short, a few feet from the point of the gun, and while riveted to the spot, lets the poker slide from his hand to the floor.

Or, detailing one phrase of a fight:

> Mercutio takes his foot off of Tybalt's sword and circles around him, passing
> by the struggling Romeo, who is being held by Benvolio and Balthazar. He
> mocks Romeo, as Tybalt struggles up off the ground, swiping his sword
> furiously in the air to get Mercutio's attention. Mercutio turns to face Tybalt
> and yawns loudly. Tybalt swipes the air again and assumes a high en guarde.
> Mercutio becomes very serious, quiets the crowd, then comes en guarde in
> a very low stance. There is a pause as the two creep slowly closer together
> until their blades are almost touching. Mercutio suddenly pulls his
> handkerchief from his belt with his left hand and throws it toward Tybalt,
> who, startled by the suddenness of the movement, rears back quickly.
> Mercutio and Benvolio laugh at Tybalt, as the handkerchief flutters
> harmlessly to the floor.

Clearly, though, it is vital for you to identify and clarify your own fight
story, and it is equally important not to overlook the clues given by the playwright within the text of the play. Textually, certain events are important to the
furtherance of the plot and each character's story lines.

Many famous plays have already written into them a clear fight story, which
only needs your imagination to flesh out. Take, for example, the famous poem
duel in *Cyrano de Bergerac*, by Edmond Rostand. Study of the text of different
translators, and in the original French, will give a very clear direction of Rostand's intention for the fight choreography.

The fight must, if it is to succeed theatrically, follow the textual clues carefully created by the author. These lines shed light on the style of the movement, the rhythm of the actual strokes, the playfulness of the action, and the
growing frustration of the character of deValvert. Rostand gives us a wonderful scaffold upon which to hang a brilliant series of cuts, thrusts, and parries.

Romeo and Juliet gives us many clues for the fight story within the text. Tybalt
is highly confrontational with his line to Romeo,

> Boy, this shall not excuse the injuries
> That thou hast done me; therefore, turn and draw.
> > (*Romeo and Juliet*, 3.1)

Referring to Romeo as a "boy," and in an earlier line as a "villain," is an insult in itself! Does Tybalt push Romeo while saying this line, hoping to provoke him? Does he slap him with a glove? In Renaissance Italy, angry words were enough to start a fight, not to mention a physical blow. How does the crowd react to this assault? This must be clear in your fight story.

Shakespeare gives us a very careful account of the fight between Mercutio and Tybalt, which could be the basis for your fight story. In act 3, scene 1, following the deadly encounters between Mercutio, Tybalt, and Romeo, a crowd gathers to hear a retelling of the fight by Benvolio, who describes the opening moments of the encounter to the Prince:

> Romeo, that spoke him fair, bid him bethink
> How nice the quarrel was, and urg'd withal
> Your high displeasure. All this, uttered
> With gentle breath, calm look, knees humbly bow'd.

Furthermore, it is clear from the text that Tybalt was blind to Romeo's peaceful overture and

> Could not take truce with the unruly spleen
> Of Tybalt, deaf to peace.

It is also clear who starts the fight, and how Tybalt begins to use swords rather than words, when Benvolio says of Tybalt

> that he tilts
> With piercing steel at bold Mercutio's breast.

Benvolio gives details of the choreography itself, not neglecting to describe the emotions of the combatants during the fray or the response of Mercutio.

> Who, all as hot, turns deadly point to point,
> And, with a martial scorn, with one hand beats
> Cold death aside, and with the other sends
> It back to Tybalt, whose dexterity
> Retorts it.

Shakespeare even builds a wonderfully theatrical surprise into the fight, and specifically mentions the wound as a thrust that is given "accidentally" because of Romeo's intervention. Benvolio says that Romeo cries aloud,

> "Hold, friends! Friends, part!" and swifter than his tongue
> His agile arm beats down their fatal points,
> And 'twixt them rushes; underneath whose arm
> An envious thrust from Tybalt hit the life
> Of stout Mercutio.

The description does not stop here, though, as chaos follows the slaying of Mercutio, and Tybalt's fate is inevitable. Benvolio says that Tybalt fled

> But by and by comes back to Romeo,
> Who had but newly entertain'd revenge,
> And to't they go like lightning: for, ere I
> Could draw to part them, was stout Tybalt slain,
> And as he fell did Romeo turn and fly.

Shakespeare has not only deliberately given us a moment-by-moment description of the fight but also clear, specific clues as to the type of sword techniques he envisioned. The following descriptions are clues to the choreography that Shakespeare saw in his mind's eye:

> "tilts with piercing steel"
>
> "turns deadly point to point"
>
> "One hand beats cold death aside, and with the other sends it back."
>
> "His agile arm beats down their fatal points."
>
> "An envious thrust from Tybalt hit the life of stout Mercutio."
>
> "To't they go like lightning."

Many clues to the style, length, and nature of a fight are hidden within the text. Never neglect them when writing your fight story! To do so is to alter the playwright's intent. Many of Shakespeare's fights contain dialogue as the combatants confront each other *before* a fight. Consider these contrasting examples:

> CLIFFORD:
> What seest thou in me, York? why dost thou pause?
> YORK:
> With thy brave bearing should I be in love,
> But that thou art so fast mine enemy.
>
> (*King Henry VI*, Part 2, 5.2)

Does this exchange denote respect or animosity? How will you show this on stage?

> RICHARD:
> How now! what means death in this rude assault?
> Villain, thy own hand yields thy death's instrument.
> Go thou, and fill another room in hell.
>
> (*King Richard II*, 5.5)

King Richard, in the last scene of the play, clearly goes down fighting, perhaps stealing a weapon, and taking one or two soldiers with him. Shakespeare is even specific in his comedies about the fencing skills of his characters. Witness this description of the imagined prowess of Viola, as boasted about to Sir Andrew by Sir Toby Belch:

> Why, man, he's a very devil; I have not seen such a firago. I had a pass with
> him, rapier, scabbard and all, and he gives me the stuck in with such a
> mortal motion, that it is inevitable; and on the answer, he pays you as surely
> as your feet hit the ground they step on.
>
> (*Twelfth Night*, 3.4)

However, it is Shakespeare's tragedies that offer us the clearest textual references to the shape of a fight scene. *Hamlet* is the best example, showing clues for the beginning and ending of several phrases. Shakespeare even shows through text the deconstruction of the style of fighting, from sport fencing to a deadly brawl. In the sword fight in act 5, scene 2, Hamlet and Laertes's initial greetings are courteous, almost banal as they perhaps salute each other:

HAMLET:
Come on, sir.
LAERTES:
Come, my lord.

Later in the fight, after Hamlet is wounded and the broken sword is discovered, the action becomes more passionate!

LAERTES:
Have at you now!
KING:
Part them; they are incensed.
HAMLET:
Nay, come, again!

It is clear from the King's line that the fight has changed. What visual quality could the word "incensed" evoke in the choreography? This must be reflected in the fight story.

Here's another example, Macbeth's famous line to Macduff:

Thou losest labour:
As easy mayst thou the intrenchant air
With thy keen sword impress, as make me bleed.
(*Macbeth*, 5.8)

This is not merely wonderful poetry, but clear reference to Macduff's inability to inflict harm on Macbeth during the preceding exchange. So, too, does Montano's line to Cassio in *Othello* give us a clue to the quality of the fight about to erupt:

MONTANO:
Nay, good lieutenant;
I pray you, sir, hold your hand.

CASSIO:
Let me go, sir,
Or I'll knock you o'er the mazzard.
MONTANO:
Come, come, you're drunk.
CASSIO:
Drunk!

(Othello, 2.3)

The fight that follows must not be a courteous, stylish rapier bout, but rather a raucous, brawling, dangerous event that ultimately shames Cassio in front of Othello.

Clues such as those above are not limited to Shakespeare's plays but are to be found in contemporary drama, musicals, and even comedies. Although the directorial concept of a play may change the locale or historical period, it's vital that you capture the core elements of the fight laid down by the author in the text.

Textual clues are the foundation of your fight story. Once you are familiar with the text, begin to add ideas from your historical research, a bit of strategy and fight logic, and you'll have the basis for your fight story. Don't forget to factor in elements of set, lights, crowd movement, some internal high points, and maybe a narrow escape. Then, not only will your fight choreography have a logical beginning, middle, and end, but it will be easier for you to stage as you have clear goals and high points to achieve in the fight.

Now you are ready to begin to conceive the individual phrases of your fight scene (Figure 2-20). To help you through this next step, there are a few tried and true techniques that many professional fight directors use daily.

Techniques of Fight Choreography

Once the fight story is written, the historical elements are chosen, and the set, costumes, and props are all lined up, you can begin to flesh out the fight itself. Below are four techniques for putting the fight together that are used by the world's most prominent fight directors.

Figure 2-20. Progression of the first phrase of the Edgar-Edmund fight from King Lear.

The challenge by Edmund.

Edmund's first attack.

Edmund, hitting Edgar's shield with both mace and sword; Edgar falling from the weight of the blow.

Edmund hammering at the fallen Edgar. North Carolina Shakespeare Festival. Edgar played by Michael Kamtman; Edmund played by Allan Hickle-Edwards.

1. *The "Still Photo," or "High Point to High Point," Technique*

This technique is very useful since it doesn't get you caught in the labyrinth of technique right away. It is a simple process. By using period illustrations, your imagination, or a combination of both, choose dramatic "poses" that will begin and end each acting beat within your fight. Divide your fight into phrases, and come up with a series of these "still photos" or "high points" that (a) take advantage of the set, (b) tell the story (as to who is winning or losing), and (c) feature the physical strengths of your performers.

When you are satisfied with these poses—and they should be as visually interesting as possible—it then remains to choreograph the "in-between" moves to get you from pose to pose! This technique is often easier for beginning choreographers than sitting down in front of an empty sheet of paper and choreographing from move number one. (See Figures 2-21 to 2-26.)

2. *The "Little Man" Technique*

For choreographers who have trouble keeping all the elements of set, characters, furniture, and props in their heads when they choreograph, the "little man" technique may be a great deal of help. This consists of using some kind of physical representation of each character, the set, and furniture as you choreograph so as not to lose track of anything or anyone.

It helps to get a blueprint of the set from the designer; but if one is unavailable, a mock-up is easy to create on paper or even on the floor. Performers may be represented by toy soldiers, beer bottles, or bits of paper with names written on them. Furniture can be created by using blocks of wood, doll furniture, or anything that comes to hand.

With these tools the fight can be blocked almost three-dimensionally, constantly keeping track of each character on stage, as well as of the extras and props. While this is a very good technique for mass battles, it can also be used for two-person fights.

Occasionally, the two techniques of the "high point" and the "little man" can be combined to help visualize the combat.

3. *The "Live Body" Technique*

Many choreographers prefer to work on their feet—and do not, or cannot, work on paper. These fight directors will take the time to work out—through

Here is an example of the "still photo" technique of detailing in the death scene from *Julius Caesar. I designed each moment to tell a story and involve the actors, then I strung the images together. Photo sequence by Bill Savage. Caesar: Mark Lazar; Brutus: Allan Hickle-Edwards; Cassius: David Colacci; Casca: Graham Smith; and Metellus Cimber: Lucius Houghton. Directed by Louis Rackoff.*

Figure 2-21. 1. The first blow has just been struck from behind by Casca, who says, "Speak, hands for me!"

Figure 2-22. 2. The group moves in, and Caesar rises.

Figure 2-23. 3. *Caesar receives multiple wounds.*

Figure 2-24. 4. *The group moves off as Cassius stabs Caesar.*

Figure 2-25. 5. "Et tu Brute?" The crowd falls back further.

Figure 2-26. 6. Brutus's stab and Caesar's line, "Then fall Caesar."

contact improvisation or by trial and error—the individual moves of a fight. Often they will use an assistant or advanced student to work out moves before having the performers do them. However, sometimes they might choose to work out the fight on the performers themselves.

This can have the advantage of input from the performers on the spot, and a kind of communal choreography evolves that may work very well. A lot will depend on the training of the performers and what kind of collaborators they are.

The best situation is when the fight director has as much as possible of the fight in his or her head and the fight story sketched out, so that there is a form for the fight. Otherwise, the process can be a waste of time, since lack of rehearsal time is one of the enemies of a good fight.

The use of this technique ensures that the fight director is sensitive to the needs of the performers and open to their comments and suggestions. Each fight scene is, after all, a collaboration to some extent since it must "fit" the performance. But keep experimentation to a minimum, unless you have an enormous amount of rehearsal time.

4. The "All in Your Head" Technique

Some experienced choreographers are able to sit down with all the research information, all the character and text information, the decisions made about weapons, costumes, concept, set, lighting, and effects, and choreograph the fight on paper.

This is very hard to do, but can be successful. It is important to be as prepared as possible before trying this, since gaps in your preparation will show up in the choreography. If you forget that the actor playing Laertes is left-handed, if you don't know that the director wants the Tybalt death to look like an accident, if you actually believe the playwright who says, "The old man is then hit on the head with a shovel!" then you aren't ready for this technique!

Choreography in this form is carefully notated and worked through from each character's perspective, leaving nothing to the imagination and taking all scenic elements into consideration. The written choreography is then used as a teaching base once you get to work with the performers.

Some choreographers can use this technique and achieve a fight that is very close to being performed exactly as written. Other choreographers will end up with a sketchier version of the fight. Either way, there will be a jumping-off

Figure 2-27. *An unfortunate end to a duel: rapiers for two, coffee for one.*

point for a fight rehearsal. It is important to be extremely familiar with the fighting styles you want to use before trying this. Beginning choreographers may have more success with the "live body" or "high point" technique.

All of these techniques are useful in planning your fight and your rehearsal time, but never forget that you are imposing your ideas on live actors, who have their own ideas, faults, flaws, and egos. Be flexible, be observant of your actors' capabilities, and never push beyond the limits of safety.

57

The Fight Director's Timeline

Though each production is unique, the following timeline is a chronological step-by-step outline of a fight director's duties and responsibilities. This timeline will help you organize your creative involvement in a show and help you interface more effectively with the performers and all the different technical departments. It begins with preproduction and takes you through the rehearsal process all the way to opening night.

Not all theaters will want you to work this way, nor do all productions demand each step listed here, as many fights are quite short and your contact time with the actors is limited. Nevertheless, it is important for you to understand that the job of fight directing is more complicated than merely staging a fight and walking away.

Read through this timeline and compare it to fight shows you may have done in the past, or use it as a springboard to plan one you will do in the future. Either way, it should help you answer most questions and anticipate problems for any play with a fight scene.

Homework and Research

Script Analysis

Read the play. Acquire set designs and costume sketches.

Talk with the director to find out specific details of the concept. What is your role in rehearsals?

What role does the director see the fights taking in the overall production? What style of fighting will best suit the action: realistic? comedic? farcical? tragic? melodramatic? presentational? surreal?

Who fights? Why do they fight? What do they fight with?—when in the play? when in history? where on the set? What is the story? What is the director's concept?

How can you serve these characters and illuminate the text?

How can you serve the performers' characterizations?

What are the major objectives and obstacles for each character?

What are the given circumstances?

Explore the sociopolitical viewpoints of the violence in the play.

Research contemporary paintings, music, architecture, and primary accounts of fights from the time.

Prepare a presentation for the cast: goals, training, safety, fight story, weapons, rehearsal time.

Fight Analysis

What is each fight scene trying to achieve?

What were the dominant weapon styles of the period?

Are there secondary weapon styles to take advantage of?

Do any characters use hidden weapons or found weapons?

Pin down the year, month, day, and hour the fight takes place.

Is it hot or cold? Does this affect the choreography?

Take into account the age, health, and psychological makeup of the characters. How can the fighting styles support these? Are they clean or dirty fighters? confident or scared?

Pick an animal image and a possible movement style for each character that fights.

What does the audience expect from the fights and how will your choreography satisfy that expectation or shake it?

Inquire about the training level of the performers, and then decide on the amount of rehearsal time you expect to need.

Preproduction Meeting

Meet with department heads to see final sketches, models, and plans for the design of the show.

Set a realistic budget for weapons purchase and rental.

Give the production team a clear idea of your concept of the fight(s) in the show. Identify problem areas that you foresee. Ask for creative input from set, costume, light, and music designers.

Set Requirements

Analyze set sketches and blueprints.

Communicate your set requirements *before* the set is built.

Inquire about floor surface treatments.

When the set is finished, walk the set yourself, looking for possible safety hazards. Check for sharp corners and protruding screws and nails.

Check for safety railing around high platforms.

Check stage or platform's rake angle.

Costume Requirements

Analyze sketches or renderings of all costumes.

Ask about any movement problems you anticipate and about how the costumes can help or possibly hinder.

Consider padding performers if necessary *before* costumes are purchased or built.

Ask about sword belts and scabbards for swords or daggers. Will costumes or props supply them?

Be aware of potential dangers such as high heels, armor, tight clothes, zippers, buttons, bare feet, jewelry, and vision-impairing headgear like wigs, hats, or helmets.

Discuss the use of blood and how it might affect costumes.

Lighting Requirements

Ask about the lighting concept during fight scenes.

Add your input based on what you have in mind for the fights.

Be careful of strong front- or sidelights in combatants' eyes, especially during sword fights.

When choreographing, use the light to focus the movement, or guide the audience's eye to highlight or hide.

Ask about low-hanging instruments.

Prop Requirements

Pin down a weapons budget.

Present catalogs and pictures of weapons you expect to use, and ask for input from all departments.

Prepare a list of prop and weapon requirements.

Inquire about weapon maintenance. Set a schedule.

Ask about gun safety. Are theater personnel trained and licensed?

Examine and collect rehearsal props.

Discuss creation and maintenance of blood effects.

Create a character weapon list, and track each weapon through the production. Ask to have offstage sword racks built (Figure 2-28). Mark weapons to help keep track of them, especially when sharing them in large productions.

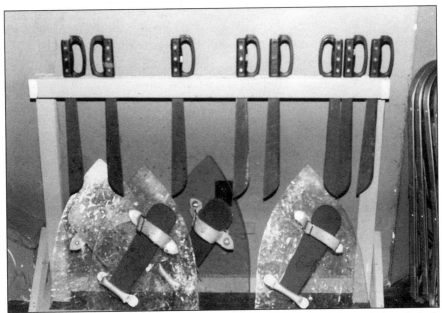

Figure 2-28. *A backstage sword rack helps organize the weapons. Label each weapon with the performer's name and, if necessary, number each weapon. Note numbers on the shields, which will be hidden from the audience by the actor's arm.*

Imaging the Fight

Decide on a dominant movement style for each character. Tie it closely to each performer's body type and training.

Detail how each character is armed.

Sit down with the set plans and all research, and imagine the whole fight, high point to high point, as you would like it to be. Do this several times until you like the ideas, flow, and story that the fight tells.

Think about patterns and tempo/rhythms. Plan the floor pattern flow of the fight. How will you draw the audience's eye? How can you misdirect the audience to mask blows, blood hand-offs, or prop switches?

Don't worry about the individual moves yet. Answer these questions:

> Is it a duel or a brawl?
> What is the opening beat?
> What story do the middle phrases tell?
> How do you see the climax or kill?
> Can you use any surprises, like disarms, crowd movement, special effects, blood bits?
> How formal or rough is the movement?
> Look for contrasts in the combatants' styles.
> What is the logic of each character within the fight?

Begin to explore the individual moves, one phrase at a time, after deciding on the basic shape and flow of a fight.

Don't forget to move the fight around the set to maximize scenic elements and to play the fight to different parts of the audience.

Finalize the fight story, write it up, and clear it with the director.

Choose, then purchase or rent weapons at least one month before rehearsals begin.

Detailing the Fight Choreography

When the fight story is agreed upon, finalize the number of individual phrases.

Title your phrases before detailing them, such as "The Salute," "The Fatal Mistake," "Mercutio's Surprise!"

Decide on the length of the phrases. Short = 1 to 5 moves. Medium = 5 to 10 moves. Long = 10 or more moves.

Choreograph your fight, move by move, building from one high point to the next, keeping the whole fight story in mind.

Build in pauses, surprises, and specific acting beats.

Don't forget to use the text! What are the playwright's images and clues to the content of the fight?

Detail the entrances and exits and the movement patterns of principals and crowds on the stage.

Work for a build in the excitement of the fight.

Choose attacks and defensive moves that reinforce the acting beats and that help tell the story (Figures 2-29 and 2-30). Are the characters fresh or exhausted, healthy or ill? Do they have a physical obstacle (Richard III or Falstaff)?

Be specific about layering in text to the choreography. Do the performers speak as they fight, or during pauses?

Is less choreography better?

Are you taking advantage of scenic elements and levels?

Can you use the furniture or props to advantage?

Fight Rehearsals

Teach the fight to the performers only after you have worked out 95 percent of the details. You need a plan! You can always change your mind later. Be decisive!

At this point, make changes in the fights based on your observation of the physical capabilities of the performers, set, lights, actors' and director's suggestions.

Figure 2-29. *Choose attacks and defensive moves that reinforce the acting beats and tell the story. Here, Hamlet (Mark Waterman) stabs Laertes (Kennedy Brown) with the "unabated" sword. From a production at the Jean Cocteau Repertory Theater.*

Figure 2-30. *A moment later, Hamlet withdraws the sword, provoking an extreme reaction from Laertes.*

Accept suggestions from the performers. Can you incorporate them? Should you?

Carefully observe how the performers learn the choreography, since this is a clue as to how it will be performed.

Work hard to make the fight choreography "fit" each performer.

Begin to choreograph other performers—the crowds and onlookers—who might be onstage during the fight.

Layer in specific crowd movement patterns that will highlight the primary combats.

Suggest specific vocal reactions to crowds and onlookers, and when their reactions would best support the main action.

Always use rehearsal costumes, especially footwear, to discover any movement problems or difficult elements, such as armor, hats, capes, helmets.

Work slowly, introducing new material as the performers master the old. Don't push for a performance too early. Tie choreography closely to acting beats.

Begin to introduce any musical elements or sound effects.

Work with pads, mats, and other protective gear.

Introduce blood bits. Use water bags to get used to them.

Pass out written notation of fight choreography to performers and staff.

Now is also the time to choose and train a fight captain who will maintain the fights and run the preshow fight rehearsals.

Check the fight for masking problems. Be sure punches, kicks, and knaps are hidden from the audience, as well as stabs and other wounds. Remember, less is often more.

Technical Rehearsals

Before technical rehearsals begin, acquaint the performers with the surprises to expect from elements such as lighting, blood effects, sound, music, and costumes.

Figure 2-31. *Here, Laertes tries to avoid a "touch" by Hamlet in the first phase of their duel.*

It is still not too late to cut choreography that looks awkward, is dangerous, or doesn't work. It is a bit late to add lots of new material and expect it to be performed safely and at performance speed.

Walk the set with the actors and have them rehearse the fights slowly, stopping to solve problems.

Make sure that the technical elements don't overwhelm the fight or make for a dangerous situation. Examples are blinding smoke effects, excessively loud music, strobe lighting, or insufficient lighting!

Carefully check for lights in the eyes. Check all platforms and levels. Recheck all props and weapons for safety.

Slowly begin to add costumes and blood effects.

Work up to performance speed as a final goal, usually reached two or three days before opening night.

Keep your temper, for as opening night gets closer everyone's nerves fray. Keep your common sense as well, and look for safety problems everywhere.

Encourage your performers when they do well, and help them keep a lid on their emotions and red-light fever!

Make sure you watch the fights from various parts of the house and balcony to check on masking and stage picture.

There are two important things that must be mentioned when talking about choreographing fights. The first and most important is that you, the fight director, must be familiar with *any* techniques that you attempt to choreograph. It is senseless to attempt to stage a sword fight if you have never taken lessons. It is dangerous to set up a boxing match if you don't know how to throw a punch. It is negligent to stage a gymnastic throw if you don't know how to teach it!

The performers depend on *your* experience and training. Don't get in over your head!

Second, and equally important, you must never fall in love with your own choreography to the detriment of the performers or the play. The trap of an inexperienced choreographer is overchoreographing! Too many moves do not make the fight better! Therefore, always try to do less or "just enough to tell the story." It is much better to stage a short fight that performers can do with relish and energy!

Finally, don't impose combat techniques on the actors that are impossible for them to perform. Whether the problem is kinetic, or one of balance or comprehension, if a technique or a phrase looks awkward on an actor, *change* it. Don't be afraid to scrap a carefully designed sequence in favor of one that is more organic for a particular performer or one that is safer!

Remember! Safety is always *the* deciding factor in creating a fight. Have the courage to cut.

Now that we have analyzed the practical side of fight directing, it's worth taking some time to study some of the more philosophical and theoretical aspects of staged fight choreography. In order for a fight to work on stage, it must have several things going for it, not the least of which is *logic*.

Figure 2-32. *It is much better to stage a short fight that performers can do with relish and energy! Here, Laertes attacks Hamlet from the floor.*

A modern-day struggle in a bus station and a formalized trial by combat must both appear to be logical not only for the characters within the fight but also for the viewing public. Furthermore, the stage picture you create with the fight is not only important to the performers but is an added dynamic for the audience. Finally, the tempos and rhythms created by the bodies and props, swords, lights, and sound give the piece a finished look and can't be ignored by a serious fight director.

Phrasing in Staged Fights

All fight scenes are built of individual phrases that complete the whole scene. This not only enables the audience to follow the action but gives the performers smaller "bites" of choreography to remember and allows for the action to build to a climax. Phrases must be designed to match acting beats in the fight, as determined by the characterizations of the performers, with the help of the director and the fight director.

As any seasoned performer will attest, three minutes of fighting is a very long time. Fight choreography need *not* be drawn out to be effective. The audience will respond to the acting of the fight more than the actual moves. The audience is interested in what the characters are doing, how they are feeling, and if they will succeed. A fight that is just a series of "flashy" moves performed at the speed of light will not be as satisfying as a well-*acted* fight performed at a moderate tempo. The most important elements of any fight are not the punches or kicks, nor the individual cuts and parries. These moves are merely the medium by which the characters are expressing themselves, and the performer's job is to interpret the moves and phrases in a fight.

Most young fight directors, or amateurs, make the mistake of creating fights that are too long and too difficult to perform, with little or no focus to the moves. These directors have the performers just "go at it"! Little or no thought is put into *how* each character can or would fight. This is, of course, vital to the success, not to mention safety, of the combat, regardless of style or period.

If the fight is looked at as a series of phrases, then each phrase should be only long enough to do its job. In other words, if a phrase is designed to show, for instance, the physical superiority of one character over the other, as in the fight between Charles and Orlando in *As You Like* It, then the first phrase need not have a strangle, a head lock, several kicks, a hit with a breakaway bottle, and then a full body slam! This is—if you will pardon the expression—overkill. Each phrase should be carefully composed to fit into the overall fight. Some phrases will be longer than others, but many more will be short. The value of a short phrase is that the performers have time to ACT!

This brings us to the obvious, and often forgotten, technique: the PAUSE. The pause is a valuable choreographic technique since it allows the audience (or camera) to catch up to the action and the performers to breathe a bit, and gives room for a necessary amount of acting, or perhaps dialog. A short, well-performed fight is always preferable to a long, complicated fight—and may appear more realistic. Real fights rarely last long, most of the action being taken up with fighters who are out of range of each other, gesturing, posturing, and threatening.

In addition, successful phrases must follow not only the accepted rules of combat, as determined by the period of the play, but also the education, morals, age, health, and previous training of the characters. No two people will fight, move, or salute in the same way. Each has a different objective and worldview that must be taken into account by the fight director.

Logical Phrasing in Fight Choreography

Not only must an entire fight scene be entertaining to an audience, but it mustn't strain the audience's sense of logic. Even stylized fights have an inherent logic to them. To work as a whole, a fight or battle must be built from logical parts, or phrases.

Logical phrasing must have several things going for it. It must be performed at a speed acceptable to the audience's eye. If too fast, the fight is a blur of movement, signifying nothing. If too slow, the audience feels uncomfortable, since they see the tricks and the choreographer's hand. Moves within phrases must also follow a logical and natural flow of the performers' bodies. I have seen performers forced to justify tremendously difficult and illogical moves in choreographic sequences.

Phrases must follow logical rules of attack and defense—either armed or unarmed—for each specific period in history. For instance, a broadsword fighter holding his left arm over his head in an Olympic "fencing" stance and thrusting across the stage is ridiculous, although I've seen such choreography performed many times.

Phrases must make visual, physical, and kinetic sense to the audience. The audience must be able to understand what is happening and what is being achieved. For instance, a small 100-pound person would not normally be able to push off a 250-pound attacker. It is also stretching logic for an unarmed "hero" character to fight off four attackers and sing an aria while wounded in both legs and carrying the heroine on his back!

We must, of course, also take into account comedic logic that will break all the rules. In comedy it is perfectly logical for a 100-pound person to send a 250-pound attacker sailing across the stage. We will believe it if the performers are involved, the movement invested, and the smaller person sufficiently motivated!

The fight must also have clear objectives, which are reached (or not) by a series of steps (phrases). Clear objectives are interesting to the audience. The audience *wants* to see what will happen to the characters. A character may have to change his or her actions when obstacles get in the way of reaching an objective. The phrase following a change in objective must reflect that change. Obstacles that might initiate a dramatic change are, for example, superstition (Macbeth), fate or accident (Mercutio), and inexperience (young Siward).

A further example might be taken from the play *Les Liaisons Dangereuses*. The character of Valmont duels with the inexperienced Danceny, with the objective of committing suicide. Let's analyze some possible choices for the first three phrases of the fight.

> Phrase 1   Danceny begins quite passionately, attempting to wound Valmont with a flurry of attacks.
>
> Phrase 2   Danceny's passion surprises Valmont, making it necessary for Valmont to fight harder than he expected.
>
> Phrase 3   Valmont's defense then slowly deteriorates as the reality of the situation grows on him.

The objective of the middle phrases of the fight (phrase 4 and 5) might be to humiliate or to avoid Danceny's attacks. Finally, it must be clear to the audience that the phrase leading up to Valmont's suicide is a choice, not an accident.

Each character *wants* to win a fight and will try different methods to achieve his goal. Therefore, the phrases must logically reflect this build and each change of action.

For instance, let us imagine the character of Macbeth fighting young Siward and break down the phrases in their fight for an imaginary production of *Macbeth*.

> Phrase 1   Macbeth allows Young Siward to exhaust himself by tripping him, easily parrying multiple blows, and running him around.
>
> Phrase 2   Macbeth overpowers Siward physically, throwing him to the floor.
>
> Phrase 3   Macbeth walks away, ignoring Siward, distracted by the war raging in his castle, and within himself, exposing his back to Siward on purpose.

Phrase 4   Finally, Macbeth draws Siward in too close, avoiding a deathblow, and kills Siward with a dirty move
before throwing him to the ground.

These choices are merely examples of how this fight could be built logically. The combat phrases would then correspond to the actors' choices and
would support the performance!

It is also important for the phrases not to be repetitive and predictable for
the audience. Although most modern audiences have very little, if any, technical knowledge of sword fighting, theatergoers are an intelligent group. If the
fight director is stuck in a series of moves that are repeated over and over, or
uses "tricks" more than once, the audience becomes aware of the choreographer's hand in the combat and ceases to be drawn into the performances. This
must never happen!

The performance of fight choreography is an art that must hide itself. The
audience must never be aware of the techniques involved or of the hours of rehearsal it took to create a fight. Above all, the audience must stay interested in
the performances and engaged in the story being told. How do you tell that
story? Here's another way.

Some fight directors use an "event list," or "beat sheet," to help them realize
their phrasing. Once the character's objectives are identified, this type of list
aids the creation of choreography and is closely associated with the "high point
to high point" technique of staging fights discussed earlier. An event list for the
individual phrases of a Macbeth-Macduff fight might look like the following:

1. Macbeth and Macduff challenge one another.
2. Macbeth and Macduff stalk each other.
3. Macbeth surprises Macduff by brandishing a hidden dagger.
4. The combatants begin close quarter fight.
5. Macduff almost loses.
6. The fight reverses, and Macbeth is slain.

Each phrase might also have an event list, such as the following:

1. Challenge (1 to 3 moves)
   a. Macbeth spits and howls.
   b. Macduff charges, but Macbeth avoids him.

2. Stalking (7 to 9 moves)
   a. Macbeth evades Macduff downstage.
   b. Both circle, looking for an opening.
   c. Macduff attacks.
   d. Macbeth trips Macduff, who falls hard.
   e. Macduff crawls toward Macbeth, forcing him upstage.

3. Hidden dagger (5 to 7 moves)
   a. See lines, "Thou losest labour," etc.
   b. See lines at end, "Lay on, Macduff." Macbeth discards shield.
   c. Macbeth attacks with two hands on sword.
   d. Grappling with Macduff, Macbeth pulls a dagger by surprise.
   e. With a near miss of a stab to Macduff, the dagger sinks into set.

4. Close quarters (7 to 10 moves)
   a. Macbeth trips up Macduff and falls on him.
   b. Both lose swords during fall.
   c. There is a struggle on the floor over the dagger.
   d. Macduff is stabbed (blood bag).

5. Macduff's setback (8 moves)
   a. Macduff struggles away on floor.
   b. Macbeth stands and kicks him.
   c. Macbeth retrieves broadsword, dropping dagger.
   d. Macduff retrieves shield.
   e. Macbeth hammers Macduff, who blocks blows with shield.

6. Slaying of Macbeth
   a. Macduff kicks Macbeth from floor.
   b. Macduff rises and throws shield at Macbeth (upstage).
   c. Macduff scrambles to dagger.
   d. Macbeth charges Macduff.
   e. Both fall to floor.
   f. Macbeth is stabbed in chest during fall.
   g. Macbeth struggles, weakening, to strangle Macduff.

    h.   Macduff rolls Macbeth off him, showing bloody dagger.

    i.   Soldiers move in to drag Macbeth's body offstage.

It now only remains to string the "events" together with interesting and safe choreography. Using the event list, or beat sheet, is a great time saver and a wonderful way to plan the phrases of the fight on paper. Show the finished product to the performers and the director of the play to get their approval and input.

Finally, let's look at fight choreography strictly from a movement perspective. Character movement across the stage, and posture, animal images, internal and external tempo/rhythms are another layer to successful staged violence.

Patterns and Tempo/Rhythms

The stage fight is forever a thing in flux—moving, liquid—neither frozen on a page nor fixed upon a spot on the stage.

It stands to reason that an aggressive fighter with murder in his eye will probably take the quickest route to his opponent—the straight line. In the same vein, an unsure, tentative, thoughtful, perhaps nervous, fighter might prefer the more oblique angle, thus forcing him out on a circle. These elementary character observations are clues to the pattern of a fight.

The characters' motivations, and their physical, emotional, and psychological relationships, drive the pattern of the fight and the tempo/rhythms. The term *pattern* is understood to be either the actual floor pattern of movement during a combat scene, on the one hand, or the pattern or structure of the phrases of the fight choreography, on the other.

The tempo/rhythms are the speed and beats of the individual "moves" of a fight. They should be carefully composed in the choreographic and rehearsal phases of the fight. Phrase tempo/rhythm should be precise, like the following:

	Tempo	Rhythm
Phrase 1	slow, smooth, and even	(6 beats)
Phrase 2	fast, light, and fluid	(8 beats)
Phrase 3	moderate, but staccato and somewhat heavy	(7 beats)
Phrase 4	starting slow, then fast	(2 beats, then 9)

Each phrase needs to have a strict tempo assigned to it. This is not only vital to the interpretation of the choreography but is an important rehearsal tool. The performers will learn the fight more quickly with a defined tempo and with clear rhythms, or beats, to the techniques whether they are sword fights or unarmed combat.

Tip!

Try a rhythm exercise with each phrase in your fight. After you've taught the phrases, randomly impose a new set of even or uneven beats, and slowly rehearse again. Uneven beats (3,5,7,9) create tension, even beats (2,4,6,8) suggest confidence. See if these new rhythm patterns help the performers find new acting impulses. This exercise often breaks up choreography in interesting ways but should be rehearsed slowly until the performers understand the new rhythm pattern. Remember, rhythms may increase (2,4,6,8) or decrease (8,6,4,2) or be random (3,8,1,12), for different effects.

The set design and playing space may also dictate, restrict, or suggest various floor patterns and tempo/rhythms. A bare, flat, wooden stage will not invoke the same images as an outdoor, multilevel, rock-strewn arena. Scenic elements may also suggest an ebb and flow to the fight, be it a duel or a battle. Elements such as stairways, archways, deep rakes, central fountains, vomitoriums, large crowds, music, lighting, and weather will make their mark on the tempos and patterns of a fight. Take advantage of them!

Movement patterns in staged combat tend to reflect who is "winning" the fight. This is not always the hero, or "good guy." Set design again plays a part, though not the only one. Obviously, a fight pattern that revolves around one character tends to feature that character. A pattern that weaves the fight through a crowd will dissipate the lead character's focus.

Tip!

Never turn the lead character upstage for too long. Actors hate it, and the audience *does* need to see facial reactions to enjoy the fight!

Basic stage pictures must reflect the ebb and flow of the fight and must be factored into the pattern of the combat as a whole. Triangles, circles, semicircles, as well as the fighter's entrance and exit patterns, are as important to the story as the individual techniques of combat that you employ. A strong upstage center entrance is more telling than one downstage left. A kill on an upper platform upstage center is more dramatic than one upstage right.

However, a fight will be too static if a character remains in a fixed position throughout a scene. Other physical relationships must be explored to maximize the story of the fight and the size of the stage. Tripping, falling, charging, escaping, rolling, wrestling, and circling change the physical relationships constantly, helping to illuminate the characters psychophysical impulses as one tries to best the other.

Stage combat, and particularly theatrical sword fights, offer the performer and fight director a wide variety of tempo/rhythms to explore.

Ideas for tempo/rhythm changes can spring from very simple or quite complex reasons, stemming from character and/or strategy. For instance, the sword work in one phrase may be very light, relying on point work, pauses, and testing moves. The next may be very hard, relying on beat parries, punching, charging, and close-quarter work.

An example of a strategy affecting tempo/rhythm is of two fighters who are trying to "psych" one another out, with lots of changes in position, changing of en guardes, and invitations in different lines. These two fighters may not actually come to blows very often at all. An example might be the Viola–Sir Aguecheek duel in Shakespeare's *Twelfth Night*.

The opposite is the scene in which the characters are too emotionally charged to take time to think but just "go for it." Examples would include Macbeth and Macduff, Romeo and Tybalt.

In all of these examples, the individual techniques involved in the fight—whether they be cuts, thrusts, parries, punches, kicks, or throws—will have an internal rhythm of their own. Too often the fight director ignores this rhythm and, because a fight is taught step by step, forgets to include a sense of rhythm, or "beat." All fight phrases are improved by using a specific "music." The simplest sword phrase of "cut 5, 2, 5, 2, 5, 2," (head, leg, head, leg, head, leg) will look much better if performed in a different rhythm. For example, if you alter this regular rhythm to "cut 5; pause; cut 2, 5, 2; pause; cut 5, 2," it is much more interesting!

Using Tempo in Rehearsals

The use of tempo/rhythm in rehearsals is a tried-and-true technique. Begin rehearsing the fights quite slowly but phrased in a recognizable rhythm. As the performers become more familiar with the choreography, the tempo steadily increases while the rhythm stays the same. The tempo should reach "performance tempo" by the week of dress rehearsals, so that the actors have a full week to practice the fight at performance tempo/rhythm. Sudden *changes* in tempo/rhythm account for most mistakes and injuries in theatrical fights.

A good fight director will always create a fight, linking the fight phrases to playable actions. These actions may take many forms, like the following:

to test	to probe	to draw out
to avoid contact	to lash out	to punish
to set up a rhythm to break it	to engulf	to overpower
to outclass	to outstyle	to outmaneuver
to draw in	to show off	to stand ground
to give the low blow	to wade through	to humiliate
to protect	to toy with	to grandstand
to puncture	to tear	to evicerate
to destroy		

Another rehearsal technique is to explore animal images to help performers create character movement, which will affect tempo changes, or rhythms, within a fight. These techniques can allow the performer to fight in a subtley different way, almost subliminally for the audience. Examples of this type of fighting are:

fighting like a
  bear, snake, gazelle, pig, dog, tiger, rat, lizard, Tasmanian devil, wasp, cat, antelope, mouse, scorpion

The Music in the Blades

In theatrical sword fights, we often hear the phrase "music in the blades," which refers to the rhythm pattern of the cuts and parries, footwork, and vocal exchanges of the performers. These sounds are not only important to the audience but are also important to the performers because they create a repeatable rhythm within the fight.

Fight directors often change or add to the sound of the steel with the sound of strikes or blows. Fight directors vary the cuts and parries in a sword fight with punches, missed cuts that hit the set or the floor; and screams, cries, and laughter that punctuate a move—all of which work to focus the audience's attention for a split second. These techniques give the fight its own audio quality and break up rhythm patterns that could make the fight sound repetitive. Here are some ideas that are often used to create rhythmic sound effects:

quick parry/riposte sections	(rhythm)
beat parries	(percussive strikes)
binds, envelopments, glissades	(slides, grinds)
blade traps	(shocks)
foot stamps	(percussive sound, punctuation)
crowd reactions	(vocal support of high points)
strikes to metal shields	(high percussive notes)
strikes to wooden shields	(low percussive notes)
running steps	(increasing or decreasing sound)

Don't neglect to use found props to make interesting music. Found props used as weapons, thrown around or dropped, give an interesting dynamic to the music of the fight. Found weapons might include:

an iron poker, wood, breakaway glass, bells, pottery, laundry, bread, vegetables, wicker, furniture pieces

A good fight director will not only look at patterns and tempo/rhythms and listen to the music of the fight, but will also create the fight around the character's motivational actions, which build to an objective, or recognizable, conclusion. The fight must be rehearsed with these acting beats, patterns, and tempo/rhythms in mind from the first day and not laid on days or weeks afterward. In this way, the fight is more organically connected to the play and to the performances from the very beginning.

Though I love hearing the musical clang of swords, almost half of my professional work is staging violence for contemporary drama. While many of the things we've already covered still apply, contemporary violence demands a different approach. Violence in plays such as *Extremities*, *True West*, *The Miracle Worker*, *Angels in America*, *Oleanna*, and *Short Eyes* demand rehearsal and performance techniques different from those in *Romeo and Juliet*.

Contemporary Violence

It's worth spending a little time examining the styles of staged violence written in plays in the late twentieth century. Western society has changed dramatically in the last half of the 1900s, and random, personal violence is on the increase. Sociologists blame this on overpopulation, economic causes, the proliferation of illegal firearms, poverty, the drug culture, and television and movie violence.

In countries ravaged by war and terrorism, people live with violence in daily proximity. Political upheavals, random bombings, hijackings, carjackings, rapes, terror squads, guerrilla warfare, and genocide make newspaper headlines worldwide. Playwrights reflect this growing trend, and they mirror conditions that are fertile for violent acts.

So how is staging fight scenes for modern plays different from working on period plays? For one thing, the nature of violence in period drama is different. Personal fights in period drama are, for the most part, arranged and formalized. The combatants know how to fight and meet at a public place in front of witnesses. They fight within a formalized set of rules—for instance, Renaissance rapier-and-dagger play in *Romeo and Juliet*. Romeo, Tybalt, and Mercutio fight in front of their friends at noon in Verona's square. All of them know how to sword fight and have had training. The same is true in *Tom Jones* (though the weapons are updated to Restoration smallsword) and the public wrestling match in *As You Like It*.

Modern characters usually have no formal training in combat, with the exception of characters such as police personnel, members of the military, and martial artists. However, while Hollywood exploits these character types, few plays use Rambo or James Bond in leading roles. Average men and women cannot rig a bus to explode and don't know how to sword fight or box. They fight more organically, spontaneously, and randomly, with little or no strategy other than a vague goal. They also rarely fight in public but act out their stories in bedrooms, motels, kitchens, seedy apartments, or lonely park benches. Modern fights on stage more closely resemble footage from an eleven o'clock news broadcast.

Have you ever seen a real fight? They are usually short, violent, and sloppy. Combatants pose and yell a lot, and few blows are usually landed. The idealized Hollywood fistfight is a fiction. The idea that someone can receive several punches and kicks, like John Wayne and Clint Eastwood, and continue to fight to the finish is a romantic falsehood. Antagonists squaring off and delivering a long series of accurate blows is simply not realistic.

As a fight director, I enjoy creating fights for contemporary plays, since it gives me the opportunity to explore new kinds of movement with the performers involved. The use of the set is vital to the success of the fight; and the props and furniture, even the doors and walls, become organically mixed into the choreography.

However, there are major safety problems in depicting contemporary violence. These fights are simply more dangerous to perform than period fights. Why? Even though swords are dangerous, there is usually about 6 feet (2 meters) between the combatants. Actors have a healthy respect for swords and keep their distance. Contemporary fights, by nature, are performed closer—much closer. The often intimate contact between the performers raises the likelihood of an accident. Unarmed acts of violence—beatings, rapes, strangulations, and even grabbing and struggling—put the actors in harm's way of being struck by flying knees and elbows. Even falling to the floor, being tackled, feigning a football match (as in a scene from *National Anthems*) is inherently more dangerous than a sword fight.

Why? The movement must appear to be more organic, natural, and ideosyncratic than period fights. Emotions well over, and a man is stabbed in *The Zoo Story*; a woman struggles with a rapist in *Extremities*; a man bloodies his lover in *Angels in America: Perestroika*; a professor lashes out at a student in *Oleanna*. These are not premeditated acts by individuals who are trained fighters.

It is more difficult to hide the choreographer's hand when conceiving fights in contemporary plays. Modern audiences instinctively know when modern characters are fighting unrealistically. The characters must move, struggle, and fight back the way ordinary people really move! Let me share with you one rehearsal technique that can help achieve a realistic effect.

Contact Improvisation

The contact-improvisation rehearsal technique is a good way to free your performers from stilted movement and to create a truly collaborative fight scene. Here are a few rules that will make this technique safe:

> Examine the scene with the director and performers and identify the high points (see earlier section entitled "Techniques of Fight Choreography").
>
> Create your high points physically with the performers in the rehearsal room. It's a good idea to cover the floor with mats and to use safe rehearsal furniture and props. If you don't have mats, protect the actors with knee and elbow pads and have them wear thick, loose clothing. Rehearse and set the high points several times.
>
> Talk over the scene and set down the rules of the improvisation. The actors will improvise the movements between the high points, getting to the first one, then to the second, and so on. Here are the *rules*:

1. All movement is to be in extremely *slow motion*. Sensitive, or intimate areas of the body should be avoided.
2. Don't deny your partner's impulses but go with them. Try to use the whole set, including the floor.
3. Work the fight from one high point to the next. These must be identified in advance.
4. Analyze your improvisation and talk over what worked and what didn't work. Do the improvisation again and re-create the sequences that work. Continue to explore new ideas.
5. The fight director must oversee each improvisation, stopping the actors only if safety becomes an issue. Edit out unsatisfactory moves and identify ones that excite you visually and help tell the story.
6. Once the exploration has been performed many times, you should agree to "freeze" the fight sequence. *Very* slowly increase the speed of the rehearsal.

The beauty of this kind of work is that the actors will create movement that is organic for them, that will feel right to their bodies, and that will naturally be more organic than any type of imposed choreography. The fight director's job is to edit and mold the shape of the fight to achieve the best result.

This technique can be very effective. There is sometimes difficulty in working in strikes (punches, slaps, kicks), and wounds that must be masked from the audience. However, if these events are treated as high points and staged before the "improv" work, then they are less of a problem.

In the case of, say, a fight with a knife, it's vital that the wound be prestaged; but if the actors wish to explore struggling over the weapon further, they may safely do so in slow motion, but should do so unarmed! Once the moves become set, a rubber knife may be substituted for a time. Only after all safety issues over the knife (or other prop) are answered may the show prop be slowly incorporated into the choreography.

I find that contemporary fights offer the opportunity for extreme physical movement: falling, kicking out, running, escaping, grabbing, and struggling combined with missed punches, thrown objects, ripping clothes, and falling into furniture. It is this physicality that excites the audience and involves the actors but that is potentially dangerous (read the section on padding!). To support this type of physical action, though, you must be sure to provide the actors with a safe playing area. Padding under rugs, reinforced furniture, no glass anywhere, and other common safety rules become more important here.

It's impossible to stage the fight in *A Streetcar Named Desire* between Stella and Stanley realistically if you depend on Hollywood fisticuffs from the 1940's. The same will be true for the struggle in *Wait Until Dark*, *Dial M for Murder*, or *The Miracle Worker*. Allowing your actors some controlled freedom in the rehearsal process can lead to wonderfully exciting, but safe, moments of contemporary violence.

Good fight directors are always looking for new and interesting ways to enliven staged violence. Sometimes the use of an unconventional weapon or prop can breathe new life into a scene that otherwise might have been quite ordinary. Look around you, and you'll find numberless items with which to fight!

Found Weapons

"Found weapons" are anything on the set that a character may find during the course of a scene that the character might pick up and use as

Figure 2-33. *An example of using "found weapons" in a period play. Here, French soldiers (Curzon Dobell, left; Alec Phoenix, right) kill an English boy (Miriam Healy-Louie) in an incident in Shakespeare's* King Henry V. *Produced by Theater for a New Audience. Director, Barry Kyle. Photo by Gerry Goodstein.*

a weapon. Such weapons would include anything from the furniture to the kitchen sink! Sometimes referred to as "weapons of opportunity," these props can often add an element of reality to the combat that otherwise wouldn't be there. Found weapons also affect the choreography in interesting ways.

I use found weapons in fight choreography from all periods in history. While found weapons are used most often in modern plays that depict contemporary violence, and are seen in film and television fights, the use of found weapons onstage in period plays is often overlooked.

A modern audience has trouble relating to sword fights. Yes, they are exciting, but probably not one audience member in five hundred has ever picked up a sword. However, if Laertes in his passion picks up a stool and hurls it at Hamlet, or if Romeo caught at the gravesite must fight Paris with an "iron crow" (crow bar), these are props that modern audiences can identify with immediately. Found props like these give a sense of reality to a fight in a period play, and they are essential to modern plays.

Examples of found props are occasionally written into such plays as *Extremities*. The woman in this play is only able to fend off her attacker with a weapon of opportunity—a can of insect spray—after which she binds her attacker with a handy electrical cord. In *I Hate Hamlet*, the character of Barrymore uses a champagne bottle in his fencing duel with Andrew. In *Dial M for Murder*, the homicide is averted when the victim "finds" a convenient pair of scissors with which to stab her assailant.

However, found weapons are often brought into the fight choreography by the fight director or as a "happy accident" during rehearsals or improvisation. I have staged fights with chairs, tablecloths pulled from tables, curtains pulled from windows, and with kitchen utensils, trash cans, books, tools, food, and even electrical appliances. I remember watching a very satisfying fight on the television show *Hill Street Blues* in which a frozen fish was used to subdue a perpetrator.

How to Choose Found Weapons

It is always important to keep in mind that found weapons must satisfy two basic principles:

1. They must be organic to the action, situation, character, and historical period.

2. They must be constructed in such a way as to be SAFE!

Accidents can happen when the prop is not thoroughly checked for safety by the fight director. If a prop is simply pulled from storage and used in a fight scene with no thought of what that prop must accomplish, you are inviting disaster!

Here are a few things to look for when checking found props.

1. There must be *no sharp edges*.

2. There must be structural integrity to the object. In other words, it must not break under the demands to be placed on it. For instance, all glass objects are out!

The above list is true for small as well as large props. I will often use furniture as something to fight with (or on!). It is important to check furniture for strength before using it, since prop tables and chairs are not always of the highest quality. I remember averting a serious fall in the Beth Henley play *Abundance* when an actor was supposed to lift an actress onto a table: the table in question was very weak and would have collapsed, spilling both of them to the floor, if I had not intervened in time.

Furniture that is fought on, or around, especially tables that are used to stand on or are flipped over, must always be reinforced. If they cannot be "beefed up" by adding bracing, they should be replaced. In a small or crowded set, I often use the convention of turning the furniture over or "flinging" it out of the way of the combatants to add space on the set: the extra room allows for increased safety; most accidents in modern plays are caused when performers accidentally run into or fall over the furniture on crowded sets.

Found Weapons in Historical Plays

Let your exploration of possible found props in period plays be as free as it would be in modern ones. What do the characters suggest? What does the set design make available to you?

If you decide in the opening scene of *Romeo and Juliet* that the servants are taking out the trash, bringing in firewood, and going to the local laundry, then buckets of garbage, firewood, and wicker baskets full of sheets and underwear might insinuate themselves into your opening brawl. If, on the other hand, the opening moments are staged in a somber funeral procession that is interrupted by Sampson and Gregory, then funeral flags and wreaths are possible props over which a fight may evolve (perhaps one of the flags is "torn" accidentally during the fight, fueling the fury). A third option might be an opening scene on "market day," with the fight placed among the stalls of the local vendors: in this case, clothing, baskets of fruit and bread, poles holding up cloth awnings, and indeed the awnings themselves might be used; perhaps a wheeled cart could add a nice "random" element to the fight as well.

Found weapons form the detritus of battle, and can help inspire choreography. In this sequence, Clifford (John Wodja) uses a tire and a can of gasoline to torture Rutland (Heath Patellis) in Barry Kyle's production of Henry VI.

Figure 2-34. 1. Clifford douses Rutland with gasoline (water) after pinioning his arms with a tire.

Figure 2-35. 2. Clifford kicks the helpless Rutland.

Figure 2-36. 3. Clifford ignites a lighter, about to complete the image of burning, before the lights black out on the scene.

Another moment to explore is the fight between Edgar and Oswald in *King Lear*. Oswald, probably armed to the teeth, finds what appears to be an easy kill in a blind old man and a madman. We know, however, that Edgar must win the fight, but what weapon can he use? I have often used a stout walking stick "borrowed" from Glouster.

In other words, as in the above examples, allow your imagination freedom to suggest prop, set, and furniture elements that will help to root the fight in the reality of the time. This will make your fights more interesting and truthful for your audience, and the audience will think you're terrifically creative! Allow your performers to experiment and improvise with found objects, and they'll often come up with vastly more interesting choices than you could have ever imagined on your own.

Group Fights and Mass Battles

Before we can consider how to stage a battle for the theater, it is worth taking some time to study what constitutes the experience of battle. Eisenhower, Napoléon, or medieval kings experienced battle in a vastly different

Figure 2-37. *The English army letting fly a cloud of imaginary arrows during the Agincourt sequence in* King Henry V. *These poles doubled as bows, spears, and swords during the battle. Photo by Gerry Goodstein. Theater for a New Audience.*

way from their fighting men. They are removed from the fight, controlling men and machines from a safe distance. Hunger, exposure, disease, and fear are the staples of the fighting man, from the front lines of Waterloo to the beaches of Normandy.

Let's take a specific example of a famous battle, Agincourt. Few commanders follow or in fact lead their men into battle. An exception to this is found in Shakespeare's play *King Henry V*, where we find the King wandering around the English camp the night before the battle of Agincourt, trying to get an idea of how his men were feeling. History tells us that after marching all day the English camped on a muddy cornfield in a rainstorm. The French were camped on a hill close by, and both armies could see each other. The night was October 24, 1415. In act 3, scene 6, through the Chorus, Shakespeare gives us a wonderful poetic vision of the mood in the camp and of the sounds piercing the rain.

Now entertain conjecture of a time
When creeping murmur and the poring dark
Fills the wide vessel of the universe.
From camp to camp, through the foul womb of night,
The hum of either army stilly sounds,
That the fix'd sentinels almost receive
The secret whispers of each other's watch:
Fire answers fire, and through their paly flames
Each battle sees the other's umber'd face:
Steed threatens steed, in high and boastful neighs
Piercing the night's dull ear; and from the tents
The armorers, accomplishing the knights,
With busy hammers closing rivets up,
Give dreadful note of preparation:
The country cocks do crow, the clocks do toll
The third hour of drowsy morning name.

The English, with approximately six thousand men, knew themselves to be vastly outnumbered. The fresh and newly supplied French numbered more than twenty thousand. How must the English soldiers have felt around their fires that night, faced as they were with almost certain death? Shakespeare paints a picture of contrasts between the two armies.

Proud of their numbers and secure in soul,
The confident and over-lusty French
Do the low-rated English play at dice,
And chide the cripple tardy-gated night
Who, like a foul and ugly witch, doth limp
So tediously away. The poor condemned English,
Like sacrifices, by their watchful fires
Sit patiently, and inly ruminate
The morning's danger, and their gesture sad
Investing lank-lean cheeks and war-worn coats
Presenteth them unto the gazing moon
So many horrid ghosts.

Finally, it becomes clear that Shakespeare's King Henry V has the common touch, for he walks among his men, giving them hope, heart, and something to fight for.

> O, now, who will behold
> The royal captain of this ruin'd band
> Walking from watch to watch, from tent to tent,
> Let him cry, Praise and glory on his head!
> For forth he goes and visits all his host;
> Bids them good-morrow with a modest smile,
> And calls them brothers, friends and countrymen.
> Upon his royal face there is no note
> How dread an army hath enrounded him;
> Nor doth he dedicate one jot of color
> Unto the weary and all-watched night;
> But freshly looks and over-bears attaint
> With cheerful semblance and sweet majesty;
> That every wretch, pining and pale before,
> Beholding him, plucks comfort from his looks:
> A largess universal like the sun
> His liberal eye doth give to every one,
> Thawing cold fear, that, mean and gentle all,
> Behold, as may unworthiness define,
> A little touch of Harry in the night.

How bleak the dawn of October 25, 1415, for Henry's army, with nothing but the prospect of being ridden down by the cream of the French aristocrats, who were mounted on fresh war horses, their armor glistening in the autumn sun. History tells us that the battle didn't start until eleven o'clock in the morning, but I'd bet that few had slept the night before or had taken the time to eat. Beyond hunger and sleep deprivation, many of the English were also suffering from dysentery, and I'm sure that not a few of them were bolstered by strong drink: hardly an idealized chivalraic image, but probably a realistic one.

After the English finally advanced into position and Henry's archers planted their stakes in the soft ground and the French began their first charge, the end of the battle took only three hours. In that time, seven thousand French combatants were killed by English arrows, axes, and broadswords, with some soldiers being crushed to death in the mêlée. Stories tell of men in the thickest part of the fighting who had to climb mounds of dead bodies five feet tall in order to swing their weapons freely. English losses were (at odds with Shakespeare who numbers them at twenty-nine) reported to have been sixteen hundred.

Nothing can prepare us for what must have been the experience of the men in that battle. Try to imagine yourself in the thick of the fighting, dripping with rain and sweat, slipping in the mud. All around you is utter chaos: arrows flying, men and horses screaming. Smoke from cannon fire obscures your vision, which is restricted to a few feet around you: the more so if you are wearing a helmet, looking out through a small slit in the steel. You would have no idea of the battle as a whole, or of who was winning or losing; you would know only of the events around you. You would have to watch your footing, since wounded men and horses thrashed about on the ground as they fell. Tripping and falling meant being trampled by the crowd, and you were being pushed and pulled within a mass of bodies, unable to turn and flee. If you were lucky, you could stay with a group of fighters who could protect each other's back and side. Often, though, you wouldn't even be able to swing your sword, since the press of bodies from all sides would be too great. Adrenaline coursing, you would do your best just to stay alive.

Personal survival was the moment-to-moment reality. The sheer physical labor of fighting in any battle—be it with swords and armor or with rifles and bayonets—is exhausting. Nor can we possibly hope ever to theatrically recreate the horror, smell, and random quality of a pitched battle. Yet that is a fight director's job!

Group fights, or brawls, battles, alarums and excursions, or any fight scene that involves more than two combatants, have unique staging problems. Shakespeare's history plays, Rostand's *Cyrano de Bergerac*, Dumas's *The Three Musketeers*, and most outdoor dramas have large multicharacter fight scenes. These scenes must give the impression of masses of armies fighting, skirmishing, giving and taking ground, within the limited confines of a stage. I use the word *impression*, because it is impossible to completely recreate a battle on the narrow confines of the stage, but it is possible to give an impression of chaos, movement, and the confusion of battle.

The most obvious problems when staging mass battle scenes are NUMBERS, SPACE, and TIME. How can you manipulate all the performers to give the

Figure 2-38. *A fifteenth-century knight fending off an attack. In a battle, personal survival was a moment-to-moment reality.*

Figure 2-39. Can you find all the mistakes in this battle scene? Combatants should be given plenty of room to fight each other, so they don't endanger other performers around them.

audience a satisfying experience of a battle? The problem of space is not just how to fill it, but rather how to fill it with sound, energy, and the sense of a real battle. Finally, rehearsal time is at a premium at any level of production, and how can you best prepare for your battle scene so as to maximize your time?

The fight director must pay careful attention to each encounter within the battle and decide whether it is a primary fight (main characters), featured fight (excellent fighters or other secondary characters), or background fight (extras, soldiers, etc.). The way these types of fights fit together is a vital safety problem, as well as a creative one.

> For safety, use chalk marks on the rehearsal floor to keep fighters in their own space and away from other weapons! Transfer the marks to the stage the first time the actors rehearse on the set.
>
> *Tip!*

The most common injury in group fights occurs when one performer strikes another whom he can't see. Individual fights must be carefully placed into the space, AND REMAIN THERE. Therefore, battles must be rehearsed very carefully at slow speed to make sure that all the pieces fit together and that no performer is in jeopardy of losing a finger or an eye from another's negligence. I regularly ask the performers if they feel that they are in danger of being hit by another performer, since I cannot see each fighter's every move.

> Rehearse the floor plan of the whole battle sequence with all of the actors many times *without weapons of any kind*. Adjust the blocking to achieve the effect you want. Familiarize the performers with their entrances and exits, partners, and movement patterns before adding choreography!
>
> *Tip!*

It takes an enormous amount of time to choreograph an extremely complicated battle scene, with multiple switching of ground, interlaced fights, changing of partners, group charges, and so forth. Therefore, when time is a problem, I suggest that the battle scene, or brawl, be kept simple. Rely on running charges offstage and on group movement rather than lots of individual fights. Keep actual engagements for the main characters or for those performers who can handle combat scenes (such as SAFD trained actor/combatants), and have the extras and soldiers running through, or framing, a fight.

A lot of "sound and fury" can be created with smoke, flag bearers, and groups of men who are carrying wounded comrades, or by marching with drum and colors across the stage, and any other "creative" use of performers and stage business to suggest the field of battle. Don't forget to add sound effects, lighting effects, and even fog to fill the space.

The Battle Story

The most important thing to help keep all performers attuned to each other in a battle scene is the BATTLE STORY. Research the accounts of actual battles before writing your own, especially if you are recreating a known event, such as the Battle of Agincourt, Hastings, or the Alamo. The battle story must be a clear, step-by-step scenario drafted by the fight director, and approved by the director, that tells the story of the fight. For instance:

> The Spanish charge the French line, from upstage center, led by a flag carrier. The flag carrier is shot as he stands high upon the ramparts, waving his flag, and he falls back into the arms of his comrades, dropping the flag out of sight. Enraged, the Spanish begin to pour over the ramparts, and individual sword fights break out along the line. The French discharge a round of gunfire into the enemy from a secondary line of musketeers. Many of the Spanish fall, some bodies landing across the ramparts, some falling backward out of sight. Two of the French are dead, one wounded. Their bodies are dragged away from the ramparts and attended by a doctor, while the French re-man the ramparts, joined by the musketeers, who discharge a second volley of gunfire (offstage) at the fleeing Spanish.

This is an example of a very simple battle story that each performer can understand. It is important that each performer understand his (or her) place in the overall scheme of the battle scene. This will help the cast work as a team and will keep them all aware of the scene as a whole and their place in it. Accidents often happen when performers do not understand the whole picture and are just out on the stage fighting furiously.

Choreography Tip!

Categorize the characters who will fight. I use a *three-step system*:

Primary Fight

This is a fight that involves the main, or title, characters, or any character with dialogue. This type of fight must move the plot along and must be placed on the stage advantageously. This fight must also be the center of focus during the battle, though not necessarily centerstage. These fights should be choreographed carefully to feature these performers and to help tell the story of the play as a whole. (Examples are Edmund and Edgar, Mercutio and Tybalt, Hal and Hotspur, Macbeth and Macduff)

Featured Fight

These are fights involving secondary characters, or performers capable of performing involved choreography safely. As a preliminary fight, it is sometimes helpful to match an experienced combatant who is playing a supporting role (or even a nonspeaking role), with a star, or primary character. This can help "set up" the primary character as a great warrior! For example, the character of Macbeth might kill one or two soldiers prior to meeting up with Young Siward. This type of fight can happen in the "thick" of battle, with many characters fighting on stage at once, or during a "cross over," with characters entering and exiting toward or away from the main battle scene.

Background Fight

This type of fight is designed to support the two main fights listed above. Choreographically, the background fight should be the simplest of the three. Moves that repeat themselves, simple grappling, stage picture, and rhythm are all important. Since these performers will probably be less experienced with weapons, I try to keep the fights easy, with perhaps a switch of terrain, to keep the audience's eye from catching on. In films, these performers have plastic weapons so that they don't hurt each other!

Once the battle story is agreed on by the staff, and the number of performers made to jive with the number of weapons and costumes, the fight director can begin to lay on the choreography. Often, some actors are recycled within the same battle to play different parts. For instance, if an actor playing a Spanish soldier in the Cyrano battle is "killed" early in the action and staggers offstage, he may cross around and reenter, potentially in a different costume at a later point in the battle. The audience is rarely aware of this kind of simple doubling, and it makes the army look bigger!

There are other staging ideas. Most battle scenes revolve around a few standard elements. What follows is a brief description of each element.

Traditional. The stage is filled with bodies that are fighting, heaving, and running to and fro. Principal fights emerge from the chaos and disappear within it. Lights and sound play a vital part in creating the tension. The movement is realistic/ naturalistic.

Stylized. This element consists of nonrealistic movement and scenic elements: slow motion, mime, dance elements, ensemble movement, stop action, surrealism, fantasy. An example would be a battle on top of a huge map of England that envelopes the armies.

Chaotic. With this element, the eye doesn't know where to look, and armies blend together. There are random, confused images. Often an element of chaos is followed by a period of clean fighting.

Battle line. One army holds a position onstage (an imaginary line, square, circle, or scenic element such as a wall, rampart, or barricade) against attack and continues to face in that direction during the fight. Individual fights may break through. The wounded are carried behind the line.

Ritual. A ritual battle is observed by others—that is, by kings, queens, generals, judges, or clergy who decide, or observe, the winner. Often there is a formality to the staging—for example, flag bearers containing the battle, a pool of light defining a battle area, where champions fight to decide the fate of armies.

Often a battle will have elements of several of the above within it. Additionally, within these staging concepts are types of military events typical to battles from any time in history:

Sortie. A small group leaving a protected area to take the fight to the enemy. The ensuing fight may happen offstage or onstage, and the group may or may not return.

Retreat. A removal under pressure of a body of individuals from a battle area. Retreats may begin offstage and come storming onstage. Retreats may halt onstage and then continue offstage. A battle line may dissolve under pressure and retreat offstage leaving the other army holding the area.

Charge. A full-scale attack of all forces toward the enemy. A charge may go offstage or may come onstage and attack a group holding the area.

Stand. As in "Custer's Last Stand," a group in tight formation trying to hold against attack from all sides. Often a major character is hemmed in with a few supporters.

March. Troop movement from one place to another. Remember that troops will look fresher and cleaner at the beginning of a play than at the end. Don't forget that characters would bring personal belongings and military equipment on the march.

Reconnaissance. A survey of terrain by one or more members of an army to determine the enemy's position. Remember, the closer the enemy, the sneakier the team must be.

Ambush. A military maneuver designed to surprise the enemy from a concealed position. The murderers in *Macbeth* ambush Banquo and Fleance. (Shakespeare refers to an ambush as an "ambuscado.")

Large numbers of performers present the possibility of staging a large stunt. For example, high falls into the arms of a group of "catchers," falling debris, rope swings over the heads of other performers, and throwing of furniture such as tables and chairs—all are exciting visuals but dangerous to the group as a whole. Careful planning and consistency is the only way to minimize risks. Plenty of rehearsal time is also vital whenever an unusual "stunt" is called for in a battle.

Paramount to the safety of the performers (and the success of the fight scene) is not crowding the available space with too many bodies. In other words, "too many actors spoil the brawl." As far as safety is concerned, when too many performers are onstage at once, the risk is increased that someone will be accidentally hit by a fist or a blade. Keep sword fighters clear of "extras" who are crowding around, so that the swordsmen may fight with some abandon, and keep the swordsmen's energy focused on each other, not the crowd.

Once all of these elements of battle story, set design, casting, assigning of the primary, featured, and background fight is done—and perhaps the fight director has allowed the cast to move through the main elements without weapons—THEN choreography can begin. Rehearse each individual fight element carefully, but don't wait too long before putting all of the elements together. The performers must get used to each other and used to where they will be on the set. They must understand and plot out how they will get to their assigned places and how they will get off. If there are "dead" bodies, plan how they are "struck"; plans must also be made to avoid stepping on the bodies. Individual moves are often altered within fights to make the overall scene

Figure 2-40. *Removal of dead bodies from the battlefield is aided here by a low cart. This prevents bodies from being lifted and gains the image of Talbot and son joined physically in death.*

safer, the timing tighter, and the stage picture more effective. Rehearse slowly and build toward performance speed only when all elements are safe.

The payoff, of course, is that dramatic or comic battle scenes are one of the most theatrical events possible. A successful battle should sweep the members of the audience off their feet and plunge them into the action of the play. The scope of a full stage battle is forever memorable to those who have staged one, watched one, or participated in one.

> CHORUS: And so our scene must to the battle fly;
> Where, O for pity! we shall much disgrace
> With four or five most vile and ragged foils,
> Right ill-dispos'd in brawl ridiculous,
> The name of Agincourt.
>
> (Henry V, 3.6)

Fight Notation

Unlike Laban notation or musical notation, fight notation is not standardized. There are several techniques used today by fight directors and teachers, each one of them valid.

The question that must be answered first when considering fight notation is: "Who is to read this?" If your notation is only for yourself and is used to remember phrases and sequences, and perhaps to keep your creation private, then a short, handwritten type of notation is appropriate. Any combination of symbols, signs, and squiggles will work as long as you understand what you mean. It won't matter that others cannot decipher your written notation.

On the other hand, notation that is meant for performers to read when trying to learn or remember fight choreography must be more accessible. It must include descriptions of placement on the stage, special business, acting beats, as well as the blow-by-blow techniques employed in the fight itself. This kind of notation is usually a combination of written English descriptions along with simple numbering systems. Most sword-fight notation techniques use the standard parry-and-attack numbers recognized internationally, which are as follows:

Parry	Target	Hand Position
prime (1)	left leg	half pronation
seconde (2)	right leg	pronation
tierce (3)	right arm	pronation
quarte (4)	left arm, chest	supination
quinte (5)	right head, shoulder	half pronation
alternate (5a)	left head, shoulder	half supination
sixte (6)	right arm, chest	supination
septime (7)	left leg	supination
octave (8)	right leg	supination

Pronation means knuckles to the ceiling; *supination* means knuckles to the floor. Additionally, standard swordplay terminology is used to describe special techniques (such as *beat parry, croisé, prise de fer, ballestra lunge, punto reverso*, etc.) used in the fight in a way that will be understood by all who read it. Definitions of these terms are to be found in the appendix of this book.

Let us look at two of the most common forms of fight notation. These are the *side-to-side*, or *ladder*, method, and the *prose* method.

The side-to-side type of choreography notation divides a page of paper in half: one half represents one partner (A), and the other half represents the other (B). Arrows are used to indicate who the "aggressor," or "initiator," is at any moment. For instance:

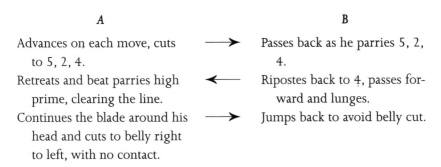

A		B
Advances on each move, cuts to 5, 2, 4.	→	Passes back as he parries 5, 2, 4.
Retreats and beat parries high prime, clearing the line.	←	Ripostes back to 4, passes forward and lunges.
Continues the blade around his head and cuts to belly right to left, with no contact.	→	Jumps back to avoid belly cut.

The advantage of this system is that you can see right away what the reaction is to any given move in the fight. You can also see the ebb and flow of the fight along the page. The choreography must only be careful to make the fight flow along the page and make the back-and-forth arrows clear for the reader.

The other form of notation is the "prose" technique, which is more laborious, but more detailed. This technique requires that the choreographer notate in prose (rather than shorthand) the details of the fight downward on the paper rather than across. The fight is arranged in phrases as in the *side-to-side* method, and the reactions to a set of moves follows immediately down the page. The following is an example in *prose* style of the same choreography as written above.

A   Advances toward B, with one advance per cut, he cuts to 5, 2, 4.

B   Passes back right, left, right; parries 5, 2, 4; but ripostes back immediately to A's 4 with a lunge on the right leg.

A   Retreats strongly and manages to beat parry B's blade with a high parry of prime, which he turns into a right-to-left belly swipe toward B, advancing strongly.

B   Caught, he recovers the lunge and jumps back to avoid swipe.

In both styles of notation, the important element is clarity and detail. Elements of the set, details of footwork, masking, body relationships, and who is initiating the action are all important to the notated choreography.

As an exercise in notation, if one is new to it, one should practice notating a simple, everyday action, and then have someone repeat it by using your notation. It isn't as easy as it sounds!

Try notating these everyday actions:

Picking and peeling an apple, then feeding it to someone

Dressing a four-year-old

Moments leading up to a "first kiss"

Brushing your teeth

Finally, good notation will reflect the whole fight and be a useful tool for the performers, stage management, and the fight director in putting together and maintaining a fight. It is also useful if you ever want to re-create your work in later years or copyright it.

Battle Notation

Trying to keep track of all the elements in a battle can be difficult at best. To notate the moves in a battle, I use two methods simultaneously.

The first technique allows me to plan the ebb and flow of large groups of people within the set. Using photocopies of the set plan, I mark major movements with different colored pens. For instance, in phase one of an imaginary battle, the main French army group sweeps onstage from up right, stopping down left center. The French are attacked by the main English group entering from offstage, which splits into two groups, one forming center and a smaller group forming left.

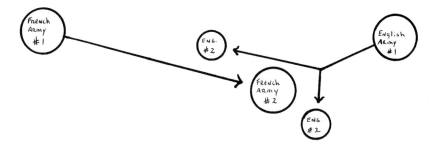

Phase two of the battle finds the French group thinning out centerstage (French #3). The English group upstage sweeps toward stage right (English #3) so that the French must fight on two sides, facing stage left and right.

Phase three of the battle shows the French group splitting in two upstage of the English (French #4) and encircling both English groups, which are forced together in the middle (English #4).

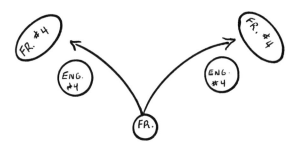

Finally, the French succeed in encircling the English group and in making them kneel and surrender centerstage. (French position #5 and English position #5).

These very simple diagrams are only a basic floor pattern upon which to base fight choreography. They don't take into account individual moments and images that identify and feature group leaders such as generals, princes, or kings. Usually group movements are led by one of these characters, helping us to follow the story visually. Often a flag or standard bearer is positioned near these characters to help identify them.

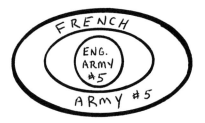

This simple mapping technique will help a fight director to create the sweeping movement of large groups on a set. It may also help acquire a large blueprint of the set from the designer and to work with "little men"—bottle caps or toy soldiers—to represent the armies. In this way a fight director can be even more specific about where the lead characters are and can keep track of large numbers of individuals.

Finally, if a fight director wishes to notate individual cuts and parries during a battle, here is the simplest way. This should help the fight director keep track of who is fighting whom and when other fights start and stop in relation to those around them.

Let's use as an example a few moves from an imaginary production of *Othello*. In this scene, we have the main characters Cassio, Iago, Montano, and Rodrigo, as well as two Italian soldiers and one Cypriot soldier, for a total of seven.

The first thing to do is to create a notation page that strings all the characters along the top and to draw lines down to the bottom as in the example below.

Now one can begin to layer in the choreography move by move and keep track of everyone. It will help to have a set sketch close by to refer to. If one studies the example below, one will see a lot of simultaneous action. One will also notice when certain characters hold, or wait, or throw focus to specific actions within the fight. Lines are drawn horizontally to indicate major beat changes and are drawn vertically to separate characters.

Cassio	*Rodrigo*	*Montano*	*Iago*	Italian *Soldier 1*	Italian *Soldier 2*	Cypriot *Soldier 1*
Enters from left and swipes at Rodrigo.	Enters, sees Cassio, avoids swipe, runs up center.	Stops Cassio near door after swipe.	Waits.	Reacts and moves down center.	Grabs and holds Rodrigo up center.	Holds stage right.
Elbows Montano in stomach.	Struggles.	Reacts and drops to floor, hurt.	Waits.	Holds; throws focus to Montano.	Restrains Rodrigo by the arms.	Holds.

(Continues)

(Continued)

Cassio	Rodrigo	Montano	Iago	Italian Soldier 1	Italian Soldier 2	Cypriot Soldier 1
Runs up toward Rodrigo.	Breaks away; hides behind Italian Soldier 2.	Holds on floor.	Moves toward Cassio as if to stop him.	Holds.	Releases Rodrigo; turns to face Cassio.	Goes to Montano, running down-stage of action.
Pushes Iago away toward stage right.	Holds.	Holds and throws focus to Cassio.	Stumbles stage right.	Holds.	Advances a step toward Cassio.	Lifts Montano to sitting position.
Swipes sword at Italian Soldier 2.	Runs down right.	Rises with help.	Pushes Rodrigo as he goes by.	Runs offstage left, yelling.	Avoids swipe and falls on back.	Helps Montano to stand.

As one can see by the above example, a lot happens in a short amount of time. This method does help one figure out who is fighting, when action overlaps, and who is waiting. One can make the notation paper as large as necessary. For large fights, I often have to tape several pieces of paper together to have enough room to write everything.

Copyright Laws for Choreography

According to the copyright laws, fight choreography, like dance choreography, becomes the property of the creator the moment it is created. In other words, even though a fight director might be paid to create fight scenes for a particular production, the producers are only paying the fight director to "rent" his or her fights for the duration of the original run of the play. They do not own the fights—the fight director does—unless there is an extra fee and a clause in the fight director's contract stating differently.

Notation and videotaping of fights is a valid method of recording the chore-ography for copyright purposes. In commercial productions of plays (i.e., *not* nonprofit or educational theater), a fight director may wish to lease his or her fights and receive a royalty based on the weekly receipts of the production— much as the set, light, and sound designers are doing.

Remember, without the fight director's approval no one should be given the right to change the fight director's choreography once it is set past open-ing night. By the same token, a theater may not legally re-create a fight direc-tor's choreography in a later production without compensation, since it would be an infringement of the copyright laws.

As one can see by now, fight directing is a complicated process. Many fight directors like to use an assistant to help them keep track of all the details, keep an eye on the performers in rehearsal and performance, take notes, and help with the myriad details. This invaluable person is called a *fight captain*.

I have worked with several wonderful fight captains over the years, and they really earn their money! Though the extra pay isn't much, the wealth of hands-on experience is unmatchable anywhere else. Where else can you get exper-ience in the professional theater, under pressure, with a certain amount of responsibility, while working with professionals? I recommend that the fight captain be a part of any production with fights.

The Fight Captain

All productions need to have a fight captain. The fight captain helps the fight director during rehearsals; and when the fight director is not present, the fight captain is in charge. The fight captain is a person chosen by the fight director in consultation with the director and stage management. The fight captain is someone who, by experience and training, is qualified to run fight calls, rehearse understudies, oversee weapon maintenance, and generally keep the fights up to speed and safe through the run of the show.

The fight captain is often one of the performers in the play, but could also be someone in stage management. The duties of the fight captain often start well before rehearsals, and might include the following:

➢ Working with the fight director to research the play and his-torical period

> ➤ Attending all production meetings and design meetings

> ➤ Working with the fight director to help create the fights

> ➤ Notating choreography and learning principal choreography

> ➤ Partnering performers during teaching sessions

> ➤ Interfacing with production staff about needs and changes on a daily basis

> ➤ Attending all fight rehearsals with principals and understudies

> ➤ Checking and overseeing the maintenance of all fight props and weapons on a daily basis

> ➤ Preparing for fight rehearsals by bringing props, cleaning rehearsal areas, leading warm-ups, and typing handouts

The fight captain must be chosen with an eye to safety; but it is equally important that he or she have the ability to deal with people and communicate well. Ideally, this will be a person who has some stage-combat training and experience in previous fight shows and who is a problem solver. Someone who is interested in grandstanding, or power plays, is never the right choice for fight captain. He or she must be someone who the entire company can respect and listen to.

Fight calls before the show are the fight captain's major responsibility after opening night. This call should be started several days before the first performance, however, to accustom the staff and the performers to it. The stage must be lit and clear and the props ready for the fight call, which usually takes place at least fifteen minutes before the half hour call.

The actors then go through the fights in a prearranged order set by the fight director. A common practice is to rehearse a fight sequence once at half speed and again at performance tempo. This gives the performers an opportunity to warm up, remember the fight and to adjust small problems. Big problems must be addressed in a separate rehearsal, when more time is available. The fight call is no place to attempt to insert understudies, and a separate call should always be scheduled.

Any changes to the choreography, any problems or safety issues that come up, unless it is an emergency, should be cleared through the fight director either on the phone or in person. Otherwise, it is the fight captain's judgment that rules the day. Often the fight captain is performing in one or more of the fights in the production. In this case, the production stage manager also watches the fight call, to check for any safety problems or inconsistencies (actor improvements) within the choreography.

It is not a bad idea to hire someone for this position during the casting process, since it will make for a tighter production and will not be left to chance.

Learning to be a good fight captain is a wonderful way to learn more about the performance or the staging of fight choreography. Fight directors are always looking for competent fight captains to use in productions all over the country. It is an important step toward becoming a professional fight director.

Below is a fight call list I generated for a production of *The Three Musketeers* at the Connecticut Repertory Theater. This list was handed out to the fight captain and stage management team. It was also posted in the dressing rooms and backstage left and right.

Note that the call starts small, with a two-person fight, building to larger fights as the fight call progresses. Because of the large number of fights in *The Three Musketeers*, this call took a full hour. Stage management and stage hands were always on call to change and move furniture, set and strike a large "island," and fly in a "grill" piece. These simple set changes are also noted on the call sheet to simplify running the fight call.

The Three Musketeers, 1995
Fight Call

1. Calais	Island preset at top for Calais
Mark, Mingo	swords, cape, knife, eyepatch
2. D'Art-Milady	Chaise longue, knives, knife
Mark, Carrie	trick, **Island reset to interior**
3. D'Art-Constance	table, pot, blanket
Mark, Nicole	**Strike Island**
4. D'Art, Const., Antoine	(downstage of Island)
Mark, Nicole, Chris	
5. Milady, Buckingham, Felton	knife
Carrie, Steve, Bill	

6. Bethune
    D'Art., 3 Musk's., Const.,
    Rochf., Jussac, Bicarat,
    Aaron, Rob
	swords, knife,
	Add Grill

7. D'Art, Jussac, Bicarat Ballroom, end Act 1	swords, diamond tags **Strike Grill**
8. Meung D'Art, Rochf., Jussac, Bicarat	table, swords, black club

9. Convent
    All 4 Musketeers, All
    Cardinal's Guards
	Add Wire
	3 stage left sheets, weapons,
	pad in pit
	Strike Wire

10. Journey #1
     Porthos, Rob, Chris,
     Christian, Kelly
	table, ax, knives, swords, letter

Journey #2
     Bill, Eric, Jimmy, Ian,
     Mark, Oliver, Steve
	barricade, shovel, hook, gun

Journey #3
     Ian, Mark, Oliver, Chris,
     Christian, Rob
	table, tray, knife, swords

11. Huguenot Battle All	**Island Down, Revolve** weapons, flag

12. Bonacieux Kidnapping
     Mark, Nicole, Moe, Aaron,
     Jason
	swords, table

13. 2 Musketeers Bill, Oliver	swords

fin

Comedy Fights

I love staging comedy fights almost more than staging dramatic ones. Why? Freedom! In comedy I have the freedom to choose unconventional props, use extreme movement styles, and highlight fights with funny sounds!

Comedy fights have their own logic, just like dramatic fights. The characters in *The Comedy of Errors* are no less serious about their situation than the characters in *'Tis Pity She's a Whore*. However, Antipholus and Dromio live in a different reality.

Comedic logic has much in common with dramatic logic. There is situation, conflict, and real fear. There are actions and consequences. However, in comedy the characters are able to drop the fear and, more important, the *pain* of a fight after it is over, and can quickly move the plot along to the next event. Think about it. Beaten servants don't really bleed, and they cry only to invoke sympathy. The Three Stooges inflict horrible violence on each other, but the consequences are quickly dropped. There may be incredible pain in the moment, but in the wink of an eye it is gone!

Comedy fights are able to break the rules of realistic fights by mocking them and by setting them up for us to laugh at. Witness the mock duel between Viola and Aguecheek in *Twelfth Night*. Shakespeare spoofs the duels of his day to the letter, complete with all the details of challenge, seconds egging the duelists on, books on fencing rules, and a pair of trembling combatants who must fight for form's sake. In real life pompous and abusive masters beat their servants black and blue, but in comedy the servant can beat the master, exposing him for the coward that he is. Comedy fights have no complicated subtext or hidden meanings. They work because we recognize human stereotypes.

Timing

SAL: What's the most important thing . . .
SOL: Timing!
SAL: . . . about comedy?

That old joke is true! Comedy fights are harder to perform than dramatic ones because they must have incredible pace *and* appear effortless. Routines that are slow enough for the audience to catch on to will never get a laugh. Physical bits that are cumbersome or heavy in any way belie the pace at which these characters live their lives.

One of the accepted rules of comedy is that comic bits and comic fights work on the rule of "three." Three is funnier than two, or four, or any even number. I refer to the individual *counts* of a physical gag, for example:

1. Harlequin loads a pistol.

2. He points it at Smereldina, who quakes.

3. He pulls the trigger, and a super ball rolls out of the barrel and bounces toward Smereldina.

The third count gives you the opportunity for the "payoff." The payoff will work if it is earned, and a three- or five-count setup usually works. The super-ball rolling out of the gun wouldn't work as well as count number one, since we don't have time to see it coming. The exception is when it is followed by a "topper," or larger third beat. For example, later in the play Harlequin aims again:

1. Harlequin pulls the trigger again, and a super ball rolls out of the barrel and bounces toward Smereldina.

2. Smereldina catches the ball and laughs at Harlequin. She tosses the ball offstage over her shoulder.

3. There is a tremendous explosion, flattening her. Harlequin looks at his gun in surprise.

Comedy fights, whether unarmed or with weapons of any kind, will work better when they are designed around a series of phrases with uneven beats, 3s or 5s.

Comic Devices

There are many standard comic devices that can work to help you create your comic fight. Most of these devices come from the earliest days of theater, back to the traditions of commedia dell'arte. Here is a breakdown of the most commonly used techniques that may be used in any combination.

Maximum-Minimum

Comedic reactions and attacks are almost never naturalistic or realistic. They will go overboard in one direction or the other, either too big or too small. Whereas a dramatic character might punch another character in the face, inflicting pain upon the victim, in comedy the victim can either (1) feel nothing or (2) experience so much pain that the play stops to allow for the reaction.

Attacks may be minimized so much that they are performed with one finger or a feather, inflicting great "pain." They may equally be performed with violent fury and enormous movement, such as a furious beating with a slap stick. Experiment with the maximum-minimum concept when you are designing your fight. It's fun to watch the characters struggle to effect an attack, for instance:

Dave	struggles with all his might to throw Bill to the ground. He lifts, grabs, and pushes to no avail.
Bill	holds his ground, aware but unconcerned.
Dave	gives up.
Bill	hooks one finger into Dave's shirt and flips him over.
Dave	performs a series of forward rolls, finally landing flat on his face.

Or take another example:

Viola	enters with an enormous broadsword, dragging it on the ground
Aguecheek	enters with a toothpick of a smallsword.

They come en guarde, Fabian helping Viola to lift her sword. Aguecheek's sword connects with Viola's bends almost in two, pressing against it, and then springs through to the other side. Viola's sword simultaneously drops down and hits Aguecheek in the foot.

This latter example takes the maximum-minimum concept into the props and juxtaposes an enormous sword against a tiny one, thus helping to create visual contrast. This type of visual contrast is one of the basics of comedy: witness the body types of three of the most successful comedy duos: Laurel and Hardy, Cramdon and Norton, Lucy and Ethel (Figure 2-41).

Repetition

Another standard timing bit in comedy is repetition. It's not enough to slap someone realistically. Try slapping someone three times—or ten times!—in rapid succession. A servant who is repeatedly beaten in a play might toward the end beat himself to save the master the trouble, repeating exactly the vocal and physical pattern of previous beatings.

Figure 2-41. *Comedic or serious? Visual contrasts are one key to successful comic fights.*

Repetition can be worked into an individual fight or phrase, taking advantage of rhythm, such as a repeated slap, kick, or ear pull, but can also be part of running gags throughout the play. The repetition of a particular move several times over the course of the evening sets the audience up to see the pattern broken. In other words, if in the play Patty slaps Peaches every time that Patty sees Peaches eating and Peaches says "Thank you," then it's a nice payoff when Peaches finally decks Patty with a punch in the nose in the final scene. The rhythm of repetition is important since the payoff is naturally set up for the audience to see.

Opposites

Using opposite reactions, attacks, and props is also standard comic fare. What are opposites? The following is an example:

> Duke [fighting twins Zeke and Deke] punches Deke in the face.
>
> Zeke reacts.
>
> Duke stomps on Zeke's foot.
>
> Deke reacts.
>
> Duke shrugs and punches them both.
>
> Both react and fall.

The following are two more examples:

> Ron preps his arm to give a vicious punch.
>
> Jim knaps, reacts, and falls before the punch is thrown.
>
> Ron looks at his hand and looks at Jim.

or

> Ron preps and throws a vicious punch.
>
> Jim reacts mildly.
>
> Ron reacts intensely to his hand hurting.

Opposites work because they hold open the element of surprise and can help create visual variety. A sword that is held backward; a gun that shoots, ricochets, and hits the person shooting; and a punch that misses the bad guy and hits the sheriff are all examples of visual opposites. Even reacting in the wrong (opposite) direction to a slap can work to great effect in comedy situations.

Takes

Successful comedians are masters at comic takes, or reactions. A fight director should work through the fight in rehearsals and exaggerate the reactions and takes, especially for the "victim": for example, early take, late take, and slow burn.

In our example above with Ron and Jim, building in a late take might look like this:

> Ron viciously punches Jim in the face.
>
> Jim knaps and turns to audience, but reacts no further.
>
> Ron walks away.
>
> Jim collapses to the floor after Ron exits.

Obviously takes can be minimized or maximized, as we discussed earlier, but can also be compounded with each other, as follows:

Late, maximum take

Early, maximum take

Late, minimum, opposite take

Slow, late, maximum take

Try these four takes as an exercise. React to a partner who is throwing a noncontact punch or slap.

Tip!

Sound Effects

Sound effects in a comic fight increase the audience's experience of the fight and lift the fight to a plane of reality where we are not concerned about the character's pain but can enjoy the situation as presented. Noises that support specific movement—such as hissing sounds when a hot iron is smashed on a hand, grinding noises when a nose is turned, cracking sounds when fingers are twisted, and similar nonrealistic and maximized effects—are part of almost every broad comic fight.

Actors' Voices

The performers themselves must have a part in creating the vocal "score" of the fight. Reacting vocally to pain, fear, and aggression is only a beginning. A fight director should explore vocal opposites, too, such as a big masculine character who reacts with a falsetto voice or a female who uses her lower register. I would venture to say that every comic fight needs support from performer vocalization. We want to hear the effect of the fight since it helps us empathize with the characters. It is important to layer in this vocal life early in rehearsals, so that it becomes integral to the timing of the fight itself.

Live and Taped Sound Effects

By far the most satisfying method of integrating sound effects into a comic fight is through a live performer. This might be one of the characters in the play or a professional musician integrated into the production concept. If the latter, then the entire orchestra of instruments can be available to you to help support your work. Bells, horns, drums, cymbals, kazoos, harmonicas, gongs, triangles, and recorders, not to mention crash boxes, crunch noises, squeaks, ratchets, "aaooogah" horns, and horses' hoof beats, are available just as they were in old radio dramas. Having a live performer to support a show is a wonderful experience for audience and performers alike.

Obviously, it is important to collaborate with this person as one directs and creates the fights in order to choose the most appropriate sound effects. One should experiment with different sounds and work with this person to achieve a consistent timing. If the production team decides to use such an artist, I suggest that the sooner the artist can be put into rehearsal the more successful this idea will be.

Taping sound effects can also be effective, and one has the advantage of multitrack recording. However, the drawback is that once the tape is set, the performers may never vary the performance by even a bit. It is very hard to anticipate the timing of a particular fight that will work for the entire run of a show and impossible for the actors to hold for laughs. A brilliant sound designer helps, as does a keen-eyed sound operator. New technology such as digital recording helps alleviate this problem, since it is much more responsive than reel-to-reel taped sound effects.

Comic Props

The imagination runs wild at the possibilities! Comedic props are allowed to stretch the envelope of realism and, because of our friend comedic logic, are allowed to exist in the world we create. Since we are talking about weapons

In this battle sequence from King Henry VI, Talbot (David Patrick Kelly) enters wearing stilts under his costume. I gave him a wooden sword five feet long to complete the image of a giant.

Figure 2-42. 1. Talbot makes his entrance in the battle.

here, and not props in general, let's be specific. What a fight director will want in a staged fight are props that are SAFE, VISUAL, and FUN!

First, it is important that the fight director choose props that will be safe to use through the run of the show. The fight director should examine them thoroughly and experiment with them to test their strength, add extra padding if needed to protect actors, and reinforce the props if they need to take repeated abuse. Don't take chances!

Figure 2-43. 2. *Talbot swipes his sword at a group of French soldiers who fall to the stage.*

Second, the fun of comic props is that you can let your imagination run free. The fight director should choose props that inspire and read well from the audience. What do I mean? How do you go about it? Let's use some of the principles discussed earlier in this chapter and apply them to prop selection.

Maximum	heavy swords, huge "boppers," giant firearms, huge explosions, enormous helmets
Minimum	an army of one, helium-filled floating stone boulders (built around balloons), sword blades of long feathers, one bullet that must be found and reused
Opposites	big guy with little sword, little gun with big explosion, limp sword that hangs to floor

What the fight director is looking for are visuals for the audience and props that will inspire the fight director and the performers to invent wonderful choreography. Surprise us! If a hanging noose is part of the scene, the fight director should consider the difficulty of a character's trying to hang himself with an elastic rope that will never tighten. The fight director should explore extremes of shape, size, and material, such as oversized props, wavy swords, and weapons made from materials like rubber or elastic that can be stretched in the fight. How about a Styrofoam® sword that is cut in half in the first stroke by the opponent?

The fight director should consider unusual weapons, or even broken ones. I remember a hilarious Viola-Augecheek fight in which Viola's sword was in pieces from first to last and in which she fought while trying to put her weapon back together.

Foam-rubber weapons, especially doubles of existing props, are an effective visual when backed up by sound effects. In other words, you can hit someone on the head with a foam-rubber hammer, but we must hear a "ding" to make it sell. Rubber food props, cleavers, axes, armor, and clubs all allow for some amount of contact on the victim. Care must be taken that blows are pulled, and land on major muscle groups and padded areas; but combined with sound-effect support, these types of props are wonderful!

Finally, the fight director shouldn't discount using realistic weapons in new and interesting ways. The fight director should involve us and find ways in which the characters can use the props realistically yet comically. How? Try staging a sword fight in which the swords never meet. Try staging a fistfight in which a third and uninterested person always receives the worst blows. Try staging a belt-beating scene where the belt never strikes the victim, but appears to, and where the attacker is convinced he's done a good job!

Comedic Logic

Most characters in comedy are driven by base motives such as greed, lust, and gluttony. Whether or not these emotions are hidden by layers of manners as in Molière's comedies or are on the surface as in commedia dell'arte, all are driven by desire!

The servant Truffaldino in *The Servant of Two Masters* lives in a world where he is beaten daily and is overwhelmed by his desire for the next meal. He will accept the beating and abuse he receives as payment for the journey to the dinner table. He is, however, the most intelligent character in the play. Comedy gives the world a new twist wherein the lowborn characters usually outwit the leaders in society. Doctors, priests, lawyers, bankers, and soldiers are usually portrayed as inept, while their sons and daughters make love and their servants abuse and manipulate them throughout the play.

Because of this reverse logic, violence in comedy can take on nonrealistic forms, and the audience will suspend its disbelief to follow along. Fight directors must take advantage of this "chopt logic," as Shakespeare says, and use it to their own advantage.

Where a dramatic character may hit once, a comic character might hit three times. While a realistic slap might occur in a David Mamet play, a nose grab, an ear pull, or a cheek squeeze might be more appropriate in Shakespeare's *The Taming of the Shrew*.

When creating comic fights, a fight director should keep in mind the above examples and shouldn't hesitate to throw in a surprise or two. The fight director should work extra hours to make comic fights appear to flow effortlessly and should explore extreme character movement with the performers. One should have fun, explore, and not forget that sage advice: *Louder, faster, funnier!*

Now, as to the specifics of the hardest type of comedy fight—the food fight—read on!

121

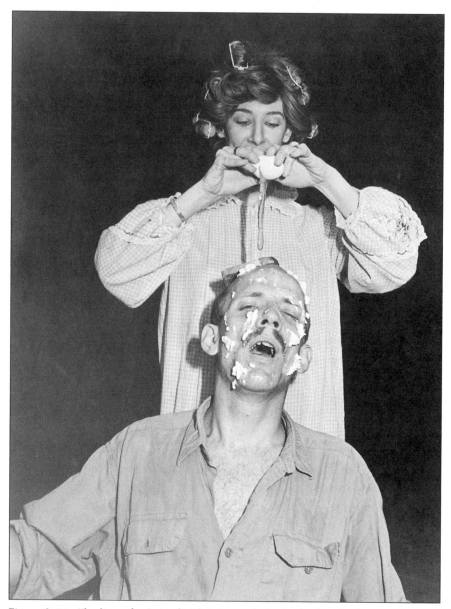

Figure 2-44. The climax of a glorious food fight between husband and wife in the play A Night at the Fights, with actress Nancy Sigworth.

Food Fights

Ah! the glories of a good old-fashioned food fight! The pie in the face! The squirting seltzer bottle! Fencing with sausages! Spitting cabbages on the end of a knife! Visions of the Three Stooges mix together with Tom Jones.

However, if one ever tries to stage a food fight, one will immediately run into lots of safety problems. Now, I grant that food fights are loads of fun and audience pleasers, but they have to be even more carefully thought out than regular fights. Why? Because food is slippery, slimy stuff and will trip up performers before you can say cream pie. If not properly cleaned up, the residue of a food fight can remain on the floor for the rest of the show, endangering the performers in later scenes.

The basic safety problem for food fights is the food itself or the containers holding it. It is also dangerous because food must be thrown at other performers, and that presumes a certain amount of control and accuracy! Sure, some of the food will miss, or be avoided, but some has to land on target or it just isn't fun! However, I have been handed (by the prop department) a cream pie made from whipped cream and contained in a glass Pyrex® dish!! In this case, the food was safe but the container was lethal.

Foremost in the mind of the prop department and the fight director should be, "What are the safest props available to get the job done?" Here is a list of some safe food props. They are, however, only safe within limits!

Safe Food Props

Vegetables

➢ Handfuls of beans/peas (cooked or raw)
➢ Heads of lettuce (leaf lettuce, not iceberg) (no dressing if salad!)
➢ Cut-up raw vegetables (broccoli, cauliflower, celery)
➢ Overcooked (limp) vegetables (as above, and at room temperature)
➢ Mashed potatoes (cold)

Breads

➤ Rolls (can be thrown at body when soft, but only when really soft!)

➤ French bread (long; best when stale)

➤ Round breads, muffins, cupcakes, sandwich bread

➤ Cakes (with or without icing)

Other Fun Food Props

➤ Spaghetti (cooked pasta with or without sauce—sauce can be ketchup)

➤ Squirt ketchup/mustard bottles (Beware of mustard in the eyes!)

➤ Fake salt and pepper shakers (replaced by black and white sand)

➤ "Hot" coffee/tea

➤ Eggs, broken first, and dropped on head or in crotch (never thrown!)

➤ "Soft" butter in plastic tubs (scooped in the hand and smeared on)

➤ Eggs, cooked sunny-side up or scrambled (can substitute dyed bread)

➤ Pizza (cold) (Note: don't forget to fight with the delivery box too!)

➤ Jell-O® (colorful; can mold into various forms, large and small)

➤ Cheese (wheels of *soft* cheese, i.e., brie, camembert, cream cheese)

➤ Ice cream (cones too!)

➤ Cream pies! (also custard, cottage cheese, Jell-O®, jam, jelly)

➤ Whipped cream in spray cans

Meat

➤ Sliced ham, bologna, salami, turkey, etc.

➤ Long hard salami (only to parry with, or to swing and miss!)

➤ Frozen turkey legs, mutton legs (similar reservation as above)

Fruit

➤ Bananas (can be peeled and squished onto someone, the peel then tossed to the floor to be slipped upon later)

➤ Watermelons (can be stabbed, karate-chopped in half, or hurled at someone; can miss and explode against the wall/floor)

Avoid such citrus fruits as lemons, oranges, grapefruits, etc. since they are harmful to the eyes, except in very controlled situations. Avoid apples, which are too hard; pineapples, which are too spikey; and pears, which are usually too hard.

Beverages

➤ Seltzer (can be sprayed from old-fashioned containers with nozzles or shaken up and squirted out of plastic one-quart/liter bottles)

➤ Coffee or tea in plastic cup (cold)

➤ Water in plastic bottles, plastic glasses, or bowls

➤ Beer or soda (shaken up; sprays all over when opened)
(Never use anything that is hot or acidic. Never use anything in a real glass container, like a wine bottle.)

Always be sure of your food props! When possible, build them out of other materials. Food props are perishable, smell bad, are a pain to store, and must be replaced after every performance, so they are an added expense to the production.

If possible, the fight director should arrange for the prop department to "create" a pizza with latex, paint, and cloth pepperoni. It will be as safe (if not safer), durable, and less expensive! If the pizza isn't slimy enough, just add a little ketchup at the last minute! The same is true for many of the above mentioned items, like the long salami, spaghetti (cut-up rubber bands glued together), the French bread, even the eggs fried sunny-side up! If one is careful, only a few very specific props will have to be real food. The rest can be fakes, though they must look real. Fake food is widely available in retail stores and novelty shops; and though most of it looks bad, it can be made to look much better with a little shading and shadowing by airbrush or by hand painting. I would much rather have to dodge a plastic tomato than a real, squishy one!

When the food fight has been choreographed, the fight director will need safe containers for the food props that will be used in the fight. Safe containers for food are listed below.

Bowls/Baskets

wood

plastic

metal

wicker, or straw

Glassware

breakaway glass

heavy plastic (never brittle)

paper cups

Styrofoam® cups

Plates/Platters

wood

plastic

metal (heavy aluminum foil)

cardboard, papier-mâché

paper

wicker

fiberglass

"Sugar glass"

Styrofoam®

clay (soft, unfired)

Cutlery

plastic knives, forks, spoons
   (available chromed)

plastic or rubber serving utensils

Pie Tins/Plates

paper (or papier-mâché)

aluminum

cardboard

pastry (commercial frozen
   crusts)

An Elaborate Food Fight

While most food fights are simple and of short duration, let us examine a big one. If the food fight takes place, say, at a wedding buffet, then one will need to create the illusion of an elaborate, professionally catered meal.

Long tables draped with washable tablecloths, bowls of fruit (plastic), carved watermelons, bread displays (some for fighting, some not), large fish on platters (rubber fish, metal platters, surrounded by lettuce and garnishes), bowls of pasta (lightly cooked spaghetti, tortellini, linguini in separate bowls), an ice sculpture (Plexiglas®), salads (tossed lettuce and vegetables, Jell-O® molds), cutlery and china (all plastic, or ceramic if you have a huge budget), glassware (plastic or breakaway glass), steaming bowls of soup, steaming pots of coffee (dry ice to create "steam"), pies (!), the wedding cake (!), and on and on to your creative heart's content.

If the tables are strong enough, one can even slide one of the guests down the length of one and into a punch bowl as a finale!

A Simple Food Fight over a Romantic Dinner

A very simple and convincing food fight can be created through common sense and the creative use of the above list of foodstuffs and containers. For instance, an argument between two lovers could erupt over a romantic Italian dinner, and the ammunition could include the following:

> spaghetti with meatballs (meatballs of sponge rubber)
>
> Italian bread (in a long wicker container)
>
> salad (chopped vegetables and lettuce in a plastic bowl)
>
> seltzer water
>
> salt and pepper shakers

And on a serving table nearby there could be

> blueberry pie (whipped cream in an aluminum pan, with a layer of blueberries mixed with blueberry jelly for color)
>
> "hot" coffee in a pot (to throw in someone's face)

127

The cutlery, water glasses, and ice cubes should be plastic, the table and chairs should be sturdy, and the wine should be in a plastic carafe. The lovers could even fight with the tablecloth after they have exhausted the foodstuffs, broken the plates, and trashed the set. The important thing is that their environment is safe!

Variety Shows

Food fights are often done in variety shows, or vaudeville nights. There are few legitimate plays that demand food fights in the course of the action. For any director planning to add one of these fights into a variety show evening, I would recommend placing the food fight at either an act break, right before an intermission, or at the very end of the show. This way, a crew can come on in the light and clean up thoroughly before the show continues. Food fights make an enormous mess; and if some precautions can be taken, such as laying down a tarp or old rug, cleanup will be a whole lot easier on the crew. When done outside, and where possible, I have even staged the cleanup as part of the fun. If the "crew" enters to break up the fight with water hoses and brooms, the fight can be drawn out, the mess cleaned up, and the place hosed down at the same time!

Commonsense Safety Rules

Some commonsense safety must prevail, too, when creating the fight. Even when using the so-called safe props, danger is created when the actors must perform beyond their ability, when the floor becomes too slippery, or when hard food props or containers come in contact with sensitive areas of the body.

For instance, a fight director shouldn't give an actor a large bowl full of stale, hard, bread rolls and instruct the actor to throw them at someone fifteen feet away. In the first place, the actor will have to throw them very hard to cover the distance; and in the second place, there is no telling where the rolls will land! No fight director should ask a performer to shove cooked spaghetti into another performer's face and put the spaghetti in a hard wooden platter! It will break the performer's nose!

Any food prop that will actually be thrown and make contact with a performer's body must be soft (spaghetti, soft rolls, ketchup, Jell-O®, cream pie), be in a soft container (paper, aluminum foil, pastry), or in no container at all, and must never hit anything other than a major muscle group (presuming a healthy performer, correct placement, and a "pulled" blow). Hard food props such as stale breads, cauliflower, and long salami should be used to flourish, attack and miss, hit things like furniture, or throw (and MISS!). I have even used French bread to "fence" with, for a comedic effect, and have "caught" a head of lettuce on the point of a dagger! (French bread needs to be reinforced with a wooden dowel run lengthwise up the thickest part of the bread.)

The important thing not to forget when getting elaborate, or even when staging a simple food fight over an intimate dinner, is that all—and I mean ALL—of the containers must be safe. That means *no glass anywhere!!* That includes plates, glasses, ashtrays, vases, bowls, pitchers, flower bowls, and so forth, and not only on serving tables but on nearby tables as well. The fight area should be kept completely glass free!

Fight directors or stage directors must be aware that as the fight progresses and escalates the floor surface will get progressively slippery. This is no joke. I staged a large food fight on board a cruise liner for a company of actors called Murder To Go, Inc. Though the performance had been carefully choreographed and carefully propped with safe food in safe containers, the performers slipped and slid so horribly on the plastic tarp laid down to protect the floor that the choreography was almost impossible to perform. Luckily, no one was injured.

So, fight directors should learn from my mistake and should keep food fights simple, without too much complex running around—and have some broad, slippery, gooey, slimy fun!

> I peseech you heartily, scurvy, lousy knave . . . to eat, look you, this leek!
>
> (Henry V, Fluellen: 5.1)

How to Work with Fight Directors

The job of fight directing is fairly new to the theater scene. When I first started directing fights in 1971, there were few professionals to look up to: Patrick Crean in Europe and Canada, Rod Colbin in New York, and certainly others of whom I was not aware—but only a handful. The standard process used to be that the local Olympic fencing coach would be brought in to stage sword fights, and a series of ex-Marines, policemen, and wrestlers brought in to stage fisticuffs.

Through the hard work of several groups in the U.S., England, and Canada, a new generation of professionals has emerged that takes the study and creativity of fight directing seriously. However, scant knowledge of how to work with these professionals is available, and I know of no masters program in directing that deals with the subject of collaborating with fight directors.

It is, however, vital that theater directors understand how to work with a fight director as a creative collaborator, much as they already work with light, set, and costume designers to create their vision on the stage. Perhaps a better name for the job would be fight designer, to fit neatly into the design team.

I have worked with directors who have spent a lifetime learning their craft and who can brilliantly discuss the fine points of lighting, architecture, period dress, and manners, but who are unschooled in the basics of physical conflict. And while it isn't necessary that directors understand every nuance of swordplay, a basic knowledge of period fencing, unarmed combat, and battles seems to me a basic tool of directing. For what we're talking about is the director's communicating the concept of his or her artistic vision to a fight director in terms that can be useful.

While it's true that I've had famous directors tell me that, "I see this fight as . . . well . . . blue!" or, "I don't care what they do, as long as they don't get hurt!" I would have appreciated more concrete clues. Because the fight director's work is interwoven within a larger production, it is important that the fight look like part of a whole, not something tacked on and separate from the rest of the story.

The following is some of the basic information a fight director needs to start work.

> ➤ A clear idea of time, place, and concept

> ➤ A set design and costume designs

> ➤ A rough idea of actor placement before the fight and after the fight (Example: Macduff enters up center, and Macbeth holds on the platform above him up center.)

> ➤ Where main action is to take place (Example: Mercutio's dead body is down left, around which Romeo and Tybalt fight.)

> ➤ A rough idea of the time allowed to create and rehearse fights

➤ The director's thoughts and feelings about how you see the style of the fights (realistic, bloody, surreal) and how you want the fight director to work with you (Examples: Attend all table sessions and present history of typical fights of the period. Explain to cast the probable length and style of the fights. Or have minimal interaction with the cast. Attend only rehearsals scheduled by stage management. Or do anything else you want.)

There are also many ways in which the fight director can interact with the production, and rehearsal time varies tremendously. The following are the three most common ways.

Method 1. All the Time

In an ideal situation, a fight director is on call for almost the entire preproduction and rehearsal periods. Fights will be blocked early in the rehearsal stages and kept up and improved incrementally throughout rehearsals until opening night. In this way, the director can see each improvement and can give direct input to the fight director daily for changes and suggestions.

Method 2. One Week Early, One Week Late

The fight director is hired early in rehearsals to block and create the fight sequences. One week (first or second) is usually sufficient time to do this. After the director's approval, the fight director leaves the rehearsals in the hands of a trained fight captain. The fights are then run, improved, and kept up over the next few weeks of rehearsal. The fight director is then usually brought back just before dress rehearsals to put the fight into the theater and to finalize the speed and such technical elements as lighting and sound. Constant communication among the fight director, the fight captain, stage management, and the director over the phone is vital.

Method 3. The Last Two Weeks

In this method the fight director is hired and given lots of time in the last two weeks before the play opens or previews.

This presumes that a great deal of work has already been done on character, lines, and general blocking by the director. The fight director needs only to quickly create and run sequences over and over before dress rehearsals. Obviously, extremely complicated sequences, experimental or ensemble work, or highly technical fights cannot be created safely in this way. The drawback here is that if the production is at all behind schedule and the director feels rushed or nervous about giving up time, it is the fights and the actor's safety that suffer.

It is clear that there are many other ways to use the talents of a competent fight director, but the above examples are the most common and allow for the most rehearsal time and artistic freedom. I have had as little as an hour and as much as twelve weeks to create fight sequences. My nightmare job was staging all the fights for *Julius Caesar* in six hours. Never again!

What isn't clear is how much rehearsal time fight sequences take to appear real, to be safe, and to have pace and truth for an audience. The director should always budget generously when planning rehearsal time to create fight scenes.

Remember that the director is the final word on what will eventually make it to the footlights. A director should never hesitate to question the logic or safety of particular sequences. The director must ask the fight director to explain anything that is unclear or awkward in fight scenes. In other words, the director should get involved in the creative process of the fight from first to last!

Finally, a tip for the director: Look for a fight director with a proven track record. Hire someone who shares your artistic sensibilities and vision and who is a good communicator. Look for someone with the company's interests at heart, not his or her own. Look for a team player, not a solo act.

While it's hard to hire a fight director based on résumé alone, here are a few additional tips that can aid in finding one.

Qualifications of Fight Directors

It is easy for anyone who has taken a weekend workshop in stage combat to say that he or she is a qualified fight director. Many teachers, students, directors, and professional performers have been exposed to stage combat

Figure 2-45. *A medieval knight astride his warhorse, wielding a battleax and shield.*

techniques. Perhaps they have taken a course at the university level, or perhaps they have attended a short workshop at a theater conference, such as the South Eastern Theater Conference in the United States. They may even have taken a three-week intensive program called The National Stage Combat Workshop, sponsored by the Society of American Fight Directors. However, it should be stressed that in all of these situations, the training is of the most basic nature and is designed primarily for performers as opposed to fight directors. It is not reasonable to expect that a person with minimal experience such as this would be a qualified fight director. One would not hire a dance choreographer who had only taken a few classes in ballet to stage dances for *Cabaret*. One would not hire a director to stage a Shakespeare play, when that person had only attended a weekend workshop in children's theater.

The only association in the United States that is testing and recognizing performers of stage combat, certifying teachers of stage combat, and professional fight masters (fight directors) is the Society of American Fight Directors (SAFD). This organization is a nonprofit corporation devoted to excellence in stage-combat techniques, education, and safety standards. It has rigorous testing procedures that applicants in all three categories must pass before being considered. The term *certified*, though, has caused some confusion in the industry; and in the interests of safety, this issue will be addressed here.

To be a *member* of the SAFD one must only pay the dues. This does not qualify someone as a fight director. To be "certified" or "recognized" only means that a person has passed one of three hurdles set by the SAFD as *minimum* standards in the industry. Let me quote from the official SAFD policy statement on membership (1992):

> **Recognized Actor Combatant:** An individual who has received basic training in at least three weapons forms, and passes a performance test with a minimum number of required moves. This recognition *expires* three years from the date of issue but is renewable through a retesting process. This does not qualify this individual to teach stage combat, or to arrange fight scenes. We recognize this person as a safe and competent performer.

> **Certified Teacher:** An individual who has extensive educational training, and has passed tests in the following areas: Actor Combatant Skills Test, teaching techniques, historical styles, first aid, weapons theory and practice, and theatrical choreography. We endorse these individuals to teach stage combat.

> **Certified Fight Master:** An individual who has completed all the requirements of an Actor Combatant and Certified Teacher. Beyond this, they must have an average of twelve years of professional experience, including a minimum of twenty Union productions, and must successfully pass an oral, written, and practical examination. We endorse this individual to teach, coach, and choreograph in professional theatre, film, T.V., and in the academic arena.

It is obvious that these requirements are quite stringent and that they need to be. Fight directing is truly a multidisciplinary art that requires a person to be at once qualified to create and then teach choreography in any historical period, given the restraints of rehearsal time, budget, and concept, *and* to understand weapons construction and purchase, first aid, and the blending of all scenic elements into a safe and effective fight.

I urge every stage manager, director, producer, and the heads of any theater or drama program or search committee who is reading this book to carefully check the credentials of anyone claiming to be a fight director. If this person is not affiliated with one of the groups listed below, then he or she should at least have training equivalent to the standards set by those groups. These groups are: the SAFD, the BASSC (British Academy of Stage and Screen Combat), the BADC (British Academy of Dramatic Combat), and FDC (Fight Directors Canada). The SBFD (Society of British Fight Directors) disbanded in 1996. (See Appendix for contact information.)

I hear stories yearly about unknown fight directors, or combat teachers, who wound, injure, and maim trusting performers or drama students. These stories include incidents of life-threatening injuries caused by overzealous and undertrained individuals working beyond their capacity. Please, in the interests of SAFETY, look deeper than a résumé and don't believe a surface recommendation from someone that "Oh, [so and so] played Tybalt once, so let's get him to stage our fights!"

Hire someone who is not only qualified technically but who has the performers' interests in mind. When in doubt, oversee the fight rehearsals! If there is a shadow of doubt about a fight director's methods or ability to communicate choreography, you'll know to look around for someone else.

How to Safely Rehearse Fights

I have witnessed this scene countless times. It is the first day of fight rehearsal. I arrive at the rehearsal studio, a bag of swords under my arm. I am met heartily by the actors and am introduced by the director. But before I can doff my jacket, nimble hands are in the sword bag, removing weapons of all types and swinging them in the air to see how they'll sound, oblivious to the people around them! Egads!

The above scene is common enough. In my years in theater and television, I have found one common thread concerning fight rehearsals: neither seasoned professionals nor rank amateurs have the slightest idea how to safely rehearse a fight scene; in short, everyone wants to "cut to the chase"!

Speed is the killer when setting, running, or polishing a fight. The *final* goal of a series of fight rehearsals should be "performance speed." The usual method, and the unsafe one, is that once the performers have memorized the basic moves, the outer shell of the fight, they then just go at it! Heave ho! Allez-oop! Caution to the wind, and let's sling some steel!

Allow me to mention that the above scene will be true in academic theater, professional theater, television, and film for all eternity. Why? Human nature. We love to jump into the fight scene fast because it makes us feel so good! Beat up the nasties and save the world—that's us. We also want to look good in front of our fellow actors and ripple a muscle or two! And if a black eye, a strawberry, or a chipped tooth gets in the way, so what?

This cavalier attitude aside, how *does* one approach rehearsing a fight? To start off, the bigger the brawl the longer the time it takes. However, one shouldn't neglect the "little scuffles." More actors are probably injured in "little scuffles" than in major combats, mainly because not enough attention is paid to those small scuffles.

> DIRECTOR: You're an actor, you work it out!
> Or
> DIRECTOR: You just try to get out the door, and these guys will hold you back!
> Or
> DIRECTOR: In this scene, Aldonza will get bounced around from Muleteer to Muleteer, until they finally throw her down and jump on her. Let's fake through it once, and see how it goes.
> PERFORMER(S): Okay!
> ME: This is where someone's gonna get hurt!

It takes some forethought to set up a decent fight rehearsal schedule and stick to it. Here are some tips on how to get through it safely.

1. **Hire a fight director.**

   No one is more experienced than a professional fight director. However, many theaters or institutions cannot afford one. In this case, assign *someone* to do it who has the time. The director usually doesn't. Find someone with experience, tact, and a good eye for detail. The less experience the fight director has, the less complicated the fights should be. Lower your expectations according to the résumé of the person in charge, and *be realistic*.

2. **Agree on the length and fight story before rehearsals.**
Don't waste time in rehearsals exploring with the performers or haggling with the director. Meet beforehand and work out problems. Each fight rehearsal must work toward a goal. Do your homework, and come to rehearsals prepared to maximize what little time there is. Work out the minutiae of each move of the fight for each character.

3. **Budget a realistic amount of time for fight rehearsals.**
If you are pressed for time, plan for short fights. Don't push the performers into complex combats, or someone will be hurt.

4. **Teach the fight in realistic sections.**
Teach the fight in phrases that your performers are capable of retaining. Don't give them a three-minute fight in a one-hour rehearsal and expect them to remember it. Go over the choreography phrase by phrase, and only run the whole fight when the phrases are mastered individually.

5. **Adjust the fight to fit the performers' skills.**
After spending time teaching the performers the choreography, there should be a period of adjustment. Now is the time to alter the fight moves or length of the fight to fit the performers. The difficulty level can safely move down, or even up, while performance is still a long way off.

6. **Alter the tempo of the fight during rehearsals.**
Slowing down the tempo of the fight during rehearsals is the safest choreographic technique I know. When working on phrases, or running the whole fight, slow the tempo down! I use these catchwords, which are common in the industry:

Tai chi: (a superslow motion technique). The partners try to keep eye contact and flow through the choreography smoothly. Centering and balance are very important. *Precision* in attacks and reactions, whether armed or unarmed, is stressed. Partnering and timing are the final elements. No emotion is allowed to interfere with the movement. Remind the partners to breathe as they work.

Quarter Speed: (one quarter of the final performance speed). The fight is now taken slightly away from an emotionless state, and the performers "mark" the moves more realistically. Difficult moves, such as kills and contact techniques, are safe at this speed. Group fights benefit greatly from this technique.

Half Speed: (half of final performance tempo). Fights may be rehearsed with some acting elements, such as full voice, but still at a reduced tempo. Precision is still the key. Balance, partnering, rhythm, masking, and control are still stressed. Half-speed fights tend to accelerate without the performer's knowledge. Care must be taken to keep a lid on a half-speed rehearsal. This tempo should only be attempted when *all* the performers are comfortable with the choreography, the props are set, the stage surface is clear, and the acting beats are understood by everyone. Half-speed fight tempo should be attained at least a few days before technical rehearsals.

Performance Speed: (the tempo goal of fight rehearsals). This is not, as some would believe, a tempo determined by "as fast as we can go!" Performance speed is a tempo dictated by the choreographer that tells the story, illuminates the characters, hides the tricks, excites the audience, and keeps one or two beats ahead of their critical eye, but above all keeps the performance safe. Performance speed should be attained only after several quarter- and half-speed rehearsals with all the elements of set, costumes, lights, props, and so forth. The performers must be thoroughly familiar with all the elements of the production, the fight choreography, and characterization. Some fight directors assert that performance tempo is really three-quarter tempo, with the added adrenaline kick that a performance gives.

7.   **Pick a fight captain.**
This person is always a company member who will stay with the production through the run, help train the performers, and keep the

fights "up to snuff" during the run. This person should maintain weapons and other fight props. This person should also be able to step into a fighting role if another performer leaves the show or is unable to perform. Pick someone who the company can respect. Pick someone who is experienced and trained. Pick someone with the company's, not his or her own, interests at heart.

8. **Prepare for rehearsals.**
    Prepare for the fight rehearsal by having a first-aid kit handy, just in case. Prepare the props, set, and special effects in advance. Encourage your performers, and help them build confidence. Have special equipment available, such as mats or pads. Assure yourself that the props (swords, guns, furniture) won't be a weak link in the safety chain. Listen to your performers when they complain of unsafe or uncomfortable choreography. Be flexible enough to change individual moves to make them more safe.

There are three separate phases that a fight goes through on its way to opening night. It is a good idea to have these phases in mind as the fight director works. Every production will have a different time frame, and a realistic approach to time use will help get the fight up to speed in time for technical rehearsals.

Suffice it to say that before rehearsals begin, the fight will have been "created." The fight director, in collaboration with the rest of the staff, will have worked out in detail all the scenic and dramatic elements of the fight, from beginning to end. There will be a clear story to tell, and the fight will have been created with the text, set, period, and characterizations in mind.

From here, the first phase of the fight rehearsal is ready to start. This is called "setting the fight."

Setting the Fight

Setting the fight means teaching it to the performers move by move. This is also a time when the fight director and director tell the fight story to the performers. This helps all of the performers understand where the fight is going.

This is also a time for collaboration, for suggestions from the director, staff, and performers themselves. Performers often come up with brilliant suggestions that can be incorporated.

The fight director's job now is to teach the moves of the fight clearly phrase by phrase to each of the performers involved in the fight. The fight director also layers in the other characters who either watch or participate in a non-combatant manner. This is also the time to plan out special scenic effects as well as sound, props, and lighting elements.

This process of familiarity with the choreography, the props (if any), and the other performers continues until the entire choreography is learned and can be rehearsed at half speed. This is where safety problems should be solved before things get too fast!

Running the Fight

Once the choreography is learned by the brain, it is time for the muscles to learn it. This phase of rehearsal finds the fight being run as a total piece. Performers need time for the moves to sink into their muscle memory and to find ways to perform the choreography with the intentions of the characters.

While still in a preproduction rehearsal mode, the fights may be fiddled with as far as small changes, tempo adjustments, phrasing, and other improvements are concerned. Normally, though, during rehearsals the fights are run at one-quarter to one-half speed, then notes are given. The fights are then run again, with the changes incorporated by the actors. Time can still be taken here for intense one-on-one rehearsals to work out problems of timing, dialogue, masking, illusion, or tempo.

As the show gets closer to production, other elements must be added in. Shoes, blood effects, and costume pieces head my list. However, set, furniture, lights, and the theater space will affect the performance of the fight. The performers will be thrown off by every new element.

Therefore, the fight must be run with each new thing in mind. The performers need to get used to costumes, blood bits, lights, music, set, and set dressings. They need to get used to the theater space itself, if it is unfamiliar.

Finally, the fight(s) must be run within the context of the play itself. Act run-throughs, or full-play run-throughs, are important steps for the performers. The performers must be able to fit the choreography into the characters they are portraying. It must not look as if the fight were a separate element of the play. There must be a seamless transition into the beginning of the fight and out of it. The fight director should not neglect details, such as how to get "dead" bodies off the stage!

The fight director shouldn't wait until the first dress rehearsal to run the fights at full tempo! If full costumes aren't available, the fight director should run the rehearsals with costume pieces, even if it is only the shoes.

Finally, as the day of production gets nearer, the last element of fight rehearsal kicks in and may overlap the previous one as well. I call it "polishing the fight."

Polishing the Fight

When the performers are clearly at ease with the choreography, it is time to polish the fight. By polishing I mean focusing. There are always certain phrases, moves, or acting beats within the fight that should be pointed up to the audience. The fight director needs to be very clear where these moments are.

Any fight, whether a sword fight or an unarmed fistfight, will look better if certain high points are brought to the attention of the audience. In a sword fight, it could be a particularly fast (but safe!) sequence, or a pause when the combatants circle for position. In a fistfight, it could be a particularly large punch or a comic moment.

Moments of focus don't just happen arbitrarily. They either spring from particularly interesting rhythmic, or visual, images during a fight or have to do directly with an acting beat for one of the characters. The fight in *Romeo and Juliet* changes focus when Mercutio is stabbed by Tybalt. That moment must be seen by the audience, felt by Mercutio, and unseen by Romeo.

Polishing sections of the fight can start as early as the first week of rehearsal, if the performers are quick enough to pick up the routines.

The entire series of fight rehearsals should be a constant process of refining the choreography so that it is safe, exciting, and kinetically involving so that it helps the story move forward. The fight director should lead the actors along, keeping the elements in this chapter in mind. The fight director should encourage the actors and keep reminding them to slow down until they learn the phrases by heart. The fight director shouldn't push for speed too early, since the result could be dangerous.

This advice will be true with professional actors as well as with less-experienced ones. The fight director may be in a situation where a fight has to be created and rehearsed by college, high school, or even community theater groups. This calls for some special handling, since performance and athletic experience will vary widely. Any fight director who works with amateurs or young people should read on!

Thoughts on Safety in School, Amateur, and Community Theater Productions

Many plays involving fight scenes are produced for elementary and high schools or for amateur and community theaters. Plays and musicals such as *Romeo and Juliet*, *Peter Pan*, *Treasure Island*, and *Camelot*, are popular, and I've even seen productions of Shakespeare's history plays produced at this level. While

Figure 2-46. *Staging realistic fight scenes for children and young performers may be inappropriately violent. Children may not have the physical skills, be emotionally prepared, nor have the discipline to perform complex naturalistic fight choreography. Use mime, dance, slow motion, and other nonrealistic concepts to indicate violence. This drawing by eight-year-old Nicole Suddeth shows a child's idealized view of a sword-and-dagger fight.*

maintaining safety margins for these types of productions is a priority, it is a given that few, or none, of the performers are trained in stage combat or weapons use. However, very effective combat scenes can be staged safely that will do justice to each individual play.

When preparing to work with these groups—conceptualizing fight scenes, gathering weapons, and props—I've kept in mind that the less experience a performer has the more nervous he or she is. To give a complicated sword fight to two fourteen-year-old actors who are playing Mercutio and Tybalt, and then to hand them steel swords to work with, is courting disaster! There are many creative substitutes for dangerous props, and many approaches to safe choreography. Even something as simple as the knife wound in the musicals *Carousel*, *Oklahoma*, or *West Side Story* can be fatal, and should be planned for early in the rehearsal process.

Since casts in school or community productions are usually large, effective use can be made of mass movement of bodies. For instance, the fight scene in *Romeo and Juliet* can be surrounded by pulsing, undulating, circulating masses of bodies downstage of the main action, thereby hiding the fight a bit and filling the stage with action. The "crowd," of course, must be coached to keep away from the swords, knives, or other props. The crowd can also be used within the choreography to frame or support a fight sequence.

I recently staged a fight between St. George and the Turkish Knight for a pageant production of *St. George and the Dragon* at the Lee Strasberg Institute in New York. The crowd supported the fight in a number of ways. At one point, the Turkish Knight was "spun" away by St. George, who grabbed the Knight's long waist sash and gave it a pull. The actor who played the Turkish Knight spun into a crowd of his followers, who caught him, bent down with him in a "group lean," and then collectively rose to fling him back into the fight. As the two main characters came together center stage and locked their (wooden) swords up high, the crowd made two circles around them, chanting and moving in opposite directions. Finally, the climax of the fight came when (1) the members of the crowd lifted St. George high over their heads, (2) he was "stabbed" from below (no contact, of course), and (3) they slowly lowered him to the floor in a "Pieta" position, giving a group moan.

This is an example of safe use of the stage, group involvement, dramatic picture, and effective storytelling with complete safety for all concerned. The two characters never fought with swords in the traditional sense, in that the blades never connected aggressively. No "cuts," or "thrusts," were ever used, leaving the audience to use their imagination.

Chase Scenes

In this same vein, chase scenes are usually pretty safe, if they don't involve too many gymnastics or running on slippery surfaces. The same cautionary rule would apply to multilevel sets, steep stairs, or chase scenes through the audience. These can be very effective but must be worked out thoroughly ahead of time to prevent and minimize risk of injury. Exciting action can be suggested with a good (and safe) chase scene. A good deal of comedy can also be found in chases by using doors, windows, group reactions, and a surprise or two.

Weapons

A word about weapons is in order whenever one is talking about young performers or amateur/community theater. I always hesitate to hand someone a metal sword, knife, or other heavy realistic prop, like a pipe or club, and would never consider using firearms in this situation. Much can be achieved without difficult and complicated choreography and without using "real" weapons. Besides, you may be asking for trouble! There is nothing wrong with giving inexperienced performers plastic, rubber, or well-made wooden swords, knives, and other props of destruction. I would never use a real metal knife to stab Bernardo in *West Side Story* in a high school production, and I would even think twice about university-level actors. By the same guideline, I would not hand a young performer who was playing Peter Pan a heavy cutlass to fight Captain Hook, but rather a lightweight, well-built, wooden or plastic mockup of a sword. This kind of thinking serves two masters: first, fights are safer; second, it usually encourages "nonrealistic" fighting that is inherently safer than realistic choreography.

Hollywood has long been known to give out rubber, wood, and plastic weapons to extras in huge battle scenes. It is just asking for trouble to give real steel to three hundred extras storming the gates of a castle! Sound effects are added later on in the editing room to give the effect of the battle. This same technique can be used onstage to give added depth to large battles or to suggest fights offstage. A sound tape made while the cast members are hitting pots and pans and sticks, yelling and screaming, perhaps overlaid with drums and

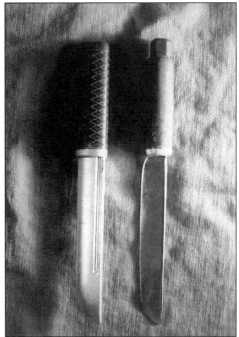

Figure 2-47. *A common French foil. This weapon is often mistaken for a safe stage combat sword. Do not use foils as a substitute for practical rapiers or smallswords. Blade design allows the foils to whip dangerously, and there is minimal hand protection!*

Figure 2-48. *A steel knife (right) and a rubber double (left). Often the steel knife will be switched for the safer rubber one before or during the fight. It's always safer to use rubber knives with untrained or young performers for extended fight sequences or for wounds and kills.*

horns, will give the effect of a huge mêlée and will be a lot of fun for the cast to create!

When young or inexperienced actors must perform a battle scene onstage rather than offstage, one should realize that they can be hurt by wooden prop swords, and one should therefore keep any choreography to a minimum. Repetitive strokes are best here, since they are easily remembered and look acceptable when done on different parts of the stage. Patterns such as "high, low, high, low" or "right shoulder, left shoulder, right shoulder, left shoulder" are easy enough for all to remember. The younger the performer the easier the pattern should be. At the same time, the more inexperienced the performer the wider the parries or defensive moves. Wide, straight-arm parries are the thing to use here to keep the maximum margin of safety. Even simple moves like ducks and belly swipes are potentially dangerous, so BE CAREFUL!

Battle Scenes

Another section of this book deals with group fights, but it is wise to keep in mind that simpler is better with young performers. The fight director must clearly have in mind the area within which he or she wants each separate combat. The fight director should use chalk or taped lines on the stage floor in rehearsal to help the performers remember! If the fight director has, for instance, four groups of fighters, they should be given as much room onstage as possible so that they don't run into each other. Positioning Group 1 upstage center, Group 2 downstage center, Group 3 far stage right, and Group 4 far stage left *should* keep them out of each other's hair. The fight director should consider simple pattern changes, too, to keep things interesting. Group 1 and Group 2 could change positions after a few moves. The fight director should make sure though that both groups have the same number of strokes! That way both fights should end at about the same time; and on a clear loud shout, that all parties are aware of, they can change positions, thus adding to the battle "confusion."

The fight director can also have escalating fights to draw out small amounts of choreography. For instance, Group 1 can run on and begin, then Groups 2 and 3 can enter and add on, finally saving Group 4 for an appropriate moment.

"Extras," or nonfighters, can add to the excitement by either running through the set (in safe areas), entering and watching, falling (carefully) onstage and dying from unseen offstage wounds, or crawling onto upper levels to cheer for their side.

Another tip for battle scenes, as well as smaller and two-person fights, is slow motion. With a change of lighting and some mood music underneath or perhaps low drums, a slow-motion fight can look *very* good and may be even more dramatic than a "real speed" fight. The fight director can work the performers carefully through every detail of the fight, perhaps using a metronome to keep them all in the same "time frame."

I have also used a technique whereby the weapons were all mimed by the company. Since young people are usually quite physical and creative, and since many of them have played "war" with pretend weapons, this technique is very natural to them. Mime also opens up a huge world of possibilities, from bows and arrows to knife throws to supersonic ray guns!

Stylized Fight Choreography

Fights in children's theater and musicals often lend themselves to a stylized approach. These types of combats can often be "danced" without need for "realism." The confrontation between Riff, Tony, and Bernardo from *West Side Story* is a good example of a fight already written as a dance. What about musicals like *Camelot*, *Carousel*, or *Man of La Mancha*? If the fight scene is approached as a dance, some of the dangerous energy of young performers is diffused. Props can then also open up to suggestive weapons—that is, lengths of plastic tubing for swords, red scarves for blood, a windmill made of actors' bodies and sheets, and other nontraditional and creative ideas.

Prop Swords and Sword Fights

Very little is to be gained dramatically by imposing a difficult and realistic battle on performers incapable of safe execution. A good rule here is: *Less is more.*

When gathering props and making swords, it is a good idea to remember that they must be safe but sturdy. A wooden sword that breaks off after two rehearsals, sails across stage, and hits the pianist in the head is not a safe prop. Likewise, a whack on the head with a "fake" wooden sword is an invitation to visit the local emergency room. Wood is hard stuff and must be treated with respect. A wooden sword must be pretty sturdy, and thick around the handle, to hold its own weight and not snap off. Edges and points must be looked after too, so that they aren't too pointy, or sharp. Rounded, blunt, and dull, dull, dull is the key here.

Another idea for swords are lengths of hollow plastic, similar to golf club liners, padded with foam and then wrapped with silver "gaffer's tape." A guard to protect the hand may be fashioned out of a large, plastic bottle cut in half, run up the blade about six inches, and taped on. These "swords" are light and easily wielded by small hands. They can also be cut short to fit!

Prop swords aren't meant for long "cut and parry" sequences. Wood will splinter and weaken from this kind of abuse. Wooden swords are for swinging around, threatening, and miming cuts, but never for actual combat. The same is true for plastic, although, since plastic is so light, some "fighting" is possible.

I refer specifically to the toy, hollow-molded plastic swords available in toy stores or those made carefully with sturdy materials. Never cut a sword out of "PVC" or hard Plexiglas® since they are too brittle and leave a very sharp edge when they break.

Maintaining a safe distance between fighters is a difficult concept for professional performers. It is almost impossible for young performers! If a fight director is staging a fight between two or more characters, the characters should be watched closely since they will creep up on each other. The fight director should try to keep them as far apart as possible, so that the "swords" can just barely touch. One exercise is to have a performer hold out his sword at full length and let the partner "cut" at it. They may then switch, with the former partner "laying it on." They should be reminded throughout rehearsal to always keep far apart.

Soft "replacement" props can be used in a number of ways. A black sock filled with cotton or fur will look like a "Blackjack," and cannot hurt the actors. I have even staged a caveman fight, using painted foam rubber rocks and soft clubs, that was very effective.

Plays that require young performers to sword fight must always be approached with caution. A play such as *Dreaming and Dueling*, about a high school romance, demands sport-fencing scenes. Here, however, performers can be encased in protective equipment, such as fencing masks, gloves, and jackets, to protect them from errant points and edges. But what about other plays? I have often staged *Hamlet* with full fencing gear in the professional theater. This could easily be done for community or high school productions. If an ambitious play such as one of Shakespeare's histories is attempted, and the use of modern fencing masks is unacceptable, why not use helmets? Even a standard like *Romeo and Juliet*, if set in modern times, can get away with protective equipment for the performers. Though it is not correct for every production, standard sports-fencing equipment is safe, stylish, widely available, and a possible alternative for inexperienced performers.

Wounds and Kills

Finally, we should have a word about kills. For inexperienced performers, realistic "kills" are out of the question—and, perhaps, inappropriately violent. Stabs, cuts, thrusts, and lunges with metal swords are technically advanced

Figure 2-49. *A "wound" from Laertes (Michael Kamtman) to Hamlet (Allan Hickle-Edwards) in a modern dress Hamlet at the North Carolina Shakespeare Festival. There is an extra margin of safety when performing sword fights in fencing masks and jackets! Director, Louis Rackoff. Photo by Bill Savage.*

illusions and are quite dangerous for professional performers, not to mention the untrained and overeager.

Rather than attempt to be realistic, "kills" at this level are better "indicated" to the audience. Control of a metal or wooden sword or knife is difficult, especially in an emotional climactic moment like a kill with the added nervousness of being in front of an audience.

The easiest way to kill a character with a sword is the tried-and-true thrust under the upstage arm pit. The sword, though, should never be aimed straight at another performer, but rather laid up against the ribs sideways for safety. As a rule, "cuts" with the "edge" of a wooden or plastic sword are safer than "thrusts" or "lunges." This way, the point is never involved in moving directly at another performer. If the "edge" of the sword is *placed* on another's stomach or leg and drawn back while carefully clearing it out of the way, with an appropriate reaction from the character being wounded or killed, it can look very effective and is reasonably safe.

The danger comes from drawing the sword up toward the face and not clearing it out of the way of the other performer or from "slapping" it in too forcefully. Another danger can come from too violent a reaction to the wound, whereby the wounded performer throws himself onto the floor or toward his partner without looking, crashing into the partner or running into the partner's sword.

Rather than risk this type of injury, the wounded performer should sink slowly to the ground or fall into the waiting arms of a few "extras," "attendants," or "soldiers," who can catch him and lower him to the floor. Swords or other weapons, of course, should be carefully dropped or otherwise cleared before falling into another's arms, since a "catcher" could be injured by these props. "High" falls or falls from platforms or near stairs, should never be attempted by those unfamiliar with the difficulty, and great risk, of these specialized tricks. Even when there are multiple "catchers," accidents have occurred when the person who was falling accidentally overshot the mark and landed on the floor. A catcher has also been known to be injured when a falling body landed on his head or neck area or when he was pulled forcefully forward and smashed faces with the catcher opposite him.

A stab with a knife should always be turned aside at the last moment and not delivered with contact. This is even true of a rubber or plastic knife. A metal knife, even dulled down, can severely injure someone if it strikes home. Metal knives should not be used, unless by someone carefully trained in stage combat.

It also goes without saying that inexperienced performers must *never* be trusted with firearms of any kind. A "bang, you're dead" pretend policy is the safest. A toy plastic gun may be used in some situations, but never other than that.

I think that many, many types of combat scenes are stageable with young or untrained community performers. But to attempt too much is to risk injury, and no production is worth that price. Careful attention to detail, not pushing the performers beyond their limits, and a little creativity can go a long way to minimize risk.

Concentration is difficult for younger performers. Attempting a complicated realistic fight scene is more than most high school students can absorb. There are certainly exceptions to this rule, but one should always keep sessions short and keep the focus on the work strong. A fight director should remember the following:

➢ Keep weapons away from head and face areas.

➢ Never use real firing guns, pistols, or rifles of any kind.

➢ Keep it simple.

➢ Use the crowd to "hide the action."

➢ Rehearse the fight from the beginning, not at the last minute.

➢ Do not use metal weapons if something else will do.

➢ Augment combat scenes with lights and sound effects.

➢ Make sure prop weapons are padded and dulled down.

➢ Pay close attention to the spacing of performers and the distance between them.

➢ Watch out for excessive energy and enthusiasm.

➢ Consider slow motion as a safe alternative to realism.

➢ Expect young actors to perform fights at least ten times faster than rehearsal speed, no matter what you do.

➢ Teach choreography over a period of weeks or months, reducing the complexity in direct proportion to (1) the age of the performers and (2) the amount of rehearsal time.

➢ LESS IS MORE!

Liability

It's human nature that accidents will happen. We do all we can to prevent them, however. Each element of a staged fight is important to the overall safety of the performers. And it should be understood that the responsibility of the safety of the performers and the audience falls directly on the shoulders of the fight director.

The last ten years have seen an increase in liability suits in cases of injury to performers and members of the audience. I don't mention this to scare anyone, but to make the reader aware of the responsibility of directing fight scenes. Fight directors are often put in difficult positions. They must teach choreography quickly, choose suitable weapons within a reasonable budget, and deal with hormonal actors who want to hit hard!

Fight directors must be sure they don't get in over their heads. If a fight director doesn't have the training in the use of a particular weapon, he or she shouldn't pretend, or misrepresent himself on a résumé. In a court of law, you might have to prove your training to a jury.

There are several things that a fight director can do to protect himself or herself and be prepared in case of a liability question. First, the fight director must be sensitive to an actor's capabilities. A fight director shouldn't make an actor perform choreography that is too difficult or too dangerous for the actor. Know when to say no! This may require that a fight director refuse to stage something that a producer or director has in mind. If in a fight director's considered opinion a particular event, move, or effect is too dangerous, the fight director must straighten his or her backbone and say *no*! That is the fight director's job! Remember, the fight director is the safety expert.

It is a good idea to always have a notation of your choreography: this way, if there is ever any question about how a move was conceived, it is in black and white. And in this way the fight director won't be caught, weeks or years later, wondering exactly how a particular punch or sword cut was staged.

Some professional fight directors even carry liability insurance. In the event of an accident and a suit, the fight director shouldn't depend on the theater's insurance company to cover him or her unless that is part of the fight director's contract. The job of the theater and its insurance company is to access blame, and they may want to deflect the law away from the theater directly onto the fight director.

Most liability law suits seek to prove negligence. Under the law, negligence has four elements:

Duty—as in your duty to stage a safe fight

Breach—specifically how you breached that duty

Cause—reason of breach, such as inexperience or drunkenness

Harm—specific harm caused by such breach of duty

The following are some tips that can help a fight director avoid a negligence suit:

1. Purchase equipment that meets or exceeds your needs.

2. Keep records of purchase, reconditioning, and maintenance.

3. Buy from recognized dealers.

4. Have dealers mount equipment. Don't buy parts and assemble them yourself unless you have experience.

5. Warn performers of the risks involved in a fight scene.

6. Rehearse with witnesses, such as stage management personnel.

7. Recognize that if a theater cannot afford to purchase safe equipment, the fights must be reconceived.

8. Keep records of your own training: hours, courses, teachers.

Acting the Fight

A performance moment from King Henry VI, Part 1. Here, Talbot (David Patrick Kelly) lifts Joan of Arc (Nicole Callender) during their encounter. Theater for a New Audience. Director, Barry Kyle.

3

*T*he most important thing, aside from safety, about any staged combat, is the STORY. To tell the story well and engage the audience, the performers must ACT the fight. This is easier said than done.

Many performers, caught up in the technique of fighting, forget that the "moves" must be interpreted much as the text of the play is interpreted. To fight without motivation, objective, and through line is just to "go through the motions," and the audience will not follow the story or the performance. Emotionally involved acting must be at the core of any conflict; and the fight

155

director, the director, and the performers must keep this final goal in mind from first rehearsal through opening night and beyond.

Every performer and director approaches the performance goal in a different way, but there are a few simple rules that cut through the different styles and that are elemental to any well-performed fight.

1. The audience must believe what each character is capable of doing, both psychologically and physiologically.

2. Character objectives drive the fight.

3. Avoid stereotypes. Character choice and movement must occur organically.

4. "Real" emotion must be kept at bay during the fight, though there is room for "real" moments during pauses.

5. Each character believes that he or she is "right" and will win the fight.

6. Neither character wants to die, even up to the moment of death (barring suicide!).

7. Breath and vocalization are an important tool and are essential to the fight.

8. Avoid the obvious, the expected, the redundant, and the repetitive.

9. Believe that the fight is happening for the first time.

10. In rehearsal, actors should explore style, character movement, posture, Laban-effort-shaping verbs, pattern, rhythm, tempo.

11. Dare to make choices (acting ones, not dangerous ones!) in rehearsals.

12. Use animal images to alter style, movement, or interpretation.

13. *Invest the movement* with reality and belief. If you don't believe, the audience never will.

14. **Safety first, last, and always!**

Performing fights in a live production is a great challenge and an exciting one. Many actors wait their entire career for the opportunity to perform Mercutio, St. Joan, or Hamlet and never get the chance.

Before launching into a fight role, an actor must understand the challenges ahead, his responsibilities in the rehearsal process, and the payoff to the audience when all goes well.

Acting the Fight

Performing a fight scene in the theater is a wonderful opportunity to grab the audience's attention! Let's face it, thrilling sword fights, rough-and-tumble fisticuffs, and exciting chase scenes are fun to perform!

But many performers don't commit fully to the process of rehearsing a fight scene and, therefore, ultimately shortchange their performance. What do I mean? Simply this. I have worked with many hundreds of actors through the years, from drama students to recognized stars. I find that the most successful performances are owing to the actor's collaboration with me in creating the fight, rather than the actor merely mimicking my choreography.

Do your homework! Make choices as to how you feel your character would move, sound, and fight, and communicate these ideas to your fight director. I often remind my students that no two characters are alike and that no two would fight the same way. Not every character is young, clean, healthy, rested, well fed, well shod, psychologically stable, brilliantly trained, and fighting in a space that is dry, level, and well lit! However, many actors fall into generalized "fight" movement no matter who they are playing.

Character Movement

How does each character fight? Well, a cursory examination of given circumstances will often give the actor a start. Here are a few simple things that will affect how all characters move and fight. Remember that each choice the actor makes will affect the physical life of the character, from the shoes he wears to his worldview.

Age

Not everyone who fights is eighteen years old. Remember that older people may not be as agile, but are sneakier. They will always have the advantage of experience and strategy. They also hold life more dearly since they usually have more to lose. Youthful fighters will throw themselves into the fray, trying to use strength and speed to advantage. Mature ones will measure their attacks more carefully, trying to avoid being overpowered and using experience to win.

Motivation

It's clear that a character who has just lost a hand at poker will fight with less intensity than one who stands to lose a kingdom. Motivation is the key to how all characters fight, otherwise how will Edgar win over the more experienced Edmund in *King Lear*, or Prince Hal beat the warlike Hotspur in *Henry IV, Part 1*? The more passionately motivated character usually wins the fight.

Health

We forget that the body's health can affect movement choices. Is Mercutio limping from an old wound? We know that medical treatment was marginal in the past; therefore, any character could have been sick with varying degrees of disability. Shortness of breath, shakes and sweats, active wounds and sores are all possibilities for the high- and lowborn and will affect movement choices.

Pain

Famous warriors and footsoldiers share a common bond during battle: pain. Fight directors often choose to use wounds during fights to add excitement or to wear a character down. In dramas, pain must be felt realistically, and the resulting change in movement patterns should be clear to an audience. A wound may mean the loss of coordination, the crippling of an arm or leg, or even impaired vision. Psychologically, receiving a wound may weaken resolve, or may strengthen it! Gunshot wounds, thrusts with swords, and a punch in the face are all clearly playable physical obstacles. Characters often enter a scene already wounded. Soldiers cut and bleeding, Saint Joan receiving an arrow in the chest and fighting on, Richard III bleeding and spent on the battlefield even before facing Richmond—these are not unrealistic images. An actor should never shy away from playing the pain of a wound, since it adds an element of truth to a performance.

Weight/Height Ratio

Just as all combatants are not youthful, not all are of idealized modern weight and height. It stands to reason that bigger-boned, mesomorphic performers will move in a convincing manner when given appropriate choreography. Physically taller, imposing physiques can also lend a menacing tone to a role. Slight performers can consider padding to add bulk, shape, and size, if necessary, to visually equalize larger opponents.

Intelligence

If your character is stupid, well, perhaps he is lucky! Intelligence will affect how a person moves and holds himself and will affect strategy within a fight. Intelligence presumes training in fight styles and a method of fighting. This is not to say that intelligent characters always win fights, since we all make mistakes. The question should be asked, "Has the character been to school? Has he received formal fight training of any kind?" The answers to these questions should help to inform an actor's movement choices. Usually the smarter an individual, the more confident that individual is.

Social Standing/Worldview

A tavern thug such as Bardolph will fight differently from Hamlet, Prince of Denmark. Saint Joan is unstoppable despite her social standing and because of her worldview. Macbeth's social standing grows from soldier to king, but his worldview degenerates into despotism and paranoia. It's important to understand where a character fits into the overall picture of the social structure of the play. It is also clear that HOW a character is treated by others onstage helps tell the story.

Psychological Health

What state of mind is a character experiencing? Is Macbeth's mind clear? Is Macduff's mind clearer? How does fear affect people? Is fifteen-year-old Danceny in *Les Liaisons Dangereuses* calm and collected as he faces his rival Valmont, or is he confused—at once elated and petrified of dying? The actor should explore how a character's psychological state can be revealed within the fight. Is the character puffed up with false bravado? Or is he calm, economical, and confident in his cause and his technique? Does the character attempt to stare down an opponent or shrink away from what may be the last few moments of life? The actor must use the sword or other props to actualize what the character is thinking, and interpret what he is feeling.

Acting Beats

What we are talking about here are strong choices! Actors prepare a role by deciding on specific character traits to play, and clearly analyzing a fight scene must be part of that process. It's important that an actor approach fight rehearsals with something other than lines learned and with clear and helpful ideas of HOW the actor's character will use a sword, attack, stand, salute, and

Images from the fight between Somerset (Geoff Cantor) and Richard (Trellis Stepter) in King Henry VI, Part 1. Theater for a New Audience. How does the stage picture (the positions of the performers in the stage space) in each photo focus the audience's eye? What does it say about the ebb and flow of the fight? Who is dominant? Who is on the attack?

Figure 3-1. 1. *A strong up-right, down-left diagonal on Somerset's entrance.*

Figure 3-2. 2. *The actors have moved center stage to begin the fight.*

Figure 3-3. 3. *It is near the end, Somerset is disarmed and helpless, with Richard standing over him, visually dominant.*

generally move through the separate beats of a fight. The actor must be specific and communicate his ideas to the fight director, so that the choreography may be responsive to them.

To help a performer along this path of creating the physical life of the fight, the performer needs to score the acting beats of the fight. The physical life must go hand in hand with the psychological and the subtextual life of the character an actor is playing. Hopefully the fight director will have divided the fight into phrases. Each of these phrases usually denotes a change in acting beats.

The actor's job is to have these beats clear in his head in order to play them; otherwise the actor is merely playing moment to moment, sword cut to sword cut, with no goal for the audience to see. What is the character's objective in fighting? It may be immediate—to kill, to crush, to overwhelm, to escape—or it may be more lofty—to rescue the kingdom, to serve God, to free the slaves.

Inexperienced performers often confuse the physical thrill of performing a fight with good acting. They stop acting, stop making choices when the fight begins, and wallow in the physicality of staged violence. A performer shouldn't let this happen! The fight is part of the destiny of a character, and the performer needs to perform it with passion! No matter whether a character is brave or fearful, adroit or clumsy, successful or shamefully killed, a performer should get involved in the details of the creative movement choices and acting beats.

Relaxation

It's a tremendously difficult job as a performer to be at once engaged emotionally in a scene of physical conflict but at the same time be aware of the fight choreography and of the need to continue to breathe and to keep the body energized but relaxed and the fight safe. There is an almost schizophrenic quality to performing a fight, since an actor must be aware of the next move in the choreography but yet play the fight moment to moment.

Only by constant and repeated rehearsals can a performer become relaxed enough with the choreography that it enters the subconscience and muscle memory. This cannot happen otherwise, and is the key to a truly relaxed, organic performance of fight choreography.

An actor should not merely depend on scheduled fight rehearsals to work on choreography. An actor should run the fight through his mind several times daily during rehearsals. The actor should visualize the fight, move by move, acting beat by acting beat, until it becomes a movie that can be played back at will. The actor should be specific and work to layer in the sounds, breath, and dialogue, as well as the individual moves of the fight. Learn to "finger fight," a method of marking the fight moves in a confined space, such as a dressing room or hallway, with a fight partner by using fingers instead of weapons to mark the moves.

Finally, a relaxation trick I use onstage is to begin to breathe with my fight partner before the first moves in a fight; in this way my partner and I are connected organically and physiologically before the opening move.

Vocal Scoring

The vocal score of the fight is as important as the individual moves of the fight. An actor's voice is an instrument of attack, a mirror of the emotions.

Many playwrights include dialogue within fight scenes; however, the "grunts and groans" are just as important.

An actor shouldn't try to layer these vocalizations on too late in the rehearsal process. An actor should experiment from the first day to create a vocal score for the character. Heavy breathing, shouting, screaming, and physical effort, as well as pain, fear, and triumph, are all human traits that help the audience become involved in the struggle.

Since these vocalizations are sometimes taxing on the voice, the actor should work with a vocal coach to help place them in such a way as not to damage the voice. Generally, an open throat and a supported voice during screams and shouts is better than a constricted one.

Partnering

Being a good partner is vital. Connecting with a partner emotionally, visually (eye contact), and physically is extremely important. Remember that a fight scene, however short, is a dialogue, not a monologue, and that it takes two to put it across the footlights.

The timing of the moves of the fight, the ebb and flow of the emotions, the sense of gain and loss of objectives is all about partnering.

To actors I say, take care of your partners in fight scenes. If they are tired, slow down. If they are tentative, help give them the confidence to continue. In general, if you take care of them, they'll take care of you, and the whole will be improved. Be a generous partner!

How to Die

Characters are always dying onstage. Actors are forever hitting the stage, bruising their knees and hips in the process, and trying not to breathe too heavily to spoil the illusion.

Perhaps an actor is playing the fourth soldier from the left who is, as they say, cannon fodder, and who dies a faceless death. In this case, less is more, and a quick grunt and collapse is what's required.

However, many major characters die on stage, some with extensive lines to say before they expire. A short list would include Romeo, Juliet, Tybalt, Mercutio, Edmund, Hamlet, Laertes, Othello, Desdemona, Julius Caesar, Cleopatra, Richard II, Richard III, and so on into opera, musical theater, and even ballet.

Figure 3-4. *Queen Margret (Pamela Gray) kills York (John Campion) in King Henry VI, Part 1. Death scenes in Shakespeare are often larger than life.*

I always find it particularly unsatisfying to see a professional play in which a performer uses a "bang, you're dead" minimalized approach to death. Not that the reverse is true either, because a drawn-out, overacted, scenery-chewing death is equally undesirable.

A good place to start detailing a death scene is some research into what actually happens to the body when it is stabbed, shot, or otherwise violated. One should talk to doctors or nurses about real-life experiences or go to the library and examine medical or pathology books. It's somewhat gruesome work, but will give an actor a realistic idea of what happens. One should examine Kübler-Ross's five stages of death: denial, anger, bargaining, depression, and acceptance.

Different styles of theater demand different approaches to death scenes. For instance, let's briefly examine two styles. The death of kings in epic drama and tragedy denotes the end of something larger than an individual life. Shakespeare writes that nature itself rebels when kings die: there are eclipses of the sun and moon, and strange animals wander the streets! Therefore, it stands to reason that the lives of epic characters, such as Macbeth, Hamlet, Richard III, and St. Joan, don't simply wink out. There is earth-shaking social and political significance in their deaths. This must be reflected in the staging and performance.

However, contemporary twentieth-century drama reflects more faceless and random violence. Even in musicals such as *West Side Story* and *Carousel* the lead characters die in senseless ways. Witness, too, the violence in plays such as *Short Eyes*, *Zoo Story*, *Woyzeck*, and *Search and Destroy*. This is the violence of the nightly news broadcast or the blurb in a tabloid. Death in these plays is neither important socially nor politically, but is no less horrifying.

Performers in these plays must understand the importance that the playwright places upon death. Few deaths onstage are romantic and self-sacrificing, with the exception of Juliet's.

Figure 3-5. *Talbot's death scene from* King Henry VI, Part 1. *Here, Talbot (David Patrick Kelly) lies mortally wounded, held up by one of his soldiers. Moments later, his dead son is brought on, adding to the tragedy of the moment.*

Finally, a bit of advice on how not to die! Don't die with your eyes or mouth open: they are invitations to flying insects! Don't die in awkward positions that are hard to hold. Don't die with your posterior pointed to the front row. The longer a dead body lies onstage, the less dead it looks; have yourself dragged off or covered with a costume, cloth, or flag.

Turning the body upstage or lying flat on your stomach is usually a better death pose than facing the audience on your back. Breath control is much easier in this position, especially if you are onstage for an extended length of time. A tip to breath control once you're dead is to expand the rib cage fully, lock it there, and breathe shallowly from your diaphragm.

An actor should carefully rehearse, script, and score a death scene and not leave it till the first preview; demand that difficult stab or gunshot wounds be rehearsed so that they are as safe and consistent as possible; rehearse blood bits until they are flawless, effortless, and create the desired effect; and work with the fight director to achieve these mutual goals.

Working with the Fight Director

Fight directors sometimes exhibit distinct personality traits. They are

➤ the bully

➤ the fencing coach

➤ the guru

➤ the buddy

➤ the professor

➤ the macho man

➤ the drill sergeant

A performer has to learn to deal with all personality types. The performer's input, though, is important to the creative process. A performer should share his thoughts and feelings about his character's fighting ability, weapon choice, and fighting style. If a performer has no training upon which to draw, then he should speak generally about how he sees his character. This input cannot help but influence the fight director.

It is also incumbent upon actors to share information about injuries and physical limitations or fears that they may have. I had an actor tell me only after opening night that he was totally blind in one eye! He had had difficulty turning to his right throughout rehearsal, and I never guessed the problem. I could have helped him with alternate choreography if he had shared this vital information.

So, if an actor has bad knees (many actors do!) or strains and sprains, if an actor has a fear of heights, or any problem whatever, he should share them early in rehearsal. If necessary, an actor should approach the fight director privately to voice these concerns. If these concerns are not addressed, or are taken lightly, the actor should speak to stage management, since the actor's body and psyche need not be put in unnecessary jeopardy.

While competent fight directors will welcome a performer's input, a performer should be careful not to overburden a fight director with too much advice. There's usually no time to talk about each move in the fight and explore alternatives. The fight director has a time problem, one that actors need to respect.

Finally, an actor should do his homework! While in rehearsals, an actor should work on his choreography just as he would his lines. An actor should come in to rehearsals knowing the fight from the day before, keep notes, warm up, concentrate, have fun!

A Final Note

Performing fight scenes is a wonderful opportunity for an actor and should be relished! Once an actor has mastered the choreography, he should work with his partner to make the fight as exciting as possible, and work to find truth in the moves of the fight. Read over the section of this book on rehearsing fights, since these techniques will help, and work to achieve a performance tempo that is neither too slow nor too fast for the audience to appreciate what the actor is doing.

If a performer anticipates a career in acting, he should train! He should seek out competent teachers and fight directors who will share their knowledge. Fighting skills such as theatrical sword fighting, and unarmed combat, tumbling, and period movement are skills that will last a lifetime. Popular martial arts can also help an aspiring actor: chief among them is aikido; but karate, kendo, iaido, judo, and pensak silat also have important qualities, not the least of which is respect for tradition and physical discipline. Parallel to physical training is research. An actor should read all he can on dueling, warfare, arms and armor, and history.

An actor should work hard to build a fight scene, train to increase his skills and strengthen his body, have fun, and perform the fight with relish, panache, and that indefinable quality of ZA!

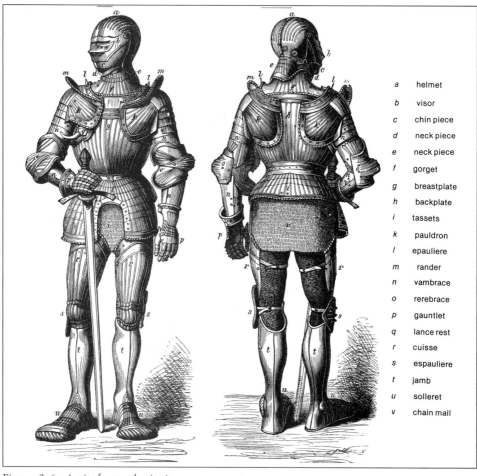

a	helmet
b	visor
c	chin piece
d	neck piece
e	neck piece
f	gorget
g	breastplate
h	backplate
i	tassets
k	pauldron
l	epauliere
m	rander
n	vambrace
o	rerebrace
p	gauntlet
q	lance rest
r	cuisse
s	espauliere
t	jamb
u	solleret
v	chain mail

Figure 3-6. *A suit of armor showing its component parts.*

A Bit of History

There is a wealth of source material to dive into to prepare a role in the theater. Contemporary roles may be researched by reading accounts of wars or personal acts of violence in books, magazines, and newspapers. These are often accompanied by photographs and illustrations that can give a performer solid clues.

Primary accounts, which are accounts written by persons who were actually present, are invaluable sources of detail. This kind of detail can be quite helpful in creating a character. Weather, location, how the combatants were dressed, time of day, state of mind, wounds and eyewitness accounts all help flesh out character choices.

Historical fights and duels make for wonderful reading. It is clear from the manuals and books on sword fighting through the ages that the study of arms has gone on for centuries. People in the medieval, Renaissance, and Restoration periods were intimately familiar with swords and sword fighting. It was spoken of in the taverns and castles. It was practiced in the salle d'armes and in the street. It was, in fact, elevated to a noble art! I translate from the preface of *L'Art en fait d'armes* by Labat, published in 1696: "The profession of armes has passed in all centuries for the most noble, and most necessary, and it is by this that the law conserves it's vigour, that enemies are repelled, and that subjects retain the respect due their Sovereign."

I thought that a cursory examination of the medieval, Renaissance, and Restoration periods in Europe might be of some value to actors unfamiliar with those periods. While this is only a brief glance at European weapons history, it may give some small perspective on the major events of the times. (Also read the section Fight Choreography Research earlier in this book.)

In medieval Europe, to achieve nobility and knighthood was to win the honor of carrying arms. The joust in the lists and the trial by combat were restricted to a select few. The possession of bladed weapons was even denied certain classes of people. The knight's sword was revered as a religious object, with carved talismans to ward (an old fencing term itself) against evil.

There is incredible detail in the arming of a typical knight in Europe in medieval times: witness the illustration of the suit of armor and the romantic names of each piece (Figure 3-6). Even mounting up and going into battle was an expensive enterprise. A knight was often required to maintain a minimum of eight mounts just for himself: A heavy warhorse that was only used in battle; a palfrey, or ambler, to ride to the field; a horse for his squire; two or more horses for men-at-arms; a horse for his manservant; another for the cook; and finally a pack horse or more to carry equipment. All of these animals and men had to be armed, of course, from the knight's purse.

There are published accounts of battles and jousts from the eleventh through the fifteenth century, detailing armor, style of combat, individual techniques such as grappling, codes of chivalry, and reams of books on heraldry. In a world with such low population density, these knights stood out and must have seemed larger than life, unapproachable, impregnable. Armed as they were with wonderful technological inventions such as the broadsword, crossbow, and warhammer, we can never know exactly how much the knights were feared. But we can come close. Their lives, however, were not as glamorous as depicted in Hollywood movies, but were harsh, dirty, and short. A knight was as likely to be cut down by dysentery as by an honorable blow struck by a worthy opponent.

By the Renaissance, the study of arms had blossomed in each country in Europe. Precise systems of rapier play and scientific theory were developed primarily in England, France, Italy, Germany, and Spain. Famous swordsmen and teachers of their day—men such as Marozzo, Capo Ferro, Agrippa, Saviolo, Thibault, Alfieri, and Fabris—published illustrated fencing manuals. Romantic names they are! Their books are still available in major libraries around the world.

The members of the rising bourgeoisie, or middle class, studied swordplay as strenuously as they studied horseback riding, dancing, and other social graces. Swords were increasingly worn by civilians and for the first time were used to settle private duels, not to mention as a defense against a growing criminal class.

A code of honor and code duellos were published. Dueling was outlawed in most countries because the cream of the upper class youth was dying, pierced by all manner of rapiers and daggers. Metalwork was improving yearly, and elaborate designs of swords began to appear. The rapier was the primary weapon, with the dagger as an accompaniment. However, various secondary styles developed, such as rapier/cape, rapier/buckler, case of rapiers, and rapier/lantern (for night fighting).

Shakespeare's characters would have been intimately familiar with these cold arms, as Shakespeare himself was. The choosing of a rapier—its size, weight, and shape; the belt and scabbard arrangement; the rapier's polishing and care—would all have been subjects of import to the Renaissance man. However, gunpowder was soon to affect the world of swordplay.

By the 1660s and the Restoration period, a new style of sword had begun to supplant the rapier. Granted, there were still some older styles around, and military and hunting weapons were still quite heavy. But the smallsword gained its ascendancy in this period, and its use was the study of the nobility and the bourgeoisie.

Short, light, and needle sharp, a smallsword was the deadliest incarnation of a civilian weapon yet. Its proponents were famous and made fortunes in their day by teaching and writing books. In France, La Touche, Labat, Liancourt, Girard, and Danet were popular, while in 1760s England a displanted Italian named Angelo began a three-generation reign of fencing masters. Until the late eighteenth century, these men led the fashion in weapons use. New types of swords were created, and courtiers began wearing them as a personal adornment at Versailles and Buckingham Palace. Enamelwork, gold and silver hilts, and rare gems were worked into the design of this subgroup of smallsword, called the court sword. Indeed, it was not uncommon for a rich gentleman to own a court sword to wear on formal occasions, a town sword to carry on daily errands that would have a more practical use, and perhaps a mourning sword, blackened of hilt, blade, and scabbard, to wear during periods of state or personal loss.

Personal dueling was at its height and gave rise to some amazing situations. One account describes two duelists who were locked in a carriage that was to circle a park three times. One duel was over a cat, another over a dog. Love affairs sparked a string of deadly encounters; in one of these encounters the challenger was found to be wearing under his shirt craftily made leather armor painted to look like skin. One famous duel was fought twice, months apart, the original winner finding himself pinned to the ground with a broken sword through his neck at the end of the second encounter. Duels were fought by all types of people over a glance, a rumor, business deals, and social snubs. Often "first blood" would settle the affair, but not always (reread the section that describes the private duel).

The Restoration period also had many interesting duelists, like the Chevalier D'Eon, a transvestite swordswoman who lived in Russia, Paris, and London. She was considered deadly, and lived to a venerable age, giving demonstrations

171

throughout Europe. Mademoiselle Maupin was also an infamous duelist, supposedly killing four men one night in a garden during a ball. In Paris and London a West Indian man named Saint Georges rose from humble beginnings and became the toast of the town owing to his legendary skills with a smallsword. Legend has it that he broke several foils over the body of one rival and could predict where he would make his next hit on an opponent.

Fencing salles were populated by the nobility, artists and musicians, military men, and the sons of the middle class. The sport of fencing became at once a social and an athletic exercise, intimately woven into the fabric of life in the major European cities. Finally, as swordplay fell into disuse, it was kept alive only by the military, in the fencing salles as a sport, and on the stage!

If an actor is preparing a role in which fighting, or fencing plays a major part, he or she will be amazed at the wealth of material available. Truth is stranger than

Figure 3-7. *Encounters such as the Alexander Hamilton–Aaron Burr duel were common, though most were not as well publicized as this one.*

fiction, and there are more interesting facts than can ever be imagined. Humans are violent by nature and have been documenting fights—whether battles in tenement hallways or the Alexander Hamilton–Aaron Burr duel—ever since the printing press was invented.

I encourage actors: if your creative juices are flowing after reading this historical appetizer, check out the sources listed in the bibliography at the end of this book. I've always believed that drama must mirror events past and present, and a careful study of history, even recent history, can only improve your interpretation. (Also, study the earlier sections on the trial by combat, the private duel, and researching period illustrations.)

On a more practical note, even the most careful planning and research cannot always prepare for that very human emotion: fear! Performing a fight in front of hundreds of audience members can be a sobering experience, one that sometimes leads to forgetting the fight! This can be very bad news to one's fight partner—not to mention the director or the story of the play.

Especially for those whose knees have ever knocked, whose palms have become sweaty, and whose eyes have glazed over before a performance, read on.

Red-Light Fever

"Red-light fever" is a term for fear, tension, nerves, or memory loss during the performance of fight scenes. Performance anxiety strikes all performers to a greater or lesser degree, and the addition of the emotional content of a climactic fight scene only adds to this problem. Performers are only human, after all, and some degree of nervousness is to be expected. The problem arises when (as on a television camera) the red light goes on and all rehearsal technique, all precision, all false energy goes out the window and the performer goes for it!

Performance anxiety can be alleviated to a great degree in rehearsals. Understanding beforehand that in front of an audience the performance is likely to be faster and harder just from sheer adrenaline rush is halfway to curing the problem. This is why most fights should be performed at three-quarter speed. The addition of an adrenaline rush usually pushes the tempo faster anyway.

No staged violence is exempt from this problem. I have witnessed performers under strain do some amazing things! I have seen invented punches, invented attacks with broadswords, flips that have driven partners into the floor,

Figure 3-8. *Red-light fever!*

noncontact punches suddenly arrive on contact, and "cues" disappear in a fren-
zied rush to attack.

   Red-light fever is responsible for many a broken nose, thousands of stitches,
and even visits to the local plastic surgeon. Rehearsal techniques *must* reinforce

the fact that the performance experience is different. Performers will be more energized by the audience and are apt to pick up the pace without knowing it.

Common sense and having your wits about you can go a long way toward keeping all your fingers and toes. It is very frightening to be opposite an actor and see a glazed look come into their eyes. That look usually means that either they have forgotten the fight or that they are conjuring up a sense memory of their hated father and about to take it out on you! This is red-light fever at its worst!

There is a school of actor training that espouses "real emotion" for every moment in the play. Unfortunately, this technique, while popular and effective in many situations, is particularly dangerous during a fight scene. The actor playing Edmund cannot *really* want to kill Edgar, or he might—and the curtain will ring down to the wailing of ambulances.

Fight scenes must be *acted* and must be consistent performance after performance. The scene must not be subject to variations of mood or emotional recall, but must be the same—always. Only in this way will the fight remain safe throughout the run of a production. The excuse that "I have to *feel* it" is only that—an excuse for poor technique. I have seen too many partners hurt by actors who "felt" it. Control is the key!

How to Get Rid of Performance Anxiety in Fight Scenes

1. Always rehearse with the performance speed as a final goal.

2. Always connect with your partner's eyes before beginning the fight and before difficult sequences.

3. Create a "fail-safe" phrase in case of memory loss. Decide either to go back to a specific point in the fight or to go to a predetermined spot near the end. Rehearse this!

4. Keep breathing! This helps to free the whole body—and besides, you'll need the oxygen!

5. Don't worry about remembering the whole fight at once; just remember the first few moves and the rest will come. Tie the choreography to ACTING BEATS!

6.   Slower is better, if you are unsure.

7.   Harder is *not* better.

8.   If you forget the moves, back away: *Don't invent!*

9.   Learn to "finger fight" the choreography backstage or in the dressing room as close to the fight as possible.

10. Don't skip fight calls or fight rehearsals.

11. Start the fight at a slow or moderate speed; this will give it somewhere to go. If the pace is too fast, it's harder to sustain it. Pace yourself.

12. In group fights or mass battles, make sure of those around you. You could hit someone or be hit! Never change the tempo of your choreography, since it will affect those around you.

13. If you are in performance and completely lost and your character must die, and you can't get out of it, commit suicide! It's safer than inventing choreography. It's coarse acting but you'll live to rehearse again.

14. Rehearse the broken blade scenario. Have the fight captain call out "Broken blade, Romeo! (or whoever)" during a rehearsal, and rehearse what you'd do in this instance. There should always be an extra sword either onstage, worn or carried by another character, or immediately offstage. Check that this safety sword is preset every night.

15. Finally, *be the best partner you can be!* A fight is not two monologues, but a physical dialogue. It is about sharing and timing and illusion.

Unbelievable, but True, Safety Mistakes!

No book on stage combat would be complete without a few horror stories of woe and mayhem. The following tales are either completely true (I can vouch for their veracity since I have counted stitches or winced vicariously in the audience) or only true by rumor and theater hearsay. The fact that it's hard to sort out reality from fiction goes a long way to exposing the grain of truth in all the stories.

So, feast your eyes upon this small collection of contusions, confusion, and combat gone awry, and learn that one should not expose oneself to similar circumstances.

Unbelievable, but True, Safety Mistakes! (via truth, hearsay, rumor, and innuendo)

1. On opening night of King Lear, an actor playing Edgar "went up," and improvised a full speed slashing headcut to Edmund, which narrowly missed beheading him. (The audience gasped!)

2. Trick arrows, supposed to arrive on target from offstage, stopped unerringly four feet from the victim's back.

3. A sword literally shattered into all its component parts and flew through the air. The fight was finished with the actor holding the bare blade.

4. A cavalry saber blade separated from its handle on a full moulinet and offered spinning death to a group of actors standing in its path. The actors dove out of the way just in time, and the blade crashed against a brick wall offstage left, ringing beautifully.

5. An actor playing Macbeth forgot to wear his "secret" dagger, thereby preventing Macduff from killing him as staged. The brave Scot allowed himself to be strangled.

6. A full lunge with a spear, supposed to be off target, arrived neatly between another actor's legs millimeters from a sensitive area!

7. In *Peter Pan* I witnessed a flying harness go awry and almost castrate the poor actor playing Michael. The actor was unconscious when pulled from the rig and walked on crutches for months. A stagehand in this production broke an arm when she was crushed against a wall by moving scenery.

8. Another actor of my acquaintance received a full blow in the face with a trash-can lid during a television fight, from a star actor full of red-light fever whose apology was, "Sorry, but you guys are used to it!" The result was six stitches.

9. During a class, an actor who was wielding a broadsword and cutting under the foot tried to help by raising the tip. The unfortunate result was a full force cut to a bare foot!

10. During an active fight rehearsal one actor overreacted to a shove, crashed against a wall, and loosed his sword, which then flew through a window and landed on the street three stories below in a shower of glass, missing (thankfully) passersby.

11. Many of my friends who joust on horseback tell of countless falls; broken collar bones; separated shoulders; broken faces, legs, fingers, and noses; knees hitting together at full gallop; and unpredictable breakaway lances that hit the face! One newspaper account held that an unfortunate jouster had a five-inch splinter (which entered through the eye) removed from his brain!

12. I have counted stitches on the head of an actor who accidentally ducked into a belly swipe with a broadsword.

13. I have counted stitches on the hand of an actor who accidentally parried too high in a broadsword fight where the partner's sword nearly severed his little finger.

14. I have worked with an actor who received a full-force blow to the back with a club, which exploded five disks in his spine. He was disabled for two years.

15. I have met a young martial artist who, while practicing with a quarterstaff, had the misfortune of shattering an overhead fluorescent light and glancing up as it fell. He is blind for life in one eye.

16. I have heard of a production in which an actor was supposed to be hanged. After careful rigging, including a safety wire, the actor jumped off a raised platform: the main wire broke, the safety wire broke, and both of the actor's ankles broke.

17. On one of the television network's shows, a strong young actor was supposed to rehearse a fistfight in slow motion, but chose to attain the speed of light. The result of his actions left his leading lady, an innocent bystander, with a blackened eye.

18. An actor in drama school was tied to a chair in a production and was being threatened with a loaded gun held by another actor. Unfortunately, the actor who was holding the gun had no instruction in its use and pulled the trigger at the wrong moment. The resulting discharge burned the face of the actor tied to the chair, partially blinding him.

19. A "hot," young, strong, handsome, daytime television actor always refused to wear any kind of padding during fight scenes, scorning them as "silly," even though the studio floors are of cement. During a par-

ticularly violent combat, he forgot his choreography and improvised a fierce grappling hold, throwing himself and his partner to the floor. Afterward, he mentioned to me that he thought that he'd come close to breaking his arm when he landed on the floor.

20. A friend of mine, after getting his first big choreography break in a movie, arrived at the studio in time to see a fight being filmed and was greeted by a severed finger flying through the air!

21. An acquaintance of mine had a job as a "bad guy" in a nighttime television show and was to be pushed into a breakaway glass case. The rehearsals went smoothly; but when the cameras rolled, the "star" hit the "bad guy" so violently that the "bad guy" lost the skin on top of his head, shaved by the top of the case, and was virtually scalped.

22. An often-told story in the theater is the one about the actor who was to sneak up behind another actor and konk her on the head with a foam rubber pipe. One night the prop was mislaid; and in her rush to complete the scene, she picked up a real pipe and bashed the unfortunate victim on the head, sending her to the hospital in a coma.

23. I remember attending a fight show many years ago in which the first performer onstage was wearing an arm cast owing to an injury received the night before, and I remember afterward meeting another cast member who had received a small cut in the eye!

24. I remember speaking to a charming lady, Lois Kibbee, whose family had been traveling performers in the early part of this century. She told me that the stage manager had always carried a loaded gun on tour in case of trouble. One night the loaded gun had been mixed up with a prop gun, with the result that during a performance her grandfather was shot dead before her eyes.

25. The following story is typical, but nonetheless unfortunate: An amateur production of *Romeo and Juliet* hired two young men who were sport fencers and who put out each other's eye while bouting without masks during rehearsals!

26. A famous actor once admitted to me that during the run of an off-broadway play, she was supposed to be slapped in the face by another actor. Although there was no fight director, the rehearsals went well.

On opening night, the actor was hit so hard that her jaw dislocated, and she passed out onstage. When she woke up, she threw everything she could lay her hands on at the actor who hit her, and the next day she quit the show.

27. On the first day of rehearsals of a new play, an actor was to be pushed to the floor by another actor. As she fell, she placed both hands behind her to catch herself. The result was that the actor who fell broke both wrists and lost her job!

28. After careful rehearsal of a Paris-Romeo fight, in which Romeo was fighting with an "iron crow" (in reality a heavy, straight steel bar), I was satisfied with the safety aspects of the scene, with one exception. The actor who played Paris had a propensity to duck a blow and then rise unexpectedly without looking, about which I warned him repeatedly. Of course, he finally rose into the oncoming steel bar and received a nasty blow to the head. Thereafter, he "believed!"

29. In a Broadway play, an actor in full armor had to fall from a height of seven feet, six inches (two meters, twenty-seven centimeters) into the arms of four soldiers. The rehearsal was unsupervised. The result was only sore arm muscles (lucky!). The possible result could have been head injury or worse.

30. Observed during a rapier-and-dagger-fight skills test, a student actor mistakenly kicked his partner in the hand instead of the leg, and drove the point of the dagger into his partner's mouth, neatly breaking off a tooth!

Those are scary examples. Don't let yourself be caught in similar situations.

Now that we have some idea of how to stage and choreograph a fight, a sense of history, and a process through which to approach the performance of a fight, it is time to look at how to arm a fight. The choosing of weapons is a vital element of the choreography process. The fight between Romeo and Tybalt would be totally different if they fought with sabers rather than with rapiers and daggers.

Further, there is that nagging problem of rust and general maintenance. Fight captains, prop people, and stage management need to know how to deal with these problems, not to mention what and where to buy weapons. Gone are the days when the prop department stayed up till morning hammering out crude broadswords out of steel bar stock that weighed as much as a small Japanese car.

No longer must actors use homemade swords, shields, and other implements of destruction. The proliferation of professional sword makers in the United States and England has vastly increased the stock of theatrical weapons available and has improved their safety a thousandfold.

Arming the Fight

4

*T*he process of arming the fight should be as carefully researched as the process of costuming the performers. What is the best way to spend what little money that prop budgets usually have?

This process is made easier if the theater or school already has either a large stock of weapons from all periods or an unlimited budget. However, money is an issue most of the time, and few theaters can afford to maintain a large stock.

Several questions must be answered before picking up the phone to purchase or rent weapons.

1. **What will the historical period and play concept be?**

   The playwright's choice of date and place must influence the style and type of weapons. Books on historical weaponry are available to help one choose weapons, and various manufacturers can provide catalogs and helpful information as to availability and historical accuracy. As a basic rule, though, if one is going to some length to provide the performers with historically accurate costumes and settings, the style of the weapons *must* match! However, a director's concept of the play can also affect the historical period or locale, and change weapon choice. Is it a fantasy or a dream sequence? Is it a ballet or opera in which opulence is important to the design? Will staging be nontraditional? Or is the setting an all-purpose "nonperiod"? One should pin the concept down before ordering anything.

2. **How many weapons will be needed?**

   One should count the number of principal combatants in the play and use this as a starting point. One should add to this number any "extras" carrying weapons. These could be soldiers, guards, or atmosphere characters. And one should add to this any ceremonial weapons. Finally, when one has a finished list, one should track the characters through the play and see if there can be any sharing or doubling of weapons, thereby reducing the number. (Tip: Don't forget to count belts and scabbards too!)

3. **What type of weapons will be needed?**

   There are many ways to approach this problem. Some productions require safe, *practical weapons*; in other words, weapons that can stand up to the abuse of stage combat rehearsals and performances and not break. These might be historically accurate swords, shields, daggers or knives, or even firearms. Also included in this list might be more modern "found" props used in a fight. As a cost-cutting measure, it is also possible to arm characters in a play with *costume weapons*; in other words, swords or other weapons that look realistic, but are merely ornamental and not meant to wield in any type of realistic fashion. These might include plastic pistols, rubber knives, and wooden swords and are much less expensive than practical weapons. Most productions have a mixture of both types, practical and costume weapons, in order to stretch the weapons' budget.

4. **What about the budget?**
    Having finalized the period in history and counted heads, one should figure out approximately how much money the weapons will cost and see if they will fit into the budget. It is usually necessary to cut weapons here and there. Principal combatants (Tybalt-Mercutio-Romeo, Edmond-Edgar, Valmont-Danceny, Cyrano-deValvert, etc.) must be supplied with combat safe weapons. Extraneous weapons are always cut from the secondary characters or "extras." Fake swords, costume prop swords, plastic guns, and other solutions can usually be found to arm the cast as a whole.

5. **To rent or to buy?**
    Outright purchase of stage weapons is cheaper in the long run than rental. If a theater plans to regularly produce plays that involve stage combat over a long period of years, the classics in particular, then it's advantageous to begin to build a stock of weapons in the prop department.

    On the other hand, if a theater has no prop storage, if budgets are tight, if it will be years until the production of another play with guns and swords, then money is better spent on rentals. Ownership of weapons carries a commitment, since they must be maintained and not allowed to rust or they will deteriorate and become useless. Sword blades become old, fatigued, and must be replaced. Weapons, especially firearms, must be stored securely, since they are a magnet to thieves. In educational situations, the cost of the weapons can sometimes be spread into an academic area, and a course in stage combat can be offered to the students before rehearsals begin for the play.

6. **Have the little things been forgotten?**
    One should not forget to budget in such items as replacement sword blades in case of breakage (a must!) and such cleaning items as oil, rags, steel wool, and polishing compound. The cost of sword belts, scabbards, gloves, and such items as blood and knee pads should also be factored in. If firearms are used, one should add in the cost of blank

ammunition, insurance, deposits, and cleaning equipment. Perishables, such as breakaways or food props, must also be taken into account in the budget.

This chapter on arming the fight will give solid advice on how to purchase or rent weapons, where to find the manufacturers, and some hints for creative weapons use. There is also a section with information on sword maintenance, not only during the run of a production, but for long-term storage. Often swords and daggers are altered by the prop department for different productions; therefore, tips on how to safely perform this type of transformation will also be given.

Finally, I have listed several safety tips about the padding of actors who must perform unarmed combat or falls. This safety equipment is often overlooked but should be planned for and purchased before rehearsals start.

I am often asked about the subject of breakaways. People seem to be fascinated with the image (often from a movie) of a chair being broken over some hapless stunt man's head. The last part of this chapter deals with the illusion, safety, and danger of typical breakaway props for the theater. The how-to's of breakaway bottles, furniture, and other props are detailed and added to the list of possibilities of how to arm a fight.

Choosing a Period Weapon

Choose a sword that fits your needs, your budget, your hand, and the historical context of the play! Before analyzing how to arm a staged fight, examine these charts on the development of swords, daggers, pole arms, and shields. The charts contain a timeline to help you choose weapons in the correct historical style for your production. The charts were prepared by Mr. Bashford Dean, past curator of arms and armor at New York's Metropolitan Museum of Art.

Tips on Historical Weaponry

Here are some other ideas that may help a fight director choose weapons for a theatrical production. It is always more interesting to have lots of choices for the performers than to arm everyone with the same type of sword or firearm. I have broken the basic periods up as follows:

(*Text continues on p. 191.*)

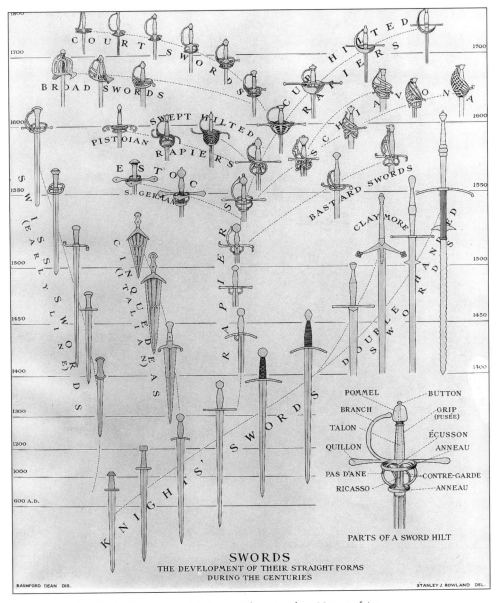

Figure 4-1. Timeline for European sword development. The Metropolitan Museum of Art.

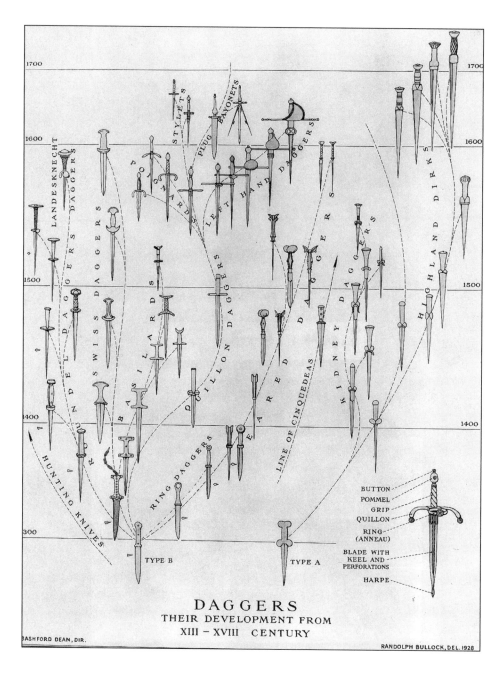

Figure 4-2. Timeline for European dagger development. The Metropolitan Museum of Art.

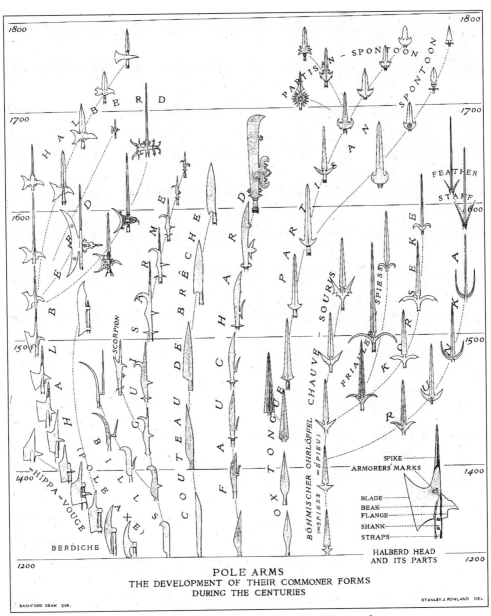

Figure 4-3. Timeline for European pole arm development. The Metropolitan Museum of Art.

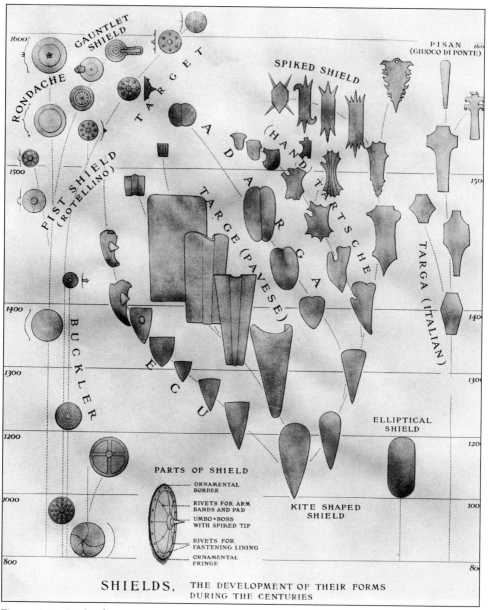

Figure 4-4. Timeline for European shield development. The Metropolitan Museum of Art.

Greco-Roman   dagger; sword; spear; gladius; javelin; bow and arrow; shield; slingshot; trident; net

Medieval   club; mace; flail; warhammer; ax; dagger; sword: single-handed, double-handed; shield: kite, round; pole arm: spear, pike, halberd, glaive, partisan, poleax, hammer, fork; longbow; crossbow; hand cannon; quarterstaff; armor; agricultural weapon; morning star; battleax

Renaissance   rapier; dagger; mace; warhammer; pole arm: pike, bill, glaive, poleax, halberd, partisan; longbow; crossbow; arquebus; pistol; buckler; shield; gauntlet; cape; lantern; falchion; poinard; agricultural weapon

Restoration   rapier; smallsword; sabre; dagger; plug bayonet; pole arm; rifle (flintlock); pistol (flintlock); hunting sword; lance; agricultural weapon

Weapons Through the Ages

An important part of choosing the correct weapons for any play is understanding the vast array of choices available. A fight director who is unfamiliar with these choices limits himself or herself as well as the performers to a single set of choreographic concepts.

Below is a list of the principal stage weapons from four periods in history. The list focuses primarily on weapons from the European and American cultures. Space prevents listing every possible weapon linked to specific ethnic groups and cultures throughout history. If a production concept places *King Lear* among the Native American tribes of the American Southwest or in medieval Japan, more research will be necessary. I have also omitted war engines such as catapults, trebuchets, cannon, and field artillery as not representative of personal combat usually depicted on the stage.

Ancient Greece and Rome

Sword   "shortsword" or "gladius" of one and a half to two feet long, leaf bladed, usually made of iron or bronze

Dagger   short, thick

Shield   round, two to three feet in diameter, also rectangular; sometimes with a locking device that enabled soldiers to interlock their shields to present a "wall" of defense

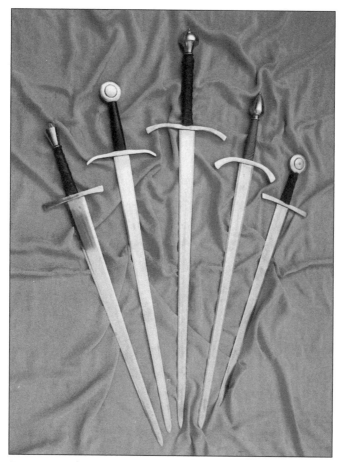

Figure 4-5. *Theatrical broadswords. These fine reproductions of medieval weapons are stage combat worthy, safe, and historically accurate. They are available in one-handed, hand-and-a-half, and two-handed styles. (Lewis Shaw, armorer)*

Spear   five to six feet long, often thrown or used at short range to attack

Sling   hand sling used to launch stones

Bow   crude bow of wood and leather

Armor   mostly leather, with iron or bronze helmets

Javelin   a light throwing spear, often carried in multiples by Roman foot soldiers.

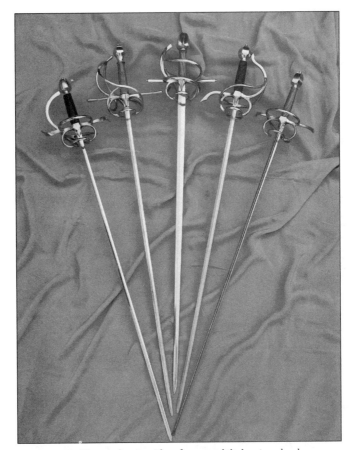

Figure 4-6. *Theatrical rapiers. These five swept-hilted rapiers also show various blade choices. From left to right: schlager, diamond schlager, "full size" diamond schlager, and épée blades. Also note the different pommel designs and handle treatments of leather or wire. (Lewis Shaw, amorer)*

Slingshot a simple missle-launching weapon made from leather or cloth that could throw stones or crude sling-bullets

Trident three-pointed, fork-headed pole arm used for attack and defense, which made its way from the field to the gladiatorial arena

Net square or circular cord net, often used with a trident to entrap, strike, or trip an opponent

Figure 4-7. *Theatrical daggers. These five Renaissance daggers would match well with a rapier for rapier-and-dagger play. The dagger was a common weapon and tool for hundreds of years. (Lewis Shaw, armorer)*

Medieval Europe, 1066–1450

Two-handed broadsword   a weapon up to six feet long, broad and heavy, used in warfare and in the "lists"

Hand-and-a-half-broadsword or bastard sword   a smaller weapon, generally four to five feet long that could be used with two hands or with one hand when holding a shield

Single-handed broadsword   a broad-bladed weapon usually used with a shield for defense

Shield   of various popular designs including kite-shaped full body, kite-shaped half body, round or rectangular, often decorated with coat-of-arms designs

Dagger (misericord, rondel, kidney)   of many designs, including common knives and broad-bladed quillon daggers used in the left hand with a single-handed broadsword (Daggers often were used to deliver the coup de grace between the chinks of armor.)

Figure 4-8. *Modest theater budgets sometimes substitute modern sport sabers fitted with épée blades for more historically accurate rapiers.*

Ax   hand axes used alone, with a shield, or in conjunction with a sword

Mace   heavy-headed concussion weapon used alone or in conjunction with a shield or sword

Morning star   heavy-headed concussion weapon attached to a short shaft by means of a chain

Flail   chain attached to a shaft (This weapon could be one-handed or quite long and two-handed.)

Pole arms   a category of arms (characterized by a length of five to eighteen feet) such as the following:

> **Pike**   spear headed and the longest of the pole arms, used in great numbers to defend groups of cavalry or archers
>
> **Halberd**   ax headed, with points for thrusting and occasionally hooks for tripping men and horses
>
> **Partisan**   broadly spear headed, often ceremonial
>
> **Poleax**   heavy ax headed and pointed, usually about four to five feet long and deadly in close-quarter fighting
>
> **Glaive**   long, single-edged cutting blade, based on an agricultural tool
>
> **Hammer**   combination of a hammerhead for concussion, a point, and a "can opener" beak for piercing armor
>
> **Fork**   various two- and three-pointed designs

Staff (quarterstaff)   long, hardwood poles with little or no sophistication, occasionally dressed with leather or iron bands at the ends

Longbow   six-foot-long bow (extreme range about three hundred yards) used by archers (more numerous than knights in medieval armies) with devastating effect. (Archers carried many three-foot arrows in quivers, and often daggers and swords as well.)

Crossbow   extreme range about four hundred yards; capable of penetrating armor at close range (The arrow for a crossbow was called a bolt, or quarrel, and was shorter and thicker than a longbow arrow. Additionally, the crossbowman had to carry a winder, or spanner, to enable him to draw the string.)

Hand cannon   an early firearm designed to launch stone or metal shot and primed with black powder and lit fuse

Warhammer   a one-handed weapon about three feet in length, with a metal head composed of a blunt hammer shape for concussion blows, and a spike, or pick head to penetrate armour or chain mail

Battleax   a heavy, two-handed weapon with a large ax head attached to a wooden shaft.

European Renaissance, 1450–1660

Broadsword   remnant of medieval broadsword design; short, thick, broad-bladed early rapier often used in conjunction with a shield called a buckler

Rapier   quintessential Renaissance sword, narrow-bladed; used for cutting and thrusting; with multiple designs (such as cups, rings, swept hilts, and counterguards) to protect the hand; civilian sword of choice

Dagger (main gauche, quillon dagger, cinquedea, eared dagger)   often a defensive weapon used in conjunction with the rapier; multiple designs, from simple crossguarded to "sword breakers" designed to trap and break a rapier blade

Longbow   (See above.)

Crossbow   (See above.)

Pole arm   (See above.)

Hand- and battle-ax   (See above.)

Shield   military shield that included large wooden, leather, or metal shields of various designs

Buckler   a type of shield used primarily by civilians and characteristically smaller and lighter than military shields; sizes ranging from three feet in diameter to only several inches; made of hardened leather, wood, or steel; used for deflecting sword blows

Cape   weighted and sometimes used defensively with the rapier to ward off blows, trap blades, or throw in an opponent's face

Gauntlet   hardened leather or chainmail-palmed heavy gloves worn on the left hand to block, seize, or deflect sword attacks

Case of rapiers   an unusual style whereby two matching rapiers were used simultaneously instead of using a rapier and dagger

Firearms   developed quickly in the Renaissance and made an impact on the battlefield and city streets

Arquebus   improvement on the hand cannon and an early matchlock rifle, from the mid–fifteenth century

Wheellock pistol/rifle   further improvement in firearms, with the advantage that it could be used with one hand; mid–sixteenth century through mid–eighteenth-century firearm

Flintlock pistol/rifle   a further refinement of the firing mechanism developed in the mid–seventeenth century that greatly improved the speed and accuracy of firearms; many varieties and styles of weapons, including derringers, hunting rifles, matched pistol sets, etc.; early seventeenth-century through early nineteenth-century firearm

Note on firearms: Though historically inaccurate, percussion-cap firearms often double for wheellock and flintlock weapons onstage (Read the chapter on firearms for further information.)

Mace   (See above.)

Warhammer   (See above.)

Lantern   used occasionally at night during robbery attempts, or duels, "bullseye" lanterns were designed to focus light forward, simultaneously illuminating a victim while blinding him.

Falchion   a type of hunting sword characterized by it's shape. Vaguely "machete" shaped, it was thick, occasionally with a saw-tooth false edge, and a curved true edge, wider at the point than the shoulder. Primarily designed to butcher animals in the field.

Poniard   (also poignard) a short dagger designed primarily for thrusting

Restoration Period, 1660s

Smallsword   final evolution of the civilian sword; lightweight, ornate, and a much smaller weapon than a rapier

Saber   advent of military saber; long, heavy—and in the case of cavalry sabers, curved

Dagger (stiletto, poinard)   basic tool of offense and defense throughout this period

Pole arm   relatively unchanged pole arm design, but more elaborate ceremonial pole arms (Cavalry soldiers carried lances, and the navy issued boarding pikes until the early twentieth century.)

Firearms   (See chapter on firearms for detailed information.)

Plug bayonet   early bayonet design which attached to a rifle by jamming it down the muzzle, creating a crude pole arm

Hunting sword   short, heavy sword designed primarily to butcher animals in the field (falchion), or longer thrusting sword designed either to kill them in close quarters as a test of hunting skill or bravery, or to deliver a coup de grace after running the animal down with horses or dogs.

Weapons Purchase

It is vital to the safety of the actors and the audience to procure practical, stageworthy weapons. This is not as difficult as it once was since several companies and individuals are now producing well-designed, safe weapons. However, because most theatrical productions do not have Broadway budgets, costs are still cut and an inexperienced fight director or prop head can accidentally buy the wrong thing.

What follows are some things to be aware of when purchasing weapons for a theatrical production.

Beware of	Look for
Swords that are inexpensive (They are probably meant to hang on a wall.)	Reasonably priced swords, sold by a reputable dealer
Swords cast from pot metal (a brittle, inexpensive metal)	Steel, bronze, or brass parts
Rusty weapons (They may be brittle or fatigued.)	Well-maintained, rust-free, used equipment
Competitive foils or sabres (They are designed to whip, and may injure.)	Theatrical reproductions that are made to withstand the beating they get from actors
Welded tangs or no tangs	Blade and tang that are one piece of metal (Examine all tangs by screwing off the pommel.) Some welded tangs are fine, but consult an expert!

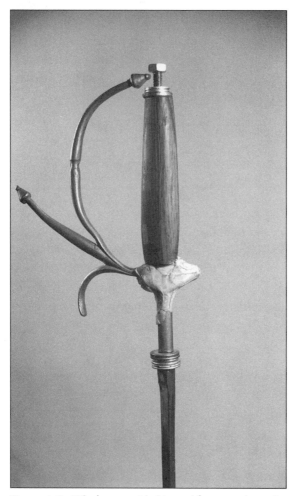

Figure 4-9. *What's wrong with this sword from top to bottom?*

1. A nut is used instead of a pommel to tighten the weapon.
2. There is a space between the nut and washers; therefore, the sword will be loose.
3. Too many washers are used as spacers.
4. The brass guard is broken. Tape covers sharp areas that may injure the hand. The right quillion is bent back.
5. Overlarge washers are used as spacers near the blade, which can injure the hand.
6. The blade is inserted sideways, preventing correct use of weapon's true edge.

I have seen many such weapons in theater store rooms. There is no excuse for giving actors unsafe equipment to use in a performance. This weapon should be thrown out!

Softwood (pine) handles	Hardwood, polycarbonate, leather, or wire wrapped handles
"Homemade" weapons	New weapons or legitimate rentals
Sharp points or edges	Filed-down points and edges
Blades that hold a bend or that are soft metal	Replacement blades before the first rehearsal
Poorly designed, cheap axes or maces not secured properly to handles	Reputable weapons dealers (Flea markets and catalogs are full of cheap imitations. Avoid them.) (See appendix for addresses.)

All fight directors have a preference as to what types of weapons they like to work with. *The person with final approval should be a fight director, not the designers or*

Figure 4-10. *Purchasing swords in the eighteenth century. Note the gentleman on the left who is trying the temper of a blade against the wall.*

prop personnel. Since cost is always a factor, care must be taken in choosing the number and style of weapons. Again, the person best qualified to do this is the fight director, who will know how much combat each character will be expected to perform. As a cost-cutting measure, nonfighting extras, or supernumeraries, can always be outfitted with costume weapons.

Creative Sword Purchase

I don't know how many times I have been in this situation. I arrive at regional theater X to rehearse the fights, and swords have not arrived, and fight props have not been built! Not only is valuable time wasted, but the safety of the overall production is jeopardized.

As soon as possible in preproduction, it is necessary to choose and order swords. This is to ensure that the fight director will get what he or she wants in plenty of time to use the swords in rehearsal.

What to order, though? Where and how? Once a fight director has chosen a legitimate theatrical weapons dealer (see appendix) and has checked the budget and counted carefully who needs weapons, he comes to the creative part.

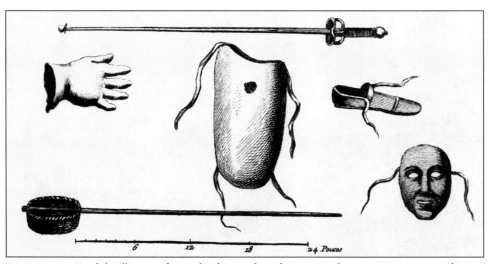

Figure 4-11. *I used this illustration from Diderot's Encyclopedie to arm and costume a scene in a 1770's fencing salle in a production of Scaramouche. Note the interesting masks, chest protector (plastron), buttoned foil, and special shoe. Below these is an example of a single stick, a wooden practice weapon popular in the eighteenth century.*

It is a good idea to choose a different type of weapon from the same period for each character. This way, a specific weapon is associated with each character throughout the play. An alternative is to give a specific *style* of weapon to each army, group, or family, such as cup-hilted rapiers to the Montagues and swept-hilted ones to the Capulets. In addition, if a particular character is from a specific country, try to give that character a type of sword associated with his country. In general, rich people owned fancy weapons, and poor ones had practical ones. There is a great deal of variety in sword styles, and this kind of matching can be accomplished without breaking the budget.

Here are some creative and safe tips to consider when purchasing weapons.

1. Give older characters older weapons. For example, an old man in a Renaissance play could have an older style broadsword. Capulet, in *Romeo and Juliet* act 1, scene 1, does in fact call for his "long sword."

2. Give lower-born characters simpler, more basic weapons. This can lead to very interesting combinations of fights. Examples of these types of weapons are farm implements, sticks, cudgels, scythes, oars, harpoons, knives, broken furniture, "homemade" weapons of all types, zip guns, chains, bottles, antenni, and so forth. The servants in *Romeo and Juliet* are usually not as well armed as their counterparts in the act 1 brawl.

   (Note: Be sure that these types of weapons are *safe*! Weapons should have dull edges and no loose parts and should be nonbreakable and practical for stage combat!)

3. Give rich or highborn characters fancy or well-made weapons. This can be as simple as giving a high polish to a sword before opening night and throughout the run of the play.

4. Decide whether to purchase or build scabbards. Almost ALL weapons had sheaths or scabbards of some type. To jam a naked rapier or broadsword in a belt is historically absurd.

5. Decide whether it is safe to have a mix of broader-bladed swords used against épée, or thinner-bladed swords. Be careful, though, since the possibility exists that the one could break the other!

6. Check the balance of heavier blades. If the weight is too far forward, replace the pommel with a heavier one.

7. Check the tangs of unfamiliar swords for size. They should never appear to have been butt-welded on. (See Fig. 4-28.)

8. Never allow the use of antique swords. Their safety cannot be guaranteed.

9. Give smaller performers smaller weapons. This is just common sense since smaller weapons are safer to wield. For comic purposes, sometimes the reverse can be true, such as giving a slight performer the biggest broadsword that can be found; but don't expect the performer to fight realistically.

10. Consider using "faked" weapons, such as rubber look-alikes, foam rubber rocks, or other weapons that will not be seen up close by the audience.

11. Consider using found objects as weapons, a cheap and choreographically interesting alternative. Use silver trays, laundry, hardwood sticks, or even costume pieces such as hats, scarves, gloves, coats, capes, and shoes to fight with. Use the furniture as well, such as chairs to throw or block, sofas to fall into, and pillows to hit with.

Finally, when searching for realistic weapons, call as many manufacturers as possible. Check their catalogs carefully beforehand and know what you want and how much you can spend. Suppliers are in the business of helping to solve theatrical production problems, and a creative way can always be found to maximize the production budget.

Remember that the choice of weapons is rooted in character. An imaginary production of *Macbeth*, for example, could have the mighty Scot armed in a number of ways depending on character, directorial concept, and style of combat:

#1	#2	#3	#4	#5
broadsword	broadsword	spear	whip	meathook
shield	mace	shield	knife	switchblade
	dagger			

These are all examples of the ways in which I have armed Macbeth in various productions over the years, in consultation with the director and the performer who was playing Macbeth.

Tip!

> The following is the most important thing to remember when deciding what types of swords to buy or rent: custom fit the size and weight of the weapon to the performer's size and ability, with an eye to the style of the sword fight that will be staged.
>
> If you want a fast, flashy, light rapier fight, use épée-bladed rapiers with simple lightweight hilt arrangements. If you want an older, heavier rapier style, order "full-sized" blades with heavier guards. If the performer playing Hamlet is slight, ectomorphic, and scant of breath, don't saddle him with a heavy weapon unsuited to his size. Another tip I've used in the past to slow an overenthusiastic performer down to a reasonable speed is to give him a weapon that is heavier than his partner's.
>
> Don't ever buy a weapon just because it looks good in a catalogue. Always keep a specific performer and fighting style in mind.

Arming a Shakespearian production can prove a daunting task on a slender budget. Here are a few ideas to stretch that dollar until it screams.

Arming *Romeo and Juliet* on the Cheap

If one is creative with the prop budget, even when it is rather small, there is usually a way to outfit the performers with safe swords. Take, for example, *Romeo and Juliet*. The characters of Tybalt and Mercutio must have swords. Traditionally they are given Renaissance rapiers of one kind or another. A production with more money might give them sets of rapiers with matching daggers. But what about a small budget show? The list of the characters who *should* have swords in *Romeo and Juliet* is daunting:

Capulet	Montague
Tybalt	Romeo
Sampson	Mercutio
Gregory	Benvolio
Paris	Abram
Prince	

Not to mention the Prince's guards, the Watch in act 5, and the angry Citizens who wield "clubs, bills, and partisans" in act 1.

However, there is always a way to maximize money. The following is a breakdown of weapons and a creative use of props for an imaginary production of *Romeo and Juliet* with a very small budget.

Romeo and Juliet

Act 1, Scene 1

Gregory	wooden knife (made by prop dept.)
Sampson	wooden (hardwood) staff (made by prop dept.)
Abram	aluminum tray of laundry, then wooden knife
Balthazar	wooden knife or hardwood staff
Benvolio	rapier A (Mercutio's later in play)
Tybalt	rapier B
Prince's Guards (4)	wooden staffs, painted and hung with Prince's colors
Old Montague	wooden broadsword, ax, or spear (made by prop dept.)
Old Capulet	large wooden broadsword (made by prop dept.)
Citizens	rakes, sticks, soft prop clubs (found by prop dept.)

Act 3, Scene 1

Mercutio	rapier A (previously Benvolio's)
Tybalt	rapier B
Romeo	rapier A (previously Mercutio's/Benvolio's)
Benvolio	wooden dagger in sheath on belt (previously Abram's)

Act 4, Scene 3

Juliet	ornamental wooden/rubber dagger or metal knife

Act 5, Scene 3

Romeo	rapier A wooden/rubber knife in sheath (for Juliet)
Paris	rapier B (previously Tybalt's)
Watch (4)	Wooden staffs with wooden spear heads (Act 1 staffs, colors removed, wooden spear heads screwed on for last act.)

In this example, the prop department only has to purchase two stageworthy swords. Then all the prop department has to do is carve three crude wooden knives which need not match, since they are for servants. Old Montague and Old Capulet receive large, fabricated, wooden weapons, which they never fight with but just flourish in the air. The enraged Citizens receive agricultural props such as rakes and sticks. If the Prince's Guards actually physically stop the fight, they can separate the families with their staffs. Juliet's "happy dagger" can be a rubber knife, realistically painted, but safe, for her suicide.

Finally, for the Guards/Watch, four hardwood dowels, dressed with flags in act 1, then with wooden spear heads in act 5, complete the prop list. (Pick interesting pole arm designs from Figure 4-3).

While not particularly historically correct, the above example *could* do in a production with a very limited budget.

The trick of Romeo's using Mercutio's sword is an old one and only necessitates Mercutio's leaving his sword onstage after he is stabbed for Romeo to pick up. Thereafter, Romeo may keep that sword through the rest of the play. Paris, on the other hand, is easily given Tybalt's sword after Tybalt's body is cleared off the stage. And voila! A Romeo and Juliet with two rapiers. However, the money was spent on SAFE combatworthy weapons, not several dangerous "wall hangers" (which are decorative swords sold to hang over your fireplace!).

Here is my point. It is wiser (and safer) by far to spend money on safe fighting weapons for principals who must fight and to be creative in other areas. One must be realistic with the budget and the capabilities of the performers. One must work closely with the various suppliers and call them on the phone and get their advice. They are experienced in helping sort out these problems and supplying information; therefore, one needn't be afraid to consult them.

When in doubt, call someone who has purchased weapons before and ask for their advice. Don't be fooled by cheap, flashy merchandise. It is difficult to judge photographs of weapons in catalogs, if you are not already familiar with the equipment.

If one tries to cut corners and buy weapons "on the cheap," the weapons will surely break at the most inappropriate time and will be, as Ralph Nader once said, "unsafe at any speed!"

While it is vital to provide the performers with safe weapons for rehearsals, it is also necessary to provide them with basic padding to lessen contact with the floor during rehearsals. Even in nonfight plays, there is often action that requires performers to be on their knees for extended periods or to fall to the

Figure 4-12. *A publicity still shot in Central Park. Note the lack of protective padding!*

ground. A box full of basic padding should be owned by every theater and drama school for the safety of the performers.

For anyone unfamiliar with the use of padding or with the kind of padding that is commercially available, the following pages should help. Most padding is easily hidden under costumes, particularly bulky period armor. Even modern plays allow for the occasional leather jacket, sweater, and overcoat that will hide this layer of protection.

If you are an actor, never hesitate to ask for padding in rehearsals, even if ultimately you won't need it in performance. Fight directors and stage managers should provide padding as standard rehearsal gear and should insist that performers wear the padding whenever there is a risk of bruising or abrasion.

Protective Equipment for Actors

Stage combat is an art that hides itself! Well then, if the audience isn't aware of strategic padding and the performer is saved from bruises and scrapes, then we've created MAGIC!

Protective equipment to save a performer from injury is often neglected in the rush to stage the fight, but can be as simple as wearing knee pads or as elaborate as padding parts of the set. Certainly performers with long-term injuries to joints or muscles, particularly knees, should be protected by wraps, braces, and padding whenever possible. Hopefully, the costumer will be able to adjust the fit of the costume to hide this protection. The audience will never know, and it is better to be safe than sorry.

It is important to remember that pads DO NOT MAKE AN ACTOR INVULNERABLE! They are only protection, not a cure-all. Don't think that you can be hit full force with a baseball bat because you have half an inch (two centimeters) of padding in your hat!

It is also very important to practice using the pads before opening night. Pads can be restrictive, and many performers do not like to wear them. There is a mistaken attitude that "the audience can see them" or that "men don't wear pads!" Many injuries have occurred from this kind of self-consciousness, for in the heat of battle, the floor comes up awfully fast! Besides, if the audience is looking at an actor's pads, that actor is not doing his job. The audience should be looking at the actor's performance!

Figure 4-13. *Another publicity shot from Central Park. This time I have lots of hidden pads under my clothes.*
Photo by A. C. Weary

Basic Padding

Performers take a lot of falls, and stage or studio floors vary widely. Padding can not only lessen the impact of a fall but can protect the skin from cuts and abrasions. There is a difference, too, between padding up because you know you are going to have some contact and padding for protection, just in case! The following are the basic types of pads and some of their applications. One should always check with an expert before attempting any kind of fall, flip, or roll. Pads do not lessen the risk of injury when performers attempt falls beyond their ability. Always turn the pads in the direction of the fall.

Knee pads   Buy the large "football" type, with a hole in the rear. These pads are used for any front fall where the knee might hit first, and are also helpful for kneeling and crawling.

Elbow pads   There are two types: small knee pads and long forearm pads that reach the elbow. Both are good and worth having. For difficult front falls, pad the upper arm with a knee pad, the elbow with another, and the forearm with a forearm pad.

Kidney pads   The "football" type, with removable foam inserts, are washable and durable and will help to protect the hips and kidneys from impact.

Athletic cup   An athletic cup is a serious piece of safety equipment widely available in sports stores. Whenever a struggling or wrestling scene threatens the groin area, male combatants should wear a cup in an athletic supporter.

Shin guards   These are used when impact on the front of the shin is expected. They are made of hard plastic, with foam backing, and are taped or strapped on. Use "football," "lacrosse," "soccer," or "hockey" types. They can also double on arms, if small enough.

Leather and Kevlar pads   These custom-made pads can help to protect from a contact cut or stab wound. Great care must still be used when performing these illusions, since the pads are not designed to STOP a blade but to protect the performer from shock or abrasion. A Kevlar chest pad can be created from a fencing jacket.

Wrist guards   Wrist guards with metal or heavy plastic inserts protect a weak wrist from falls or other impacts.

Custom-made Padding

Actors take enough abuse without adding bumps and bruises. Taking a few moments to create custom pads will often lessen actors' burdens and will allow them to perform with more freedom.

It is also possible to make your own pads for special applications or to pad something for which a commercial pad isn't available. For this purpose, "high density," or "closed cell," foam is a very good product. It is to be found across the country in camping supply stores and is used under sleeping bags. It comes in three-by-six-foot (one-by-two-meter) sheets and is easily cut and molded to fit. Do not confuse this with low-density foam! Low-density foam is usually yellow in color, thicker, and used for pillows. Some suggestions follow as to how to make custom padding from high-density foam:

Protecting the shoulders.   Cut a large piece of foam that will cover the shoulders and backbone and sew or attach with duct tape to a light T-shirt.

Protecting the coccix.   Cut a double layer of foam to fit the performer, glue together, and sew to underwear.

Protecting the head.   Cut a small piece of foam and hide it in a hat or cap.

Protecting the hips.   Cut a large piece of foam that fits around the waist and hips. Sew a long strip of Velcro® or a cloth belt into the waistband to secure it, or attach it to heavy underwear.

Hiding pads under costumes.   Custom-cut pads are easily hidden in costumes, whether modern or period. Pads can be sewn in permanently or sewn onto a T-shirt to be slipped on under the main costume. With especially boney performers, protecting the protruding bones of the spine, shoulder, hip, coccix, and elbows is very important if those performers are to absorb falls.

Hiding pads under rugs.   Cut a piece of foam the size of the rug that a performer is to fall on. If there are no rugs on the set, ask the designer for a small area rug. Stair falls, as in such plays as *Black Comedy* or *Noises Off*, also feel better with a layer or two of foam under the rug. This trick is a *must* for extended physical contact and floor work in plays such as *Extremities*. Tack the foam to the rug with a few stitches, so that it can't slip out from underneath.

An actor should never be shy about using pads for protection. A box of standard padding (knee and elbow) should always be available in the rehearsal space and should be part of standard procedure from the first rehearsal through closing night.

Figure 4-14. *Always pad under rugs if performers will struggle for long periods of time on the floor!*

Breakaway Props

Breakaway props are a staple item on television programs and in films. Breakaways that look like the real thing have clobbered many a star and, more often, a bit player or stunt person—in other words, the bad guys. Any evening on television you can see various "hard" objects flying through the air and smashing down with force (and overlayed sound effects) on heads, backs, arms, and into stomachs.

Since cost is a major factor for breakaway props, only productions with large budgets can afford them. They come under the category of "perishables" since they must be replaced every night. At a cost of approximately twelve dollars each for a "sugar glass" bottle, it rapidly becomes costly to break up the bar! Handmade (by union carpenters) balsa wood chairs or tables can cost upward

213

Figure 4-15. *Breakaway glass shatters magnificently!*

of five hundred dollars each. Custom-made sugar glass and balsa wood French windows cost about fifteen hundred to three thousand dollars!

Since safety is our main focus, let's look at the commercially available breakaways, their uses, and their potential safety problems.

Breakaway Glass

Also known as "sugar glass," this is the popular term for the breakaway bottle that is well known in the film and television industry. Made in olden days of thin, hardened sugar, today's bottles are made from resins. What most people don't know, however, is that many types of glass breakaways are available. A short list would include the following:

Glasses	tumbler, wine, mug/stein, highball, shot, champagne
Bottles	wine, whisky, gin, beer, in colors that include clear, amber, and green (complete with fake labels)
Vases	small (twelve inches high, four inches wide) and large (sixteen inches high, eight inches wide)
Ashtrays	small (four-inch diameter) and large (eight-inch diameter)
Pitchers	beer type

Breakaway glass is also commercially available in sheets, precut to size. The larger the piece, the thicker the glass must be to support its own weight. A large sheet of glass can be one-quarter to three-eighths of an inch thick. This may not seem like much, but can slow an actor down considerably when going through it!

The most common misconception about breakaway glass is that it is completely safe. This is not true. Breakaway glass can injure performers in many ways. The thicker the glass, the sharper an edge it can hold and the greater the potential for danger. Breakaway glass objects should not be treated as toys!

The Dangers of Breakaway Glass

Breakaway glass shatters magnificently! In short, the pieces go everywhere—all over the floor and furniture, down your shirt, and into your ears. Great care must be taken when the use of a breakaway is indicated by the script, the director, or the fight director. What follow are rules for handling breakaway glass and suggestions for avoiding accidents.

1. Never hit a performer in the face with a glass breakaway! The shards can land in the eyes, and the face is easily injured.

Figure 4-16. *A "rum"-style, green-color, breakaway bottle.*

Figure 4-17. *A "whiskey"-style, light brown, breakaway bottle.*

2. Never hit a performer with the thick end of a breakaway bottle. The base of the bottle is the thickest part and can injure a performer.

3. Never grab the breakaway with too much force or it will shatter in your hand.

4. Never swing the breakaway too hard or it may break on the upswing or the downswing, fly apart, and hit someone unintentionally.

5. Never use a breakaway in a confined space, such as a live performance at a party or intimate theater, or close to other performers or audience members who may be injured by flying debris.

6. Never hit a performer swinging a breakaway toward downstage, since the debris will land in the audience.

7. Avoid hitting a performer on any area of exposed skin since the shards may cut. Only hit areas protected by costumes or padding.

8. To minimize breakage and scattering of debris, wrap the breakaway with some clear adhesive tape before use, or create a large paper label and glue on at front and back.

9. Never fill a breakaway bottle with liquid! Its impact will be much greater because of the added weight. If liquid must be used, fill the bottle with only an inch or two. Never fill the bottle with hot liquid since it will melt the breakaway glass.

10. Always close the eyes at the moment of impact.

11. Prepare in advance to deal with the great amount of small glass shards onstage. These shards can be very slippery and must be cleared off the stage in some way. This becomes dangerous when the fight must continue after the bottle breaks since the mess will affect footing. Rehearse this carefully and thoroughly!

12. When using breakaway bottles, always aim to make contact with the widest part of the bottle, usually the middle.

13. Whenever possible protect the hand that is holding the breakaway with a glove, since the remainder of the bottle (such as the neck) can injure the attacker.

14. When building large breakaways, such as windows, never use any metal fasteners, such as nails, screws, hinges, and so forth. It is much safer, and recommended, to use glue, putty, and other soft, nonabrasive fastenings. Always use balsa wood, Styrofoam® or other low-density material for the window mullions and casements.

Greenware

There is an alternative to breakaway glass that many people overlook. It is cheaper than buying commercial breakaway glass, but it has limited applications.

Greenware is a term used in pottery for items that are dry but not yet "fired" and that are therefore reasonably brittle. Greenware is mainly used when the performer is not required to be struck with the prop, but when, say, a vase of flowers must be broken during the action. I repeat that it is important not to substitute greenware for breakaway glass since hitting a performer with greenware is much more dangerous. The weight of greenware can be substantial, and therefore it is not to be used on the body.

Many plays require that props be broken. Often a fight director will choreograph a sequence in which items are broken to augment the "danger factor" of the fight. Greenware is perfect for situations in which props are knocked over, thrown, or struck with swords or other props. The greenware shatters nicely, and the pieces are not particularly sharp. The pieces do not make much of a sound, though, and this can be somewhat disappointing.

A good example of the use of greenware is in productions of I Hate Hamlet. In this play the character of Barrymore must sweep a lamp off of a table, breaking it in an attempt to urge Andrew into fighting him. A lamp is quite an expensive prop to break every night, and one solution is to have the base of the lamp made from greenware. The lamp hardware and lamp shade can be reused each night.

One final advantage to greenware is that it can be purchased locally. Every city has a pottery, and arrangements can be made to have the local pottery make greenware for a theatrical production at a fraction of the cost of shipping it in from elsewhere or of purchasing breakaway glass. The other advantage is that the scenic artists for the production can paint greenware in a way that matches the set design.

Balsa Breakaways

Balsa is a tremendously versatile wood material from which many props can be constructed. All kinds of candlesticks, tool handles, chairs, stair railings, and tables can be made of balsa. The list can go on to include props not usually made from wood, such as fake metal tools, knives, ski poles—in short, almost anything can be made from balsa and then painted to look like the real thing. For years performers have been hit, poked, and smashed over the head in unending variety with these props.

However balsa is not as safe as it first may appear to be! There is a common misconception that balsa has the same consistency as Styrofoam® and is as soft. While it is true that a thin piece of balsa is laughably weak, this is a very tough material. Consider that the Kon Tiki was made of whole balsa trees and weathered the storms of the Pacific Ocean!

We are lulled into this false sense of security because the material itself is so lightweight and because film stunts look so easy! A major reason for this is that stuntpeople usually don't mind taking a bit of a tap—or often what would be described as a hell of a hit! What isn't so obvious is that the balsa prop has often been prescored by a stunt coordinator to break more easily and in the direction required.

If one were to purchase a balsa two-by-four board and attempt to break it over the head of another performer in a fight scene, it would send that person to the hospital. Balsa is that tough!

If balsa breakaway props are to be used onstage, they must be very carefully built and precut, or scored, to safely break the same way every time.

The problem usually surfaces with bigger pieces of balsa. The aforementioned two-by-four must be precut to break, with either a saw or sharp utility knife. The cut may be hidden by painting over the raw wood. Never fill the cut with glue to hide it, as I saw one person do! Only a quarter inch of solid wood should be left to actually break. It is always a good idea to make several cuts on the prop for safety insurance. The more complicated the prop, like chairs and tables, the more cuts required to make it break. A breakaway chair may have some twenty cuts in it.

The use of heavy breakaway props is NOT RECOMMENDED without trained supervision. Such props are just too dangerous to play around with. However, small breakaways can be used successfully if safety rules are followed and common sense is applied.

If one is to be hit with a breakaway balsa prop, one should pad oneself in the area to be hit. Soft pads, covered by hard plastic soccer type pads to take the initial blow, are a necessary margin of safety. Nothing is infallible, though, as I learned on a television set in New York, when I was to be hit on the back by an actor with a balsa two-by-four but was hit square in the head!

Safety Rules for Balsa Breakaways

1. Never hit a performer in the head or face with a balsa breakaway.
2. Always precut, or prescore, balsa before using it on a performer. The maximum safe width is one-quarter inch. When in doubt, cut it thinner! Rehearse the strength of the break before trying it on the actors.

3. Use padding under the costume or body armor to protect the "victim" performer from the hit. It's a good idea to overpad the area to be hit since the performer who strikes the target might miss and hit another area of the body!

4. Be aware that the pieces of broken balsa may fly across the stage or into the audience. Practice the hits in rehearsal, and stage them in such a way that the flying debris will land in a safe area.

5. If constructing large balsa breakaways, never use any metal fasteners. Only use glue, paste, soft putty, and so forth. Always consult an expert during construction.

6. Never strike a performer in a vital organ or other sensitive area with a balsa breakaway.

7. Every piece of balsa has a slightly different density and grain. Be careful when building props and set pieces since the way in which they are built will affect the breaking point, or tensile strength.

8. Do not carve "fake" knives of balsa and use them to stab performers. Do not be fooled by balsa's light weight. If sharpened down to even a dull point, balsa can do a lot of damage.

To put this into perspective, in the film and television industry, "taking" a balsa prop on the body is considered a *stunt*, and the performer is paid accordingly. The use of large balsa breakaways such as chairs or tables is therefore *not recommended* for amateurs, drama students, or most professionals. Only under very tight control, and with *professional supervision*, will this kind of gag be safe.

Sword Maintenance

It is no surprise that, since most weapons are made from metal, they rust. Oxidation, however, is not the only problem facing the rapier or broadsword. I have observed mishandling in the form of throwing weapons to the floor and stabbing them into cement walls as well as leaving them out in the rain! Old age, metal fatigue, pitting, and loosening are also part of the life of the stage weapon.

Figure 4-18. *An illustration showing the amazing detail of a Renaissance rapier.*

From the moment of purchase, the theater department or production company should appoint someone to maintain its weapons. This person is usually the prop head or the fight captain. Theatrical weapons are a major investment and when well treated can last for decades. By the same token, if left to rust in a box or if tossed into the corner of a humid prop storage room, weapons will be dangerous to use in a few months!

Here is a maintenance schedule for an average stage weapon during its useful life.

After Purchase or Rental

Check for broken or missing parts.

Oil the blade.

Check the tightness of the pommel.

Number, mark, and assign weapons.

Daily, During Rehearsal or Performance

Check for loosening and if necessary hand tighten the pommel.

Check for pitting and if necessary file by hand or machine.

Check for rust and if necessary use steel wool or oil.

Check for metal fatigue and if necessary replace the blade.

Check for breakage and if necessary replace defective parts.

Count weapons, especially during large shows.

Lock weapons away for overnight security.

Weekly, During Rehearsal or Performance

Inspect each weapon for rust and looseness.

Derust and oil blades, hilts, and pommels.

File by hand or machine (broadswords especially).

Check for stripped threads.

Tighten loose pommels.

Before Opening Night

Spend time with each weapon, making sure it is tight and secure.

Polish all parts on a bench grinder fitted with a buffing wheel. (Be sure to wear protective equipment when using a grinder. Always follow manufacturers' instructions and safety warnings.)

Check scabbards, belts, and frogs for damage; polish leather.

A light coat of oil on a blade a half hour before the fight scene helps the blade pick up the light. (Do not oil handles!)

Postproduction Long-term Storage

Loosen pommels.

Remove rust, stains, or burrs by hand or machine.

Replace broken parts.

Discard old or suspect blades or save them to make into daggers.

Heavily grease, wax, or oil metal parts.

Store in a secure, moisture-proof box, trunk, or storage area, with date and inventory.

No one can say exactly how long a sword will last; but when a sword is badly treated, its safe useful life is reduced to weeks or months! Treated with a little intelligence and a fair amount of elbow grease, a sword will be ready to serve many productions for years.

Taking care of rust and loose pommels is not the only job necessary to keep swords safe. The edges of a sword take the most abuse during rehearsals and performance. Heavy weapons take an especially hard toll and can pit and nick as deep as a quarter of an inch (one centimeter). A deeply pitted broadsword blade can become as sharp as a saw!

Edge Maintenance for Bladed Weapons

While most épée-bladed weapons do not usually, if ever, need filing for burrs, almost all broad-bladed swords do and on a regular basis. Burrs and shards of metal collect along the edge of the blade, making it dangerously sharp. The shards that are created by a heavy blow can fly off the blade and enter an eye or can cut the skin. This is true of any heavy-bladed weapon. I have been injured by a metal shard from an ax that cut through my costume and buried itself in my thigh!

The following is a list of weapons that should be regularly checked and filed:

➤ broadswords, bastard swords, cavalry sabers, cutlasses, Roman swords

➤ axes

➤ pole arms, if used to fight (halberds, pikes, etc.)

➤ maces

➤ machetes

➤ wide-bladed daggers or knives

All heavy weapons are subject to pitting and burrs. The softer the metal, the greater the maintenance required. However, filing usually rids the blade of all burrs, making it safe for the next night's performance or rehearsal.

The following is a description of the proper way to file a broad-bladed sword, ax, or pole arm.

Hand Filing

Hand filing is very easy if it is done often. During rehearsals or performances, when burrs become bad, or *at least once a week*, the blade should be put in a vise to hold it steady and burrs or pits should be filed down. You should purchase a fine-tooth metal file and keep it with the weapons for emergency filing. You should always wear gloves and protective goggles. Both sides and edges of the sword blade, ax, or other weapon should be filed. If you are filing, push the file away from you along the blade and periodically check for burrs. Do not overfile—you could be sharpening the blade! After you finish each edge, go down the length of the blade again to flatten it further. Then oil or lightly grease the weapon.

Machine Filing

Machine filing requires the use of an electric bench grinder to file down burrs and pits. This will save an enormous amount of time if many blades need

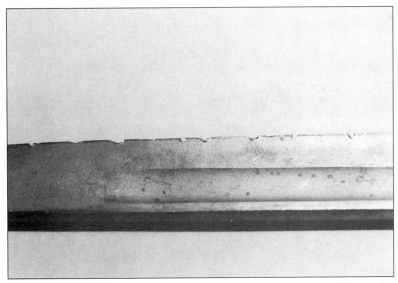

Figure 4-19. Broad-bladed weapons often develop deep pits that must be removed as a regular part of weapon maintenance.

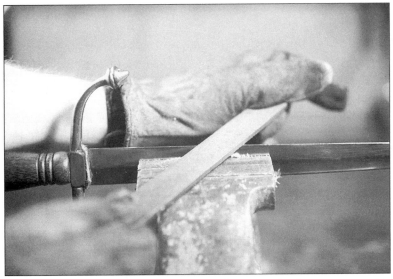

Figure 4-20. Hand-filing burrs off a broad-bladed dagger. Note that the weapon is secured in a strong vise and that gloves are worn for safety.

Figure 4-21. *An eighteenth-century engraving showing the process of blade making using water-driven stone wheels.*

work. It is also more dangerous and *should not be tried* by someone unfamiliar with a grinding machine.

If you are working with a bench grinder *always wear goggles, gloves, and protective clothing.* Do not wear loose clothing, ties, scarves, or anything that can enter the machine. Tie back long hair. *Follow the manufacturer's instructions.* Hold the blade, pointing to the left of the machine, and lightly bring it across the stone. Repeat with the blade pointing right. Pay particular attention to large divots in the blade, as well as obvious burrs. Hold the blade carefully and firmly, but use a light touch. Bearing down too hard will damage the blade and will possibly draw it into the machine.

Check for large burrs, wire brush to finish, then oil the weapon. This is a difficult procedure, so if you have any doubts about your ability to perform it safely, hand file your blades.

Care of Rapier (Épée) Blades

Épée, schlager, and "musketeer" blades usually need less care than broader-bladed weapons since they pit much less and do not require repeated grinding

Figure 4-22. *Always follow safety rules when using electric grinding machines to maintain weapons!*

or metal filing. They do, however, suffer from rust problems and need periodic care. Humidity, salty air, handling, and time all contribute to the amount and depth of rust on épée blades.

The following are some ways to remove rust.

1. **By Hand:** Using either steel wool or emery cloth, rub the length of the blade by hand, taking special care of the fuller or "blood" gutter. Do not use sandpaper or other extremely abrasive material. After the blade is cleaned, oil, wax, or otherwise polish and protect the blade. Special polishing blocks, available at fencing supply houses, also do a fine job, since they mold to the form of the blade and "erase" the rust.

2. **By Machine:** First, remove the blade from the hilt assembly. Then, making *sure* you are wearing PROTECTIVE GEAR, such as GOGGLES, an APRON, and GLOVES, proceed to slowly run the blade its full length

Figure 4-23. *Machine cleaning an épée-bladed rapier on the wire wheel. Great care must be taken in performing this procedure. Gloves, goggles, and safe handling of the weapon will ensure that injuries are prevented. Note that the grinder guard has been removed.*

across the wire wheel on a bench grinder. BE VERY CAREFUL! Do not attempt to do this without safety precautions and training on this machine. The wire wheel sheds wires at a high velocity, and you MUST be protected. Go over all three sides of the blade, paying particular attention to the fuller. Do not press too hard since you can burn and stain the metal.

When finished, use a cotton wheel to buff the blade to a high shine. Jeweler's rouge, available at hardware stores, is a good medium to

Figure 4-24. *The shower of sparks thrown off a stone on an electric grinding machine is dangerous! Always use protective eye wear.*

achieve a high gloss on blade and hilt assemblies. Be very careful when buffing small hilt parts, and use locking pliers rather than your fingers, since those parts get very hot, are hard to hold, and can be drawn into the machine.

Do not attempt to get into small interior areas with the machine. If you lose control of the piece, it can fly away, possibly injuring you. The grinder can also suck your finger into the wheel, tearing the skin and breaking bones!

3. **Deep Rust:** Deep rust and pitting on a blade usually mean that the blade has been neglected too long and is too old to be deemed safe. To test for this damaged condition, bend the blade in your hands away from your body; if the blade holds the bend, then the metal is probably fatigued. When in any doubt, hang it over your fireplace, throw it away, use it for a tomato stake, or cut it off, blunt it, and use it for a dagger blade.

Rust must be removed whenever it appears! Depending on weather conditions, handling, humidity, and other factors, I have seen rust appear on swords that were cleaned every day! One must keep ahead of the rust and be especially sure to remove rust before any long-term storing of weapons.

Polish swords prior to opening night so that they will look their best. **_Tip!_**

Replace all épée blades three days before opening night, keeping rehearsal blades in reserve in case of breakage.

How to Customize and Replace Sword Blades

It is easy to keep sword blades in shape, and even switch a blade into another sword, if you know a little about how blades are threaded and constructed.

Sword blades are divided into three basic parts. The first part, called the *foible*, is the thinnest half toward the tip. The second part, the middle of the blade downward toward the thickest part of the blade, is called the *forte*. Finally, the part of the blade that extends inside the handle and usually screws on to the pommel is called the *tang*.

Tangs are divided into three component parts. Let's take a sword apart by unscrewing the pommel and examine the tang. The following are the elements to look for:

1. **Sword shoulder.** This is where the "blade" itself ends and the tang begins. The shoulder should be at right angles to the tang, but not in a

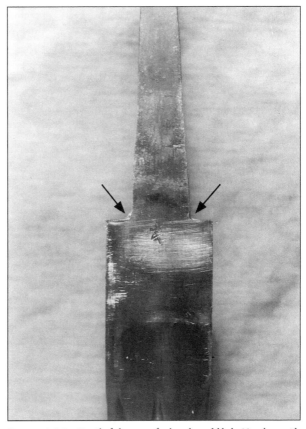

Figure 4-25. *Detail of the tang of a broadsword blade. Note how wide the tang is in relation to the width of the blade. Also note that the shoulders are square to the tang, but that the corners are slightly rounded, not sharp.*

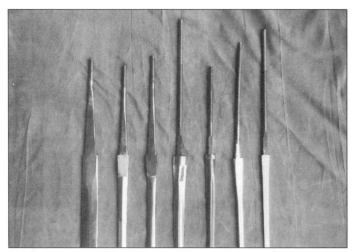

Figure 4-26. Detail of rapier blade tangs. Note that they are all one piece of metal, and threaded to receive pommels. From left to right are (1) a full-size custom rapier blade; (2) a diamond schlager; (3) a schlager; (4) a "musketeer" épée blade; (5) a "dry" épée blade and two sport blades not recommended for stage combat; (6) a saber blade; and (7) a foil blade. Photo by Lewis Shaw.

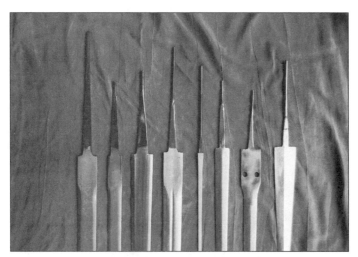

Figure 4-27. Detail of broadsword and dagger-blade tangs. From left to right (1) a hand-and-a-half, or two-handed, broadsword blade; (2) a custom, single-handed, broadsword blade; (3) a commercial, single-handed, broadsword blade; (4) a "super" blade; (5) a cut-down foil blade (safe for daggers); (6) a "dirk" blade; (7) a "main gauche" style blade, and (8) a wide dagger blade. Photo by Lewis Shaw.

hard right angle. Often the shoulders are mismatched, especially in wide-bladed weapons such as broadswords. One can correct this discrepancy by using a metal file.

2. **Tang.** This is the long section of the blade that extends through the handle. It should be straight and free of rust and cracks.

3. **Threads.** This is the end of the tang upon which the pommel screws down. It should be free of rust and have clean threads. The threads

Figure 4-28. *Detail of an unsafe broadsword blade. This blade came from an inexpensive sword and is dangerous. Note how thin the tang is and that half way up there is a poorly dressed butt weld. A weapon with this blade would not last through one rehearsal and would be very likely to break on contact with another weapon and fly across the*

233

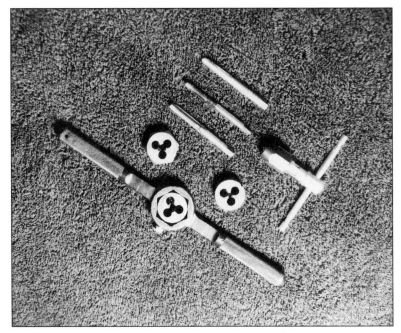

Figure 4-29. *A tap- and die-set. The die holder is in the lower left corner, and above are two alternate dies. Above them are the tap wrench and three taps. The most common sizes needed to work with épée blades are (American) 12 × 24 inches and 1/4 × 20 inches, and (European 6 × 1 mm).*

should not be smashed down, and they should not extend beyond the end of the pommel. A minimum of five complete turns will ensure safety.

Very often prop departments overlook the fact that a sword blade must fit properly into the weapon. I have seen many a weapon whose tang extended one to two inches (three to five centimeters) beyond the pommel, thus creating an unsafe situation for the performer. The hand is easily cut by this unsafe arrangement. To identify this problem, one should look for multiple washers used as spacers. (See Figure 4-30.)

Before attempting to cut sword blades to fit or remounting a blade into another weapon, a basic knowledge of threading is necessary. There are four basic thread types to be aware of:

American

1/4 × 20 inches	(wide rapier and épée blades)
12 × 24 inches	(many sport saber, épée, and foil blades)
5/16 × 18 inches	(some broadsword blades)

European

6 × 1 millimeters	(many épée, musketeer, and dagger blades, as well as blades marked "France Lames")

Figure 4-30. *A tang whose threads extend past a pommel can be sharp and can cut a performer's hand. Use the method shown in the next photo to shorten the tang so that the pommel covers it completely.*

Figure 4-31. *Cutting new threads on a sword tang with a die and a bolt cutter. First, thread the correct-size die down the tang as far as it will go. Measure and cut the tang to the new length (wear goggles for safety!). Now you can run the die back up the tang, which cleans and straightens any threads damaged by the cutting process.*

235

Many competition blades have 12-by-24-inch threads, the smallest of the three. The sword blades of most European suppliers (France Lames, e.g.) have 6-by-1-millimeter threads. It is also possible to purchase blades unthreaded—a good idea if one has a large stock, since one can cut them to fit one's needs.

A good repair kit should always include a set of taps and dies in the four sizes listed here. A "tap" is a device that will make a threaded hole in a pommel, and a "die" is a device that will thread the tang. One will also need a tap wrench and a die holder. Hexagonal die holders are superior to round ones. These items are not expensive and are well worth the investment.

Cutting Blades to Size

It is easy to cut a blade down to size if it is too long for the handle/guard arrangement. Working with épée and shlager blades is particularly easy. Such cutting should always be done when the tang is too long for the weapon. One cuts a tang in the following way:

1. Measure the tang and mark down on a piece of paper the optimum tang length.

2. Dismantle the weapon by unscrewing the pommel. Lay the component parts nearby.

3. Wear protective gear, especially gloves and eye protection.

4. Put the blade in a vise, tang pointing up.

5. Run a die down the tang threads as far as it will go. Cut new threads if necessary.

6. Measure the tang and determine where to cut it.

7. Use bolt cutters or a hacksaw to cut the tang to size. If using bolt cutters, be aware that the cut end will fly across the room. (See Figure 4-31.)

8. Run the die back up the tang to clean the threads.

9. Remount the weapon and check it.

It is also an easy job to mount different pommels onto swords. It is important to first determine the type of threading of the tang. This can be done by running a die *carefully* over the threads to see which one fits. One must not damage the threads by forcing the die over them.

One should next determine the threading of the new pommel by running the taps into it to see which one fits. Again, one should be careful of the threads and not damage them by forcing. If the pommel has a smaller threading than

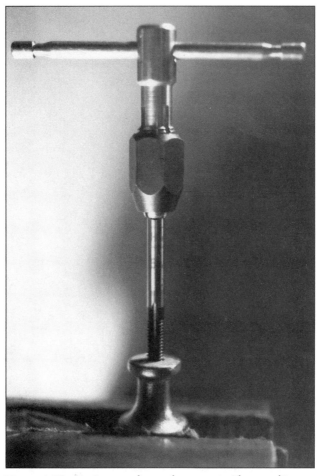

Figure 4-32. *Tapping a sword pommel to a new size. The pommel is secure in a strong vise, and the tap is screwed in slowly, cutting new threads as it goes. This is also a good way to clean old, or smashed, threads, but make sure you use the correct tap size!*

237

that of the tang, it is no problem to tap a larger thread into it. Simply place the pommel into a vise, and carefully cut new threads into it by using the appropriately sized tap and tap wrench. Use cutting oil and cut slowly, reversing the tap every two turns to clear debris. Clean the new hole by spraying WD-40 oil into it.

It is, of course, impossible to downsize a thread size in a pommel. It is sometimes possible to purchase inserts from a hardware store that will, for instance, fit into a 1/4-by-20-inch hole and make it into a 12-by-24-inch hole.

Figure 4-33. *Maintenance and customizing tools include the following (from left to right): (1) a 1/4-inch chisel to enlarge wooden handles for larger tangs; (2) a round metal file for shaping; (3) a small triangular metal file for shaping; (4) bolt cutters for cutting tangs to size; (5) a crescent wrench for loosening or tightening pommels with flat surfaces, such as sabers and foils; (6) adjustable pliers for loosening or tightening irregularly shaped pommels and for general use; (7) a fine-tooth metal file to maintain broadsword blade edges.*

It is however very common to downsize a tang to fit a smaller pommel. If the tang size is, say, 6 × 1 mm., and the pommel is 12 × 24 inches, simply place the blade in a vise and carefully screw down the 12 × 24-inch die. It is advisable, however, to retap the pommel rather than remove metal from the tang.

Recycling Existing Sword Stock

Customizing swords and remounting blades is an easy process, and one that can save money. For example, if a theater is mounting a production that will use smallswords, and there are already rapiers in stock, perhaps the blades can be remounted! The pommels must be loosened, and the blades should be pulled out and examined for damage, age, and wear. If they are still in good shape, one need only purchase smallsword guards. The blades can be mounted into the smallsword guards, and the handle, and perhaps even the pommel, can be reused for a fraction of the cost of buying completely new smallswords. One should place the blade in a vise, and assemble the new parts onto the tang to see how they fit. One may have to shorten the tang or cut new threads and may have to use a small metal file to open the new guard to make it fit the shoulders of the blade. One should work slowly and carefully, making sure the finished product is tight and feels good in the hand.

One should start with blades that are in good condition and remember that if the tangs of the blades are cut shorter to fit a different guard, they can never be extended again.

The addition of a new handle made of exotic wood or of painted gold or silver, or even a handle that is wire wrapped, will improve the looks of existing stock. All of the manufacturers listed in the appendix of this book will be glad to sell parts for a sword. So, if a new wire-wrapped handle or a fancier pommel will dress up a sword, one can spend a few dollars to achieve a great effect.

Finally, using a little elbow grease before opening night, and on a regular basis during the run of a production, will always make old swords look good— and good swords look great! Careful polishing before opening night always makes blades, hilts, pommels, and even scabbards stand out under the lights. A highly polished blade under theater lights has the added benefit of looking razor sharp!

Figure 4-34. Cleaning and polishing equipment to use with an electric grinding machine. At bottom are gloves and eye protection. Above them are a cotton wheel for polishing, using the bar of white jeweler's rouge above. At top on the left is a wire wheel, which can remove rust and minor blemishes on metal, and on the right is a stone wheel for taking nicks out of broad-bladed weapons such as broadswords and axes.

Figure 4-35. Cleaning and polishing equipment to maintain swords by hand include (from left to right): (1) Neverdull, a commercial metal cleaner useful on weapons and armor; (2) a rust "eraser," available at fencing supply houses. A quick and dry method of keeping ahead of surface rust; (3) Locktite, a liquid compound that will help keep pommels locked on once tightened down. A good product if your weapons tend to loosen during the run of a play; (4) WD-40, a spray-on oil, good for general cleaning; (5) Clenzoil, a protective compound for storage of weapons and rust prevention; (6) a pad of steel wool, a wire wheel, and a wire brush, which, when used with oil, can remove surface rust efficiently.

Figure 4-36. *Weapons storage area. Note that some weapons are stored on "peg board," and that others are stored in thick tubes, point down. All swords are arranged by historical period. They are also easily visible to check periodically for rust. To reduce metal strain, all of the pommels have been loosened.*

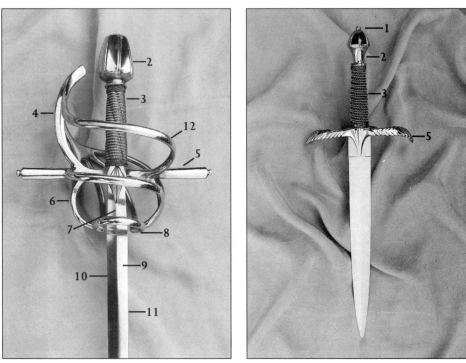

Figures 4-37 and 4-38. *The parts of a sword or dagger. From top to bottom:* (1) *pommel nut;* (2) *pommel;* (3) *grip;* (4) *knuckle bow;* (5) *quillons;* (6) *pas d'ane;* (7) *riscasso;* (8) *guard;* (9) *blade;* (10) *true edge;* (11) *false edge;* (12) *counter guard. Armorer, Lewis Shaw.*

Stage Blood

5

*W*e are all used to seeing blood in movies, on television, and in the evening news programs. Popular culture in the late twentieth century seems to have us awash in blood effects from television cop shows, Westerns, kung-fu flicks, and science fiction, action, and horror movies. In theater, however, there seems to be a movement to minimize the use, or abuse, of blood. (In this chapter, when I refer to "blood" I'm of course referring to stage blood—to the illusion of blood—although this illusion does appear real to members of the audience and even to some performers, who may react emotionally to what appears to be, and in a sense is supposed to be, blood.)

Perhaps blood effects have lost their shock value, or it may be that stage directors are tired of using blood or feel that dramatically it is more effective not to use blood effects. It certainly is easier to leave such effects out of a production than to deal with the blood bags, timing problems, and laundry hassles. Besides, once one has shown blood early in a play, one has to keep it up throughout the production, and even escalate its use. If one uses blood in the act 1 brawl scene of *Romeo and Juliet* and continues to use it in the act 3 scenes for Mercutio and Tybalt, then by the time of Paris's death and Juliet's suicide, the use of blood may have lost its impact.

Certainly there are times when blood must be used to get the required effect. Plays such as *Sweeney Todd* or *Titus Andronicus* cannot be produced without gallons of it. However, when dealing with blood in the theater, the principal of LESS IS MORE holds true.

First let's look at some of the most common ways to use blood in the theater, before we focus on how to make some of these special effects.

Blood Delivery Systems and Simple Tricks

1. **Blood bags, large or small.** These are usually hidden in pockets, hands, on props, on the set, or taped to a performer's body.

2. **Squeeze bottles.** These are small plastic bottles hidden in the set where performers may get to them. Sometimes other performers squeeze blood onto their fellow performers or into their mouths (an example would be the blinding of Glouster in *King Lear*).

3. **Blood sponges.** These are small sponges set in leak-proof containers hidden on the set where performers can get their hands/fingers into them to receive blood. Common hiding places for these are under tables, behind bars, in book shelving, on the upstage side of furniture. The sponge/cup device is refilled before the show each night by stage management, the prop department, or the running crew.

4. **Explosive devices.** Explosive squibs fall under this category. These are small explosive charges under a performer's costume designed to simulate a gunshot wound. A small blood bag is placed over the charge, and the blood is released when the squib is set off. THIS IS A HIGHLY SPECIALIZED EFFECT AND SHOULD NOT BE USED WITHOUT

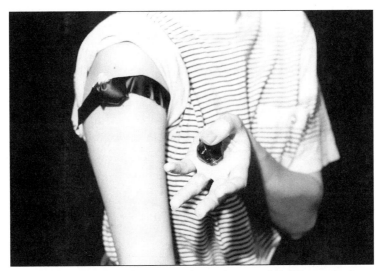

Figure 5-1. *The performer's sleeve is rolled up to show a small blood bag taped to her skin which can easily be broken by the victim and will bleed down the arm. The performer also holds another bag in her palm, which she will break on the outside of the costume to add volume to the effect.*

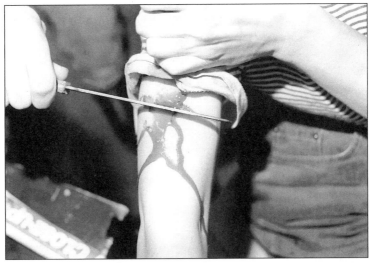

Figure 5-2. *The effect, a moment after breaking the bag, of a wound with a (dulled) knife.*

EXPERT SUPERVISION. I have also used a compressed air charge to blow blood onto a wall, or curtain, as during the fight in *A Small Family Business* on Broadway. This is relatively safe and can be an effective delivery system but should not be aimed at performers.

5. **Hydraulics.** With this system, battery-operated pumps, surgical tubing, and high technology go into the hydraulic delivery of blood. This method can be very effective and has been used in productions of *Agnes of God* to produce the stigmata effect in the palms. This is a very expensive delivery system, one that should be designed and built by a special effects professional and that is often accompanied by makeup prosthetics. Inexpensive alternatives replace the battery pumps with squeeze bulbs or with syringes.

6. **Impregnated props/set pieces.** This is a delivery system that is based on the performer hitting or being hit by a prop or set piece built with a soft section impregnated with blood. Contact with the soft area will leave a bit of blood on the performer.

   Example 1: A performer is slammed into a table. The wood in the table in a certain area has been replaced with high density foam, painted to look like wood, and impregnated with blood. As the performer rises after hitting the table, he is seen to have blood on his forehead.

   Example 2: A performer appears to be hit with a rock by another performer. The rock is really made of foam rubber that is impregnated with blood and that appears to draw blood immediately. To complete the illusion, the foam rock could quickly be switched for a real one that is dropped on the stage to further the reality of weight and texture.

7. **Prop switch.** This is a simple illusion whereby a clean prop is switched for a preblooded one.

   Example 1: In *Romeo and Juliet*, Mercutio is seen to use a handkerchief during the play prior to act 3, scene 1. After being wounded by Tybalt, he reaches into his costume with the clean handkerchief to "check" the wound and pulls out a prebloodied (dry makeup made to look wet) double to show the audience.

A simple pump device on the arm is used to simulate the cutting of the wrist. This inexpensive trick is made from an eyedropper and is hidden by the long sleeves of the performer. The opening in the eyedropper is sealed by a tiny amount of candle wax.

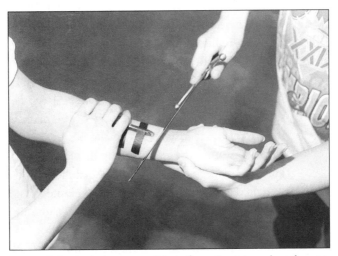

Figure 5-3. 1. At the moment of the knife cut, the victim grabs at the wrist, squeezing the blood out of the squeeze bulb.

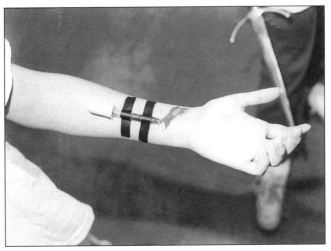

Figure 5-4. 2. The effect of the simulated knife cut a moment later.

Example 2: Mercutio is passed a double handkerchief by Benvolio within which is tied a small blood bag that Mercutio breaks.

Example 3: In *Othello*, Emilia is stabbed by Iago, falls to the bed, and retrieves a piece of prebloodied sheet material to hold to her chest.

8. **Trick knives.** A "blood knife" can be made by the prop department by removing the handle of the knife and replacing all or part of it with a squeeze bulb. This bulb can either be custom-made from latex or built around a commercially available squeeze ball found at drug stores. A thin length of surgical tubing is then placed around the end of the squeeze ball and glued to the edge of the blade, either all the way to the tip or about halfway down the blade. The whole weapon is then painted to hide the new rigging. It works best when there are two knives, a real one made from metal (dulled!) and a blood knife that is switched at the last minute. The blood knife must be dull on the edge, and the blood mechanism must be cleaned and checked with every performance, since stage blood tends to clog up over time. The thin tube where the blood exits the knife must be especially clean and after loading may be sealed with a thin film of wax so the knife will not leak accidentally. Blood knives may be created by rebuilding a metal knife or fashioned entirely out of wood, plastic, or other malleable material. Remember! A blood knife is made to create the illusion of *cutting*. Serious injury can result if a performer is stabbed with even a dulled blood knife.

9. **Body armor.** Body armor blood bag devices that one can actually stab and that will bleed can be made by taking an impression of the performer's body part (chest, back, leg) and molding half-inch (two centimeters) polycarbonate material in that shape. The resulting form is then lined with padding and fitted with straps, and a leather pad is glued permanently on the front near the area to be struck. A blood bag is then taped into position over the target and a layer of Styrofoam® is laid over it (so the knife has something to stick into). Finally, the costume is put over it all. This type of armor allows a performer to stab a knife into another performer with *relative* safety, the knife appearing to stick into the victim and blood leaking from the wound. This type of advanced blood delivery system should not be tried by amateurs and

Figure 5-5. *This performer is wearing body armor under his T-shirt. There is a blood bag taped to the T-shirt, through which the knife has gone. Do not try this trick without expert supervision!*

may be used by professionals only under strictly regulated guidelines and supervision.

Since many of these illusions depend on custom-made blood bags, let's look at how those bags are made.

How to Make Blood Bags

Blood bags constitute the most common and least expensive "delivery system." Bags are easily made up by the prop department and are either worn by the performer, handed to the performer at an appropriate moment by another performer, or hidden on the stage where they can be picked up at a convenient moment.

In Shakespeare's day, real pig's blood was put into "bladders" and used with great effect. Modern times however call for modern methods. One of the least successful was the common practice of using stage blood to fill "caps," or capsules, made of gelatine. This is an unacceptable method since the true purpose of a gel cap is to melt—and melt they will in your pocket, palm, or while waiting to be picked up. You are therefore left with a soggy mess instead of a neat leak-proof package.

The simplest handheld or body blood bag is made from a plastic bag. This can be formed in many ways and made up prior to the performance each time. These bags may be large or small and are hard to beat. Here's how to do it.

Small Blood Bag

1. Purchase a box of the most inexpensive plastic sandwich bags.
2. Pour the blood mixture into one corner of the bag.
3. Twist the bag closed, and tie a knot.
4. Work the knot down tight close to the corner where the blood has pooled in order to make as taut a package as possible. Try to work all the air out of it.
5. Trim off the excess plastic.

Large Blood Bag

1. Purchase the most inexpensive plastic sandwich bags.
2. Pour in a large amount of blood mixture.
3. Carefully seal across the top of the bag with tape, leaving a tiny opening.
4. Carefully squeeze out any remaining air.
5. Seal the bag.
6. Tape the bag onto a backing (leather, wood, plastic) so that it is a tight fit.
7. The bag should feel tight and be able to break open easily.

It is unusual to make blood bags bigger than sandwich-bag size since the bags become unstable and are likely to break under their own weight. If more blood is needed than can be held in one sandwich-sized bag, multiples can be used. If the assassination of Caesar needs to be particularly bloody, several of

How to Make a Small Blood Bag

Figure 5-6. Step 1. Pour enough blood mixture into a small plastic bag to fill one corner.

Figure 5-7. Step 2. Twist the excess plastic tightly.

Figure 5-8. Step 3. Tie a knot in the bag and pull it tight.

Figure 5-9. Step 4. Cut off the excess plastic.

Figure 5-10. Step 5. The blood bag is finished.

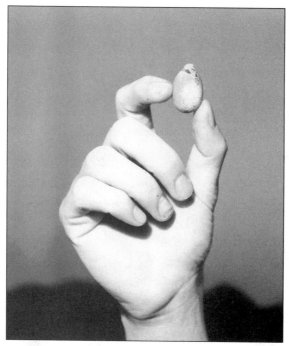

Figure 5-11. *A small blood bag made from a plastic grape. The hole in the top is sealed with candle wax. This can be hidden on the set or placed in the mouth. The hole in the top of the grape makes the blood more "directional" than a plastic bag. TIP: Fill grapes with a small syringe.*

these bags can be taped to his body, or he can wear an undershirt fitted with pockets designed to hold blood bags.

Blood bags of this type must be very well constructed, and the performers must rehearse many times to make sure that the physical activity leading up to the release of the blood will not make the bags burst too early. It is tremendously embarrassing for Caesar, or Bernardo, or Tybalt to be leaking blood through his costume before the appropriate moment.

Breaking Blood Bags

Breaking blood bags, as they say, is easier said than done. A small blood bag held in the hand can be "slapped" onto the body to break the bag and get

How to Make a Large Blood Bag

Figure 5-12. *Step 1. Pour a large amount of blood mixture into a plastic sandwich bag. Prepare a backing. Here, I am using an elastic band with velcro closure.*

Figure 5-13. *Step 2. Seal the bag to the backing with tape. Squeeze out all excess air.*

Figure 5-14. *Step 3. Use tape to create a tight bag. Check for leaks.*

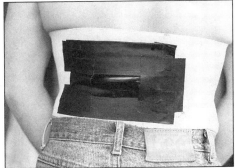

Figure 5-15. *Step 4. Secure the bag to the performer. This should be done as closely as possible to the moment the bag is broken.*

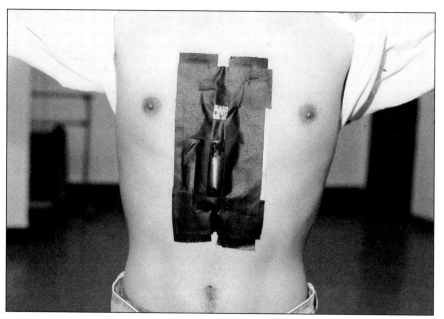

Figure 5-16. *A large blood bag taped to a performer's chest. This size bag needs not only to be broken, but "milked" of its contents. Bags taped directly to skin can be painful when pulled off!*

the required effect. Larger body bags may have to be squeezed to get them to pop, and some rehearsal is usually in order.

Handheld blood bags sometimes squirt blood in strange directions, and rehearsal with water bags usually solves this problem, though water does run faster than blood. The bag must be held firmly, and the hand should be opened only at the last second before impact with the body. Often, larger bags must be "milked" of their contents by pressing, squeezing, or otherwise manipulating the spot with the hands. One shouldn't leave this vital part of the illusion until final dress rehearsal, since it is more difficult than it would appear.

Blood from the Mouth

Performers sometimes must look as if they are bleeding from the mouth, either because they have been hit in the face during a fist fight, or perhaps stabbed and are hemorrhaging internally.

The makeup industry would have you believe that the purchase of a dry powder in a gelatine capsule mixed with the saliva of the performer will allow for a wonderful effect. Years of observation and experience permits me to tell you that the only effect possible from these devices are pink teeth and repeated chewing motions as the actor tries to get up enough "spit" to make them work.

It is much more satisfying to build a blood bag for the mouth that has stage blood in it. Obviously this must be a nontoxic blood mixture so that the performer isn't poisoned. A syrup-based blood is appropriate here rather than a soap- or chemical-based one (see blood recipes later in this chapter).

The most common solution to this problem is to use a small premade blood bag of the "sandwich bag" type, slipped into the mouth at a crucial moment. This can become a problem when the performer must fight with a full bag in his mouth, or must speak while dying, since the empty bag gets in the way of vocal production; in addition, a bag in the cheek gives the performer a vaguely "chipmunk" look. The bag is best left out of the mouth until the last possible moment. Masked by a handkerchief and given to the performer by another performer, the bag can be slipped into the mouth during a coughing fit; otherwise it can be palmed.

It occasionally happens that an actor must perform an entire fight scene with a blood bag in the mouth. This can be dangerous since it could be accidentally inhaled during the physical exertion of the fight. One should be careful if one attempts this, but one should try to avoid it.

The "bag in the mouth" method of blood delivery also necessitates discarding the empty bag once it has been burst by biting it open. What does one do with this bit of plastic? Well . . . hopefully it can remain in the mouth if the character is dead until the actor is taken offstage. In the wings it can be safely spit out. However, if the performer must bleed from the mouth and continue speaking, the only answer is to ball up the remains with the tongue and stick it under the tongue or up along the gums at the roof of the mouth, to be removed at the first opportunity. Another option is to spit it out during a coughing fit or while wiping the mouth area.

Other options to the plastic bag in the mouth include hiding a squeeze bottle in the performer's pocket, or hiding on the stage a blood sponge for dipping fingers and smearing blood on the lips and chin. Another option is using a squeeze bottle, which can be hidden on the set or palmed by another performer on the stage and squirted directly into the mouth at an advantageous moment in the fight (during a fall or a stumble into the crowd); in this way the performer has nothing but a bit of liquid in the mouth and no plastic to recycle.

The rule about blood in the mouth, as elsewhere, is that less is usually more. Rarely is a great gusher of blood very effective, and can even have the opposite effect on the audience. I have found that a small trickle of blood from one corner of the mouth is very effective. Another trick is that of a sudden "cough" that sprays blood out of the mouth, even sometimes onto another performer. In a production of *King Lear* years ago, I had the character Oswald killed on a set of stairs, where he fell upside down, so that his head was at the bottom. After his death at the hands of Edgar, and during the subsequent scene, the blood from Oswald's mouth would slowly travel downward by gravity toward his forehead, giving a most startling and satisfying effect (and it also had the advantage of keeping the blood off the costume).

Figure 5-17. *This performer has a blood bag in his mouth and has broken one on his head just above the hair line. Always be careful not to let blood run into your eyes!*

Blood on Costumes

Blood is the nightmare of costumers and wardrobe personnel. I remember a production of *Romeo and Juliet* in which Juliet was to stab herself in the chest and leave, according to director Michael Langham, exactly three drops of blood upon her dress. Unfortunately, Juliet wore a white wedding dress! How to remove the blood every night was the subject of frantic production meetings. The solution was a removable panel of white satin that was replaced for *every performance* with a new panel! An extreme, but workable, solution.

Blood is a difficult, if not impossible, substance to remove from costumes. It is a daily chore that must be factored into the running of the show, must be planned for carefully, and must be kept up by wardrobe people. During the delivery of blood, care must be taken that other performers don't get accidentally sprayed or don't kneel in the blood on the floor.

I have worked with many professional costumers in my career, and they all have different approaches to the "blood problem." When possible and practical, the simplest choice is to just double the costume. If the production can afford to replace, say, one white shirt for one performer after each performance, then it's possible to bloody up the shirt with abandon. This approach often works with *West Side Story* if Bernardo and Riff are wearing inexpensive white T-shirts with blood bags underneath for the rumble scene. T-shirts are often cheaper to replace than to launder.

However, what if the director wants Hamlet to be stabbed while wearing a (white!) modern fencing jacket and to bleed onto the stage? The solution is usually severalfold:

1. The material may be treated with a waterproof substance such as Scotch Guard to reduce penetration into the fibers.

2. The use of a soap-based blood recipe is vital.

3. Immediate immersion of the article in cold water as it comes offstage helps reduce staining.

4. One may be able to wash the article with bleach. (Note that many fabrics cannot be bleached.)

White, natural-fiber costumes are the most difficult to deal with. When possible, performers should wear colored costumes and ones that have been treated to resist staining.

Another trick that I have used successfully is to have a tearaway section of the costume, or an area of the costume that can be revealed by say, removing a coat or cape, that shows the audience an apparently fresh bloody wound. The wound, however, has been permanently painted onto the costume and made to look fresh and wet. It is, however, dry, cannot stain other performers, will not leak, and requires no maintenance. This process will also work for makeup prosthetics hidden under costumes.

Whenever possible one should try to keep blood off of the costumes. It is just as effective to have a character who has been stabbed or shot reach to that part of the body and come away with a bloody handkerchief or hand (easily washed!). We will suspend our disbelief thus far. One should bloody the costume only when absolutely necessary, with the understanding that it will be expensive and will get onto other performers accidentally.

To reduce the possibility that blood will soil the costumes, and to make the performers as confident as possible, the blood "bits" must be worked in far in advance of opening night, ideally with the cooperation and supervision of a member of the costume department.

Blood Rehearsals

It is important that the performers get used to dealing with all the little bags, bottles, and sponges necessary to create a satisfactory illusion. When these props are mishandled or used awkwardly, the audience is aware that something is amiss.

Your key ally in the rehearsing of blood bits is WATER. The blood bags, bottles, and sponges are filled with good old H_2O, and the bags are broken over and over again in rehearsal with no damage to people or costumes. All of the problems can be worked out this way with minimal mess and expense. Prop personnel can get used to making the devices, and performers can get used to delivering them, hiding them, and breaking them.

I have also found that occasionally a blood bag filled with water will look like blood onstage under lights. This can solve a major cleaning problem. Depending on the color of the costume (dark blues, reds, and purples are best) and the color of the lights, and depending on the distance of the audience from the stage, the costume wet with a burst water bag *can* look like blood. Directors should try this out for themselves.

Only after several successful rehearsals should the rehearsal water bags be replaced with stage blood. Performers should wear old clothes supplied either from their own wardrobe or the costume department.

The first blood rehearsal should be in the rehearsal room rather than on-stage, and a member of the costume staff should be present to take notes and solve any problems. The second stage blood rehearsal should be onstage under lights, to check the texture and color of the blood from the audience's vantage point. This onstage rehearsal need not require performers, since samples of cloth can be used that have been stained with various blood recipes.

It is also important to rehearse the types of wounds intended to make the blood flow. The various knife or sword stabs and the cuts, blows, and gunshot wounds should be carefully worked out so as not to injure the performers. It is irresponsibly dangerous to aim even a dulled knife at a performer with the intention of breaking a blood bag with it. Many people have been injured in this way. If necessary, performers should be protected with a garment made of leather under their costumes. Ideally, a knife or sword wound will be inflicted with minimal or no contact, and the wounded performer will break the bag with his own hand pressure. All wounds should be carefully worked out for safety.

Finally, during a technical rehearsal, blood must be used with all elements of performance: lighting, costumes, special effects, and so forth. A close watch must be made on the stage to make sure that blood bags or bloody performers don't drip onto the stage. If overlooked in rehearsals, this small problem can have a ripple effect over several scenes and can potentially create a slipping problem or stain a costume several scenes after the fight.

Blood on the Stage

Understand from the beginning that blood will get on the stage, creating slippery conditions. One should allow for this in blocking and should have a stagehand or character in the play clean up with a moist towel followed by a dry towel as soon after the incident as possible.

Another common problem is that other performers get bloody by falling or kneeling near wounded characters.

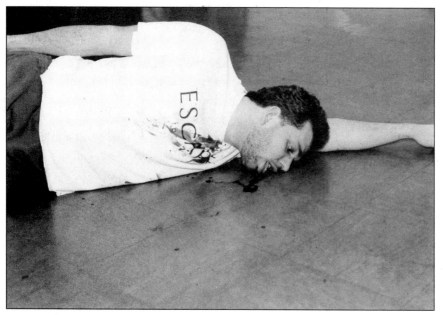

Figure 5-18. *Blood will get on the floor and must be cleaned up during a blackout or it can become a safety hazard.*

Finally, one should be aware that if blood is not cleaned up one runs the risk of staining costumes in later scenes. Long dresses that touch the floor, long capes, and even furniture pieces can be stained in this way. One should try to arrange for either costumed characters or stagehands to clean up during scene changes.

The use of stage blood can make for a realistically scary moment of theater. However, many plays are directed in other than naturalistic ways. Dance pieces, experimental theater, and "concept" productions of known plays sometimes demand a little creativity!

Alternatives to Blood

Yes, there are alternatives to blood. The obvious method is to use none. Absolutely none. We should allow our imaginations to work wonders and our disbelief to be suspended.

However, some creative props may help the audience engage in a death scene better. Taking a cue from the Chinese opera, the use of long red silk can work wonders. I used this technique in a production of *Rashomon* at Smith College. As each character died, they would use long red silks in different ways. The character of the Thief pulled one out of his collar and wrapped it around his neck before throwing the remaining six feet (three meters) of it up in the air. The Wife committed suicide and unfurled from her stomach area a twelve-inch-wide (thirty centimeters) roll of red silk that we allowed to roll down a raked area of the stage, thus presenting a very dramatic picture.

Other representational props can have a similar impact. In a production of *Henry V* for the Theater for a New Audience, directed by Barry Kyle in New York, the actors dropped red feathers during the battle of Agincourt to denote fallen Frenchmen. This was further enhanced by hundreds of red paper poppies falling from the grid onto the armies. The death of York in this production was accented by having his dead body lie on a red English battle flag.

Lighting designers have for years been known to put death scenes in pools of red light. I have also seen red strobe lighting effects (with slow-motion fights), pin spots on the face, and pulsing and throbbing red lighting pools into which the death scene is placed.

These alternatives to real stage blood are sometimes much more effective than sticky stage blood in getting members of the audience to use their imagination and suspend their disbelief. It has the other advantage of being kind to costumes and set. It is always worth considering an alternative to stage blood, which can be a labor-intensive, messy business. However, if one wishes to make stage blood, the recipes are below.

Blood Recipes

There are three types of stage blood that one can use. The first is what I call "mouth blood." This is made from natural products and can be safely used in the mouth.

The second, which has a soap base, I call "costume blood" because of its desirability for use on costumes. The third type is commercially available stage blood of various types.

Mouth Blood

To make "mouth blood," mix the following in a large sealable container (use rubber gloves, since the undiluted dye stains skin): either one bottle of clear Karo® syrup (or light maple syrup) with two teaspoons of red food coloring (more or less depending on the color desired) or one bottle of clear Karo® syrup with enough ketchup to get the color desired. Peanut butter, Hershey's® chocolate or cocoa, and tiny amounts of blue food coloring are ingredients that are often added to improve consistency or color in both mouth-blood recipes.

Costume Blood

Mix together the following: (1) Woolite® with red tempera paint or red food coloring or (2) liquid dish soap, such as Dawn® or Palmolive® with red tempera paint or Close-Up® toothpaste or red food coloring.

Commercial Blood

Stage blood comes premixed from several makeup suppliers. It is usually quite good looking and flows well. It can be purchased by mail from large

Figure 5-19. *Commercial blood can be purchased from makeup and theater supply houses. Two Kryolan products are pictured here, Filmblut and Magic Blood (an "A-B" type).*

suppliers such as Alcone Inc. or from houses such as Bob Kelly. It is marketed under such commercial names as "Reel Blood," "Stage Blood," "Technicolor Blood," "Filmblut."

So-called A-B blood is a two-part blood available under the commercial names "Magic Blood," "Zauberblut," or even "A-B Blood." As the name implies, this blood depends on a chemical reaction between part A and part B to create the illusion of blood. This can be a very effective trick, especially when creating the illusion of a knife cut on the skin.

Here's how A-B blood works. Part A is applied on the performer's skin up to a half hour before the effect. Part B is applied to the weapon—say, the edge of a dull knife. It is important that Part B stay wet, or the illusion will not work. When the wet knife blade is drawn across the skin, the chemical reaction creates a (more or less) red color that can be very startling. This is a useful effect in intimate surroundings, close to an audience, since they can plainly see there are no tricks! A-B blood is hard to remove from the skin and almost impossible to

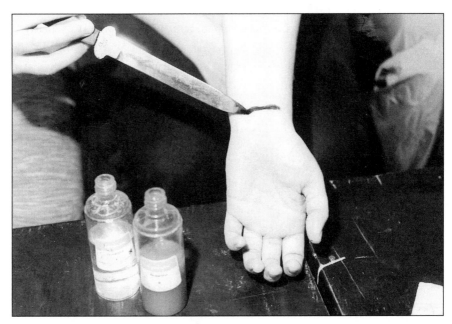

Figure 5-20. *Commercial "A-B" type blood works well up close to an audience and shows the moment when the skin is cut. If you need flowing blood, then add a blood bag or pump device. Adjust the mixture of A to B to get the correct color. It helps if the B mixture remains wet.*

remove from cloth. These products are available from Alcone Inc. and Zeller. These products should not be used near eyes or mouth.

Psychological Aspects of Blood

The impact of violence and death on the audience is well understood by playwrights. However, we often forget the psychological impact of maiming, violence, death, and blood on the performer. Most performers can justify stage violence through character, and remain somewhat emotionally detached from it. However, the addition of blood sometimes triggers emotional upheaval in an actor. It is often difficult to know just why this happens. It can be empathy for the character or even an event in the performer's life that is recalled when blood is seen.

My advice is to forestall any problems that may arise by discussing the use of blood with the cast long before it is brought into use. Particular attention and care must be paid to performers on the first day the blood is used, and any problems must be anticipated, identified, and discussed with the director, fight director, and performer(s) involved. It is a good idea in particularly emotional and violent scenes to clear the rehearsal hall to only those directly involved.

This is a sensitive issue for the company, the staff, and particularly the performers. It is not a subject to be swept under the carpet but must be dealt with carefully and without embarrassment. If the appearance of blood continues to trigger unwanted emotions, certainly its use should be discontinued.

Firearm Safety

A publicity still with Steven Earl-Edwards using long-barrel Western-style pistols with blank loads. Despite appearances, we were aiming very far off target for safety! Photo by Jim Manley.

6

Guns are scary! However, they have a magnetic allure that draws people to them. Modern playwrights have placed guns into the center of many scenes, because guns represent power! Period plays that are placed conceptually into modern times often find that a firearm or two replaces the swords and knives of previous centuries.

While swords, knives, and other cold arms are dangerous, nothing beats a firearm for instant destructive power. Because I have found that most actors and stage directors know very little about guns, this chapter would be very useful to study before staging a gunshot.

Firearm responsibility and firearm safety head the list of things to memorize and post around the rehearsal hall and backstage before attempting anything with the performers. Following that, I have put in some historical and technical details that may help directors decide what type of firearm to rent or purchase. Finally, if directors can't find a professional who can help, there are some tips on how to stage *basic* gunshots.

Because firearms are so dangerous, I urge directors to hire an expert before trying to stage firearm scenes. Sometimes playwrights include in their plays events that are difficult to stage safely—for instance, Hedda's suicide in *Hedda Gabler* or the shots in *Search and Destroy* and *The Kentucky Cycle*. I further urge directors to rent or purchase firearms from a reputable theatrical-firearms dealer, someone who is fully licensed to do so, and not try to save money by using "Uncle Bob's pistol."

Firearm Responsibility

It is very expensive to own or rent a handgun, rifle, or black-powder weapon, but more important it is a serious responsibility. Major injury or even death can result from the mishandling of firearms. It is the responsibility of the producer, director, fight director, prop personnel, and, finally, stage management to rent or purchase quality firearms and OVERSEE THEIR USE. It is important for the whole company to know where the guns will be kept, who may handle them, and who will load and clean them.

NO ONE must be permitted to handle guns who does not directly use them onstage. Neither should guns be allowed to be placed on a prop table for long periods of time offstage where anyone might handle them. Ammunition and firearms should always be stored separately, in locked areas. And it goes without saying that live ammunition (real bullets!) should *never* be allowed in the theater.

One should create a fail-safe travel plan for each firearm in the production. In films and television, a prop person is always there at the end of a "take" to relieve the performer of the weapon. For theatrical productions, it is wise to have a member of the prop department or stage management offstage to receive the gun from the performer immediately upon the performer's exiting the scene. It is also wise not to load the gun until a few minutes before it is needed onstage and not to *overload* the weapon. One should *only* put in the num-

Figure 6-1. *Always treat a gun as if it were loaded.*

ber of blanks needed that night, and perhaps one extra, in case of misfire. The gun should be immediately unloaded after it comes offstage, and stored in a secure area.

Production staff and performers should be trained to always hand a gun to someone else "breached," that is, opened to show that it is unloaded or loaded. For a revolver, the cylinder is unlocked and thrown open. For an automatic, the "clip" is shown empty, and the slide is opened to show what is in the breach (the clip may be empty, but if there is a round in the breach, the gun will still

Figure 6-2. *A revolver, showing that the chambers are empty. Always check to see if a gun is loaded, even if only a short time has gone by. Learn to breach firearms and check yourself to see if the chambers and barrel are clear.*

Figure 6-3. *A hand-off of a revolver, showing to the person receiving the gun that the weapon is not loaded.*

fire if the hammer is cocked and the trigger is pulled). For rifles and shotguns, the same procedure must be followed. One should learn where the safety switch is on guns and use it!

When using firearms, it is important to remember that the production staff may be liable for damages should faulty equipment be purchased, careless handling or training occur, or any other problem arise from negligence, thus injuring or killing someone. Check with your local police department about gun permits, since local laws vary.

This chapter is dedicated to Jon-Erik Hexum and Brandon Lee, two young actors killed in gun-related accidents while on the set. Don't be the next statistic! Firearms are potentially deadly.

➢ Always consult an expert!

➢ Always treat a gun as if it were loaded!

➢ Never use firearms without supervision!

➢ These rules are for the safety of all those involved in the production.

Gun Safety in Performance

Guns should always be treated as if they were loaded!

All firearms should be considered dangerous. A false sense of safety can be created by thinking that the firearm is unloaded or that it is "merely" loaded with blanks—and, therefore, a plaything. People are drawn to guns and want to handle them. Unsafe handling of firearms can lead to tragedy, as in the deaths of two young actors, Jon-Erik Hexum, in 1984, and Brandon Lee, the son of Bruce Lee, in 1993.

During rehearsals and performance, firearm safety etiquette must be taught to prop personnel, performers, and staff, and then followed religiously.

These are some simple safety rules to follow when handling firearms:

1. Before handling, always breach (open) the gun and show that it is unloaded. This is true of pistols and rifles, whether revolvers or automatic weapons.

2. Always use fresh blank ammunition of the correct size (caliber or millimeters) for the weapon. Never interchange blanks!

3. Never load the gun until just before it is used.

4. Never fight or struggle over a loaded gun—it may go off unexpectedly near the body, face, or ear (Figure 6-4).

5. After a gun has discharged onstage and is removed from the stage, it should be *handed* to a prop person or management, not placed randomly on a table or in a dressing room.

6. Use blanks only under the supervision of a trained expert.

7. Unload unused ammunition after every performance.

When discharging weapons onstage, it is important to remember a few simple rules. However, these rules do not cover every eventuality; so, again, one should always consult with an expert before purchasing or using blank ammunition.

Figure 6-4. *Never struggle over a firearm loaded with blanks!*

1. Never aim directly at the face, head, or body of a performer.

2. Always aim off line, either up- or downstage of the victim.

3. Always maintain a minimum of twenty feet (seven meters) between the end of the barrel and the person being shot.

4. Be aware that automatic, or semiautomatic weapons will eject hot shell casings at high velocity. Keep other performers clear of their trajectory. Do not allow the casings to fall into the audience.

5. Never clown around with firearms. Do not hold them to your head, look down the barrel, or put them in your mouth. Never point them at another person in fun.

6. Wear ear protection whenever possible. The larger the caliber weapon, the louder the report. Commercial ear plugs, cotton, or wax placed in the ears will help protect against hearing loss.

7. Do not wave the weapon around unnecessarily, since it may accidentally discharge.

8. Never discharge a weapon at close range, as in a struggle, grappling scene, or wrestling match.

9. Do not cock, put your finger on the trigger, or otherwise ready a gun to fire, until the last possible moment. Learn where the "safety" button is on a firearm and use it!

10. Always use fresh blank ammunition purchased from a licensed firearms dealer, preferably a dealer familiar with theatrical guidelines.

11. Never attempt to "plug" the barrel of a firearm or otherwise make it "safe" for the stage by altering its mechanics. To do so may cause the weapon to explode upon discharge.

12. Never attempt to alter "real" bullets to make them into blanks.

13. Always use the smallest charge or blank load possible to do the job. The larger the load, the greater the danger factor.

14. Check and recheck that the gun is unloaded *every* time it is used, and only load the weapon at the last moment. Unload the weapon between shows, and clean.

15. When firing a gun offstage to simulate a shot onstage, it should never be fired toward curtains, props, or other flammables, and never discharge the gun toward offstage personnel. Individuals firing offstage guns should wear ear and eye protection.

16. Whenever possible, use a "prop" gun (either a rubber, plastic, or non-firing, unloaded, metal one) for performers who must wear or brandish a gun. Policemen, military personnel, cowboys, gang members, and so on are obvious choices. If the gun must fire during the course of the play, use a *second* gun that resembles the prop gun. Conceal the loaded weapon on the stage or have it within easy reach offstage. This method of weapon use is safe and reduces the possibility of accidental discharge. The person discharging the weapon must be able to receive the weapon close to the moment in the play that the shot will happen. This method of using a second gun eliminates the need for wearing a loaded firearm or stopping to load it, not to mention struggling with one.

17. Never allow loaded firearms in the hands of inexperienced performers, especially young persons. The fight director and the director are responsible for determining who may safely handle these props. If there is any doubt about a performer's reliability, use an offstage shot. If the proximity of the performers to each other or the audience is such that a dangerous situation may occur, use an offstage shot.

18. Never allow live ammunition (real bullets) to be anywhere in the theater building. They may mistakenly be used in a weapon with deadly effect.

19. Maintain all firearms by cleaning them between performances. Cleaning kits are available at all gun stores. Unburned gun powder is very corrosive and will damage the weapon over time. Always have a mature, experienced individual perform this function, making sure that the weapon is unloaded before attempting to clean it.

20. Never point a firearm (even when unloaded) toward the audience. It makes the audience nervous and is a serious breach of firearm safety.

Stage directors and fight directors should always take the time to learn about and train the performers in proper firearm safety for the stage. Not to do so is a serious breach of safety rules and is asking for trouble!

Figure 6-5. *Guns should never be left on prop tables loaded and unsupervised. Unload the guns and keep them in a secure place.*

Types of Modern Stage Firearms

Pistols

Pistols, or handguns, are the most common type of firearm in the theater. They are used in many types of plays and musicals and can be deadly if not properly handled. It is important to choose the right weapon for one's theatrical production and the right weapon for the experience level of the performers. It is unrealistic to expect performers, amateur or professional, to automatically know how to handle firearms. Most people are unfamiliar with the rules of gun safety, so that a safety session is usually necessary for everyone involved with firearm handling in the production.

Below is a list of the most common types of modern pistols and period reproductions that may be used on the stage. Most are available for rent or purchase from reputable theatrical-firearms rental houses (see appendix).

Modern pistols are either revolvers, which have a rotating cylinder holding six to eight rounds, or semiautomatics, which have a "clip" that can hold a similar number of rounds. The clip usually fits inside the pistol's handle. Revolvers are more sturdy and reliable than semiautomatics and should be the first choice in most theater situations.

Modern stage pistols break down as follows:

Plastic

Never use a "real" firearm when plastic will do. If a pistol is never fired or if the age or experience level of the performers is such that a loaded weapon is too dangerous, then plastic is always the answer. If an actor must be disarmed or if a pistol is fought over, plastic is safer. If a pistol is worn in a holster or belt

Figure 6-6. *These are not real pistols, though they appear to be. At top is a "BB" gun made to look like a .45-caliber Colt. Below is a plastic toy cap gun. Never use real firearms when plastic or dummy ones will do the trick.*

and never drawn, plastic is safer. If a performer must be struck with a gun, "pistol whipped," or knocked out with a gun, plastic is the answer. (These types of blows that simulate being struck with the barrel or grip of the pistol are quite advanced, potentially dangerous, and should be noncontact blows.)

If the weight of the plastic pistol is a drawback, drill a hole in it and fill it with sand. Plug the hole, and you have solved the weight problem. Plastic pistols, such as water pistols, can look quite real, but if the color or paint job is unrealistic they can be repainted in the scene shop to look quite menacing.

Starter Pistols

Starter pistols are available in sports stores because they are widely used to begin foot races. They are inexpensive and reasonably safe. They feature solid or plugged barrels, rugged construction, and do not usually require a firearms license. Starter pistols are commonly .22 or .32 caliber and accept "crimp," or "blank," loads. They are manufactured in such a way that they *cannot* chamber a live bullet, which makes for an additional layer of safety.

Figure 6-7. *A starter pistol, broken down to show its parts. This model is a five-shot, .32 caliber, double-action revolver. Most starter pistols are .22 caliber and give plenty of "bang" for theatrical needs.*

Because the barrel of a starter pistol is usually plugged, the gas column and sparks created by the shot escape backward toward the person firing the weapon. Care must be taken that this will not discharge into the face or into flammable material, such as hair or costumes.

It is a common fallacy that when the barrel of a starter pistol is plugged the weapon may be placed close to, or even on the body of, the person being shot. This is not true and is very dangerous. The starter pistol, if discharged onstage toward a performer, must follow the same rules as a weapon with an unplugged barrel.

Starter pistols are usually revolvers and can hold four to eight shots. They are metal and therefore corrodible and should be cleaned and checked after every performance by a stage manager or other qualified individual. A starter pistol is often the weapon of choice when firing offstage to simulate a shot onstage.

As with any loaded firearm, the starter pistol should never be "fought" over, struggled with, or disarmed violently to the floor, since it may accidentally discharge or be broken. Ear protection should be used by anyone in close proximity to the discharge (see "Gun Safety in Performance," discussed earlier in this chapter).

Cap Guns

Cap guns have come a long way since the 1950s. Today, realistic replica firearms such as pistols, rifles, and submachine guns, may be purchased. These weapons resemble the "real thing." They look and feel right, but the difference is that they cannot chamber either live bullets or traditional blanks. These are not real guns.

These weapons only allow a special type of "blank" bullet to be used. This bullet, although it looks like the real thing, is actually a "cap" bullet. The sound created by these caps is acceptable in most theaters, but is not as loud as a standard .22-caliber blank. Various types of pistols are available, including older designs like the Luger, Colt .45, Walther PPK, as well as more modern styles such as the .38 Police Special, .357 Magnum, P-08 German Parabellum, and many others. These pistols are made of metal and therefore have an authentic weight and feel onstage.

The semiautomatic pistols using the "cap" bullets are manufactured in such a way that they eject a shell casing much as a real automatic pistol will. Care must be taken that no performers are in the path of this projectile and that the casings will not bounce or fly into the audience.

These weapons are sometimes called "blowback" models, and the caps are referred to as "plug fire." The manufacturer recommends various safety and cleaning procedures, which should be read and followed.

As with any firearm, all safety procedures must be followed.

Real Pistols

Why use a real pistol? Theaters use real pistols for many reasons. It may be a question of authenticity, or perhaps the prop department already owns them. Real guns can be safe to use onstage if *all* of the safety rules are strictly followed. Real pistols may be rented or purchased in many different styles and calibers. It is relatively easy to purchase blank cartridges of varying intensity, so that the level of discharge is controllable and the report is not too loud for the performers or the audience. Ownership of real pistols usually requires the theater or an individual to have a city, state, or federal weapons license.

To be absolutely safe, a real pistol should be altered so that it cannot chamber a real bullet. Weapons rented or purchased from large theatrical rental houses are usually altered in this way. This will minimize the danger of someone's loading a live round by mistake or as a prank.

It must be understood, however, by the full cast and production staff that great care and rehearsal time must be spent so that the discharge of the firearm is as safe as possible. Only use a real firearm when nothing else will do, with mature performers and staff, and under trained supervision.

Revolvers

There are two types of revolvers: double- and single-action. For theater productions, a single-action revolver is far safer than a double-action one.

A pull on the trigger will not fire a single-action revolver. The hammer must be cocked fully back and the trigger pulled before the pistol will discharge. To fire a double-action revolver, you need only pull the trigger. This will cock the hammer and drop it automatically. In the hands of a nervous actor a double-action pistol is more apt to discharge accidentally, or early, especially in a highly charged emotional scene in which a character has his finger on the trigger for a space of a time.

As far as safety with handguns is concerned, one should use a single-action revolver rather than a double-action one for firing a "blank" cartridge onstage. Further, revolvers are always more reliable than semiautomatics.

Be aware that the performers and staff must be knowledgeable about gun

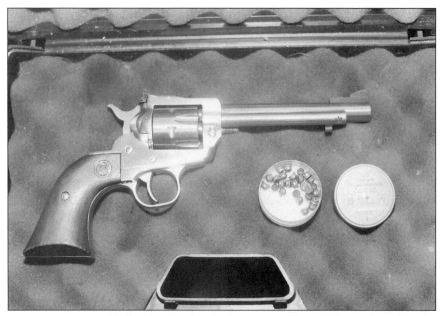

Figure 6-8. *A .22-caliber long-barrel revolver, also showing a tin of "crimps." These are the smallest type of blank load available for .22-caliber firearms.*

safety rules and must follow them to the letter. The real gun will discharge a concentrated gas column and sparks when it is discharged. A minimum distance of twenty feet (seven meters) must be kept between the shooter and the victim, not to mention that the pistol must never be pointed toward flammables or the audience.

Performers and staff personnel must practice breaching (breaking open the pistol) and loading procedures. Be aware that the cylinders in different types of revolvers turn in different directions. Some revolve toward the left, some toward the right. Be sure that you know which way your pistol revolves, since this will affect how you load. If you are unfamiliar with how a weapon should be loaded, opened, cleaned, or otherwise handled, consult an expert and don't fool around! Most accidents happen when people think a gun is unloaded.

Semiautomatic Pistols

Semiautomatic pistols are designed to be able to rapidly fire a clip of ammunition. A semiautomatic will fire each time the trigger is pulled; the action of

Figure 6-9. *A .38-caliber revolver used for stage, fitted with restrictors that prevent the loading of real bullets. Below the pistol are blank rounds shown from top and side view.*

the gun ejects the spent cartridge at high velocity while seating the next round in the barrel. Semiautomatics are much more dangerous to use onstage than revolvers are, because semiautomatics are much more complicated machines.

While there is nothing really wrong with using a semiautomatic pistol onstage, especially if it is not fired, here are several reasons for my trying to avoid them whenever possible.

1. They eject hot shell casings at high velocity that are potential hazards. Performers or members of the audience can be injured if struck by these casings, which can travel up to fifteen feet (five meters) away from the weapon.

2. A semiautomatic pistol is apt to jam after the first shot. Because a blank round of ammunition doesn't have the compression of a real bullet, the slide mechanism that ejects the shell casing usually doesn't have the necessary power to fully eject the cartridge; therefore, it has a tendency to jam.

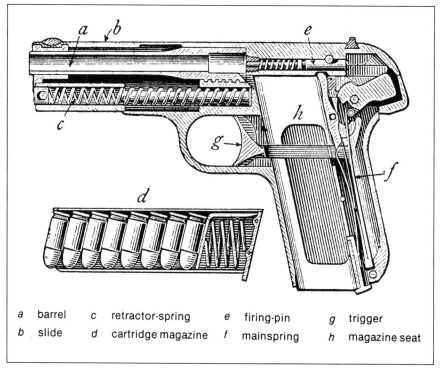

| a | barrel | c | retractor-spring | e | firing-pin | g | trigger |
| b | slide | d | cartridge magazine | f | mainspring | h | magazine seat |

Figure 6-10. *A semiautomatic pistol in cross section. Each time the trigger is pulled, an empty casing is ejected and a new round is seated.*

3. Many injuries occur when the weapon is handled with the ammunition clip removed. There is a mistaken idea that if the clip is out, the gun is unloaded. However, there is the possibility that there is still *one round of ammunition in the breach*; and if the breach is not checked, accidents can happen. Most people unfamiliar with guns will not check the breach, and the newspapers are full of stories of accidental shootings.

4. Semiautomatics are usually of high caliber, such as 9 millimeter or .45 caliber. This means that a large amount of powder must be used—in other words, a full-load blank, which creates a big bang but is more dangerous to handle. Reducing the load, say, to a half-load or a quarter-load blank inhibits the ejection mechanism so that the weapon will usually not fire more than once before jamming.

These are a few of the reasons that I recommend the use of revolvers on the stage. They are much more reliable than semiautomatics, and they are available in a variety of styles and calibers. Chrome and nickel plating, blued finish, snub-nosed and long barrel are just a few of the styles available.

Automatic Pistols

These are pistols like the Uzi and Mac 10 that have the capability of emptying the clip completely when the trigger is depressed. These are, quite literally, MACHINE GUNS, and as such are banned by law. It goes without saying that these weapons are far too dangerous to consider using onstage.

Modern Reproductions of Period, or Historical, Pistols

Some plays such as the *Kentucky Cycle* and *Cyrano* and many outdoor dramas utilize period firearms. Pistols of this type were usually muzzle-loading, black-powder weapons used before the invention of the closed-bullet cartridge, generally prior to 1890.

When choosing weapons for plays in this period it is important to realize that you have several options.

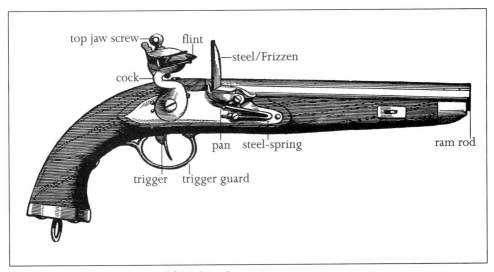

Figure 6-11. *A drawing of a typical flintlock pistol, noting its parts.*

Option 1

The safest and easiest type of period pistol is one that looks to the audience like a flintlock, or percussion cap, pistol but has been altered by a gunsmith to accept modern blank cartridges. This type of weapon is able to chamber one round, usually of .22 or .32 caliber. Much more reliable than traditional black-powder firearms, a weapon such as this is far preferable in most theatrical situations.

Option 2

Muzzle-loading black-powder reproductions of period pistols are easily obtained. Kits are even available for moderate cost, and the prop department can build and finish the weapons to taste. Muzzle loaders come in a variety of styles, from dueling pistols to rifles, but require a knowledge of black-powder safety rules. Black powder is an explosive material that upon combustion creates a large amount of flash and smoke. The volume of smoke has been known to set off fire alarms in some theaters; therefore, black-powder firearms are not usually used in enclosed spaces. Black-powder loads should be used outdoors or in large well-ventilated theaters, under professional supervision.

Black-powder flintlock, or percussion cap, pistols are of large caliber (.44, .45, and even .50), notoriously unreliable, and often will "hang fire" (discharge after a delay of several seconds) or not fire at all. All of these situations are dangerous to performers and the furtherance of the plot!

One should use these types of firearms only after careful planning, with professional supervision, and after the staff and cast have been thoroughly familiarized with black-powder safety rules. (Read the section on black powder.)

When a small amount of "bang" is enough to give the audience the idea that the gun has been fired, here are two loading tricks that can be used:

1. With percussion-cap pistols, do not load anything into the barrel at all, and just use the percussion cap itself to make a noise. Be aware that occasionally the cap will shatter and fly through the air.

2. When using flintlocks, or percussion cap firearms, prime them as usual, then *loosely* ram down the muzzle a piece of flash paper, with perhaps a small dusting of black powder. This will give a "pop" of the primer, as well as a muzzle flash, but will greatly reduce the amount of smoke from the weapon. Avoid jamming the flash paper down with any force, since it may get stuck, and be so compressed that it will not fire. Be aware that accompanying the muzzle flash will be a certain amount of projectile material exiting the barrel.

    Follow the safety rules concerning proximity of performers and flammable materials to the muzzle. If more "bang" is needed to "sell" the shot, an offstage weapon may be timed to coincide with the onstage firing.

For more information, read the section on black powder firearms.

Rifles and Shotguns

The use of rifles and shotguns onstage is rare. This is partly due to the danger of using weapons of large caliber. If a rifle must be discharged onstage, the safety rules listed elsewhere in this book must be followed to the letter; and the distance between performers must be expanded as the caliber of the firearm increases.

The safest rifle to use onstage is the single-shot, breach-loading .22-caliber rifle. This rifle uses a relatively small load, and, since the mechanism is not automatic or semiautomatic, it is more reliable. These rifles should also accept the .22-caliber "crimp" blank load for maximum safety with adequate "bang."

As with all firearms, such safety maxims as Don't struggle over a loaded weapon, Protect your ears, Keep audience safety in mind, or Don't let performers or flammables get too close to a firearm must be followed carefully.

Shotguns onstage are another matter. Because of their large size, a shotgun shell "blank" is extremely loud and dangerous. Even a small-gauge shotgun is extremely dangerous onstage, since the amount of flying particles exiting the muzzle is enormous, including the paper or plastic "wad" used to pack the powder down in the shell.

Shotguns are sized by "bore," or "gauge" (an old term of measure). The larger the bore, or gauge, the smaller the diameter of the inside of the barrel.

I do not recommend using a shotgun loaded with a blank shell onstage for any reason. I have occasionally used a small (twenty) gauge shotgun *offstage*, firing it into a clean metal trash can for an extreme effect. In this case, ear and eye protection is a must for any persons near the discharge, since the sound is amplified by the can. When using this technique, the muzzle of the shotgun must be level with the top of the can.

Blank ammunition shotgun shells should be available from a dealer and can be ordered in full, half, and quarter loads.

Single-Shot Rifles and Repeating Rifles

By far the safest types of rifles to use onstage are the single-shot breach loaders, which work by manipulating a bolt on the barrel, thus opening (breaching) the chamber. These rifles can only fire one blank at a time, which when spent must be ejected by breaching the gun again (the simplest and safest design for theater).

Breach loaders may also be repeating rifles, the blanks loaded into a clip, or internal feed system, within the rifle. Repeating mechanisms are either bolt action, lever action, or pump action, and are all manual. In each case the rifle must be "cocked" between shots, thereby ejecting a spent casing while cocking the firing pin or hammer, and seating the next round.

The rifle is then ready to fire again. Because clips are designed to hold real bullets, the reduced length of blank ammunition may cause the clip-feed mechanism to jam, or foul.

I recommend that the smallest caliber weapon possible be obtained if it is absolutely necessary to use a rifle onstage for firing a blank round. I further recommend using a single-shot, breach-loading model.

Automatic and Semiautomatic Rifles

Semiautomatic rifles are designed to use the power of the exploding gunpowder to eject the spent cartridge and to seat the next one, thereby reducing the time between shots. In theory, a person could shoot as fast as he could pull the trigger until the ammunition ran out.

In theater applications semiautomatic rifles are not very reliable. They usually do not have enough power to fully engage the ejection mechanism of the weapon, and they are very apt to jam after the first shot. While it is possible to professionally alter a semiautomatic to make it less likely to jam (but never 100 percent), I try to avoid them.

If it is absolutely necessary to use a weapon such as an M-16, Uzi, AK-47, Mac 10, "Tommy gun," or even a modern hunting rifle, contact an experienced dealer and discuss the problem. Only use these types of firearms under trained supervision.

I do not recommend that fully automatic (true "machine guns") or semiautomatic weapons be used onstage except in very rare circumstances. The large caliber of these weapons makes for an unacceptably loud report, which is hard on performers and audience alike. And there are legal problems involved.

When you have decided what type of firearm to use and have arranged to rent or purchase it, you also need to decide what type of ammunition to use. It obviously must be of the same caliber as the weapon, but there are a few more tricks that you may not know.

Before you order any ammunition, and certainly before you rehearse any shots, you should read on and make an informed decision about what type of blank round you will need!

Blank Ammunition

Blank ammunition is available from many firearms dealers, who should be contacted directly by the theater. Refer to the listing in the appendix for addresses and phone numbers.

It is important to know something about blank ammunition before calling and ordering, however. Here is some basic information about blanks that may help one decide what to buy for a theatrical production.

Always purchase new blank ammunition for each production from a respectable theatrical dealer. *Never* use blanks commonly available in hardware stores for nail guns or in sport stores for dog training; these types of blanks are often manufactured with dangerous wadding. Never use a blank that is open-ended and has a cardboard wad visible in its end.

Remember

Always buy "wadless" blanks, since a blank with a wad is extremely dangerous!!

.22-Caliber Blanks

.22-caliber blanks are the most common size used in theaters, and are the safest because they use the smallest amount of gunpowder. They also are the most easily obtained and are usually available locally rather than through special order.

There are two common types that you will need to know:

1. **"Crimps":** These are the smallest blank loads commonly available. They come in boxes or tins of fifty to a hundred, are inexpensive, and are just loud enough to give a solid "bang" without much danger to the ears. They are identified by their design, which crimps the ends of the blanks to create more compression. Crimps are often used in starter pistols and can be bought in some sports stores. Crimps sometimes have an acorn design stamped on the bottom of the casing (see Figure 6-8 on page 278).

2. **"Shorts" or "Longs":** These are also easily obtained, and have an increased amount of powder—therefore, more "bang." If possible, experiment in the gun store by shooting all three types of blanks to determine the right one for a particular theatrical production. Shorts are louder than crimps, and longs are the loudest of the three.

.32-, .38-, .45-Caliber, or 9-mm. Blanks

These larger-sized blanks are best bought through the mail at an experienced theatrical firearms dealer. Modern manufacturing techniques have improved the safety of theater blanks. Old-style blanks that use heavy wadding material are very dangerous onstage because the wadding becomes a projectile. Modern large-caliber blanks are made with parafin or crimping techniques to increase the compression of the powder, thus creating an adequate "bang."

These blanks come in boxes of fifty, are usually color coded, and are relatively expensive but worth it for the safety factor.

Here are some terms that one will need to be familiar with when ordering blanks:

> **Full Load.** This means that the blank has a full amount of powder load as if it were a regular bullet. This type of load produces a loud

sound and can create a large amount of muzzle flash and projectiles. This type of load is the most dangerous to use onstage.

Half Load. This is half the amount of powder of the full load and is a common choice for theater.

Quarter Load. This is a quarter of the amount of powder of the full load and is the most common choice for small theaters.

Hollywood Load. This type of blank has a full-powder load to which is added a material designed to give additional muzzle flash. Used mainly for movies and television in *outdoor locations,* this type of blank is supposed to look more "awesome." Theater productions should avoid this type of load because of the increased muzzle flash and the increased projectile material exiting the weapon.

Figure 6-12. *A wadless .38 caliber blank load. Note the crimped end.*

If you are in doubt as to which type of blank load to purchase, err on the low side. Pick the quarter load, as opposed to the full load, for the safety of all concerned. A large-caliber, full-load blank that discharges in an enclosed theater is *very*, *very*, *loud!*

Blanks also come in smokeless, black powder (smokey), and flash (very dangerous indoors).

Tip!

Rifle, or Shotgun, Ammunition

It is important when using blank rifle, or shotgun, ammunition to purchase fresh, professionally manufactured blanks. One should *not* try to save money by making the blanks out of bullets or by emptying the pellets out of shotgun shells. To do so is to invite an explosion.

Figure 6-13. *These should never be allowed in the theater! From left to right: a live .22-caliber round. This is a "real" bullet capable of killing someone. Note the difference between it and the crimped blank in the previous photo. At center and right is a wadded blank, another very dangerous round. Note the open end showing the cardboard wad.*

These large-caliber blanks are obtainable on special order from theatrical firearms dealers. Loads can be altered to fit one's requirements; however, lowering the load on blanks used in semiautomatic rifles will adversely affect the discharge of spent shells. These types of blanks are quite expensive, costing up to $1.20 U.S. each in 1994.

If you must discharge a rifle onstage, I recommend a .22-caliber, bolt action, single-shot model. Ammunition for this is obtained as listed above, and either the "crimp" or the "short" or "long" blanks should fit the breach. One should remember to always buy wadless blanks!

Below is a short list of common cartridge sizes for rifles, both current and early twentieth century. This list is both for single-shot, repeating, and in some cases semiautomatic and assault rifles.

Large rifle ammunition:

Size/Caliber	Weapons/Country
7.62 mm × 39	(Warsaw pact) AK-47, AKM (USSR)
7.62 mm × 51	(NATO) M14 (US), L1 A1 (GB)
5.56 mm × 45	M16 A1 (US), AR 18 (US)
9.00 mm × 19	Uzi (Israel)
.45 cal.	Thomson SMG (1928) "Tommy Gun"
.303 cal.	Short Magazine Lee-Enfield 1902-WW2 (GB)
.30–06 cal.	US Model 1903 Springfield WW1, also US M1, WW2

These types of firearms are very dangerous and should not be used in theaters except under expert guidance and training.

Shotgun Blanks

Shotgun blanks are available from theatrical firearms dealers and sometimes from gun shops. They can be special ordered to reduce the amount of powder load. It is important to realize that the wadding used in shotgun shells to compress the powder will exit the barrel at high velocity and can seriously injure a person unlucky enough to be struck by it. I do not recommend the discharging of shotguns in enclosed spaces such as theaters.

Figure 6-14. *A 12-gauge shotgun blank, showing two views. Note that the gauge is marked on the end of the casing.*

If you need to discharge a shotgun for effect offstage, always fire into a clean metal trash can. Never place the muzzle of the shotgun in contact with the sides or bottom of the can. A person who is discharging such a weapon should wear eye and ear protection.

Here are the basic sizes of shotgun shells in ascending order. Be sure of the gauge of the weapon before ordering!

22 gauge	Remember! You can special order
20 gauge	quarter-, half- or full-load
16 gauge	shotgun blanks. Be sure of what you want before ordering.
12 gauge	
10 gauge	

Dummy Bullets

Dummy bullets are bullets that have been drilled out and that contain no gunpowder or priming materials. They are perfectly safe, will not make a "bang," and cannot possibly be shot. Unlike "blanks," even at close range dummy bullets appear to be real, since they are not just empty casings but include the bullet. Dummy bullets are available from the theatrical firearms dealers in all calibers, sizes, and gauges. Never make your own dummy bullets!

Dummies can be a nice touch to a production when a character must handle the weapon, or perhaps when a character must be seen to load, or unload, a firearm. Because they look like real bullets and have the approximate weight of real bullets, they can be very convincing to an audience. Dummy bullets may easily be chambered into all types of guns (except starter pistols and weapons with chamber restrictors or blocked barrels), with complete security.

An example of their use might be in the play *Hedda Gabler*. Early in the play, with her grandfather's pistol, Hedda shoots at Judge Brock. The pistol can be loaded with a blank cartridge before the show, and Hedda can safely shoot offstage.

Hedda might later be seen to reload (with dummy bullets) her grandfather's pistol in full view of the audience; and later, when she puts the gun to her head to commit suicide, an offstage gun supplies the sound effect. She might even play with the bullets during the course of the drama.

In this example, the audience's belief in the pistol is strongly reinforced. The audience sees it shoot, sees it loaded, and hears it go off, thus killing Hedda.

> Never attempt to make your own dummy bullets by pulling the bullet from the cartridge, emptying the powder, and forcing the bullet back into place. This is extremely dangerous, since the primer is left in the end of the cartridge, which can still fire.
>
> Always buy dummy bullets from a reputable theatrical firearms dealer.

Black-powder Firearms

Prior to the invention of the bullet cartridge, rifles and pistols used loose black powder. This is a highly volatile substance, especially on the stage, and special training and knowledge is required for its use. The modern "blank" cartridge is so much easier to use that I recommend firearms that can chamber this load. Many productions set in periods prior to 1890 require the use of muzzle loading black-powder firearms.

Figure 6-15. Detail of the firing mechanism of a percussion cap pistol. The hammer is in the "full cock" position. To the right is the "nipple" onto which the percussion cap will fit. When struck by the descending hammer, the resulting spark will travel through the nipple, vent, and into the barrel igniting the main charge.

Figure 6-16. Detail of the firing mechanism of a flintlock pistol. The descending hammer and flint (missing in this photo) strike the steel frizzen, creating a spark, simultaneously opening the pan and igniting the primer charge.

I have eliminated one major category, the wheel lock, as unsuitable theatrically, since reliable weapons are unobtainable.

Black-powder firearms break down into three distinct categories:

1. **Percussion Cap** (early-nineteenth to late-nineteenth centuries). This weapon was loaded with powder, a wad, and a projectile (though not for stage). A small explosive "cap" was then set on a nipple that, when struck by the hammer, sent a spark through the nipple and into a hole in the barrel, thus igniting the main powder charge. This was the method of fire used in the American Civil War, and for stage purposes is the most reliable.

2. **Flintlock** (early-seventeenth to early-nineteenth centuries). This weapon is muzzle loading, just as the percussion-cap one above. The firing mechanism involves the striking of a piece of flint rock against a steel bar, the resulting sparks falling into a pan of loose black powder and the spark (hopefully) moving into the barrel through a small touch hole near the pan to ignite the powder in the barrel. For the stage, this weapon is cumbersome and is not as reliable as the percussion-cap one. It causes a large amount of smoke, and a flash of powder near the face of the performer firing it. It's slow to load and requires delicate handling. Each flint only lasts about twenty firings.

3. **Matchlock** (early-fifteenth to mid-seventeenth centuries). This is the oldest of the three listed firearms. The matchlock relies on a long, slow-burning fuse, or "match," to set off the powder in a pan, which then will ignite the main charge in the barrel. These weapons are few and far between. Theatrically they are the most unreliable and dangerous since a constantly burning match must be kept lit until the weapon is discharged. I do not recommend these firearms for theatrical productions, except in the hands of accomplished experts, or reenactors.

Since all of these firearms are muzzle loading, they *cannot* be altered to refuse to accept projectiles. Great care must be taken that nothing solid is ever put into the barrel!

Some theatrical firearms dealers can supply authentic-looking weapons altered to chamber modern blank cartridges. This is an extremely safe, easy, and effective way of using older (-looking) firearms. Contact Center Firearms in New York City (listed in the appendix) for more information.

Black-powder rifles and pistols are much larger in caliber than modern guns. Many of the black-powder weapons are .50 caliber or larger which makes quite a large barrel! Consequently these rifles and pistols require a lot more powder than modern guns do. The result, obviously, is a great deal of danger if one of these weapons is overloaded with powder. Black powder, itself, does not burn as efficiently as modern gunpowder, and burning powder will exit the end of a barrel and travel a good way across the stage—sometimes more than twenty feet!

This propensity for burning debris is possibly the most dangerous aspect of black-powder weapons. Their larger caliber only compounds the problem.

The following are some things to look out for when using black-powder firearms:

1. How much powder do I load?

    Always consult an expert! Before using a black-powder weapon on-stage with the performers, run a test firing session without performers and determine EXACTLY how little powder will suffice for your production. Suppliers sell small, brass, powder measures that will help you always use the same amount of powder.

2. What is a wad, and how is it used?

    The "wad" historically was a piece of cloth that was jammed down the barrel to seat the powder and compress it and upon which the ball could rest. The theatrical application is different! The ball, or bullet, will of course NEVER be used. However, the powder MUST be compressed or the gun will not "go bang" but will merely fizzle weakly. A wad, therefore, must still be used. However, *do not use cloth of any type as wadding.* Cloth does not completely burn away, and you will send burning cloth across the stage if you do this! An adequate alternative to this is thin Styrofoam® plugs, cut to fit the caliber size. I recommend nothing thicker than a quarter inch (1 centimeter).

    This wadding should burn completely away when the gun is fired. *Never* put anything solid into the barrel since it will act like a bullet and will sail through the air when the gun is fired. NEVER leave the ramrod in the barrel accidentally because the ramrod will also become a flying projectile. Many were killed in wartime this way—when, in the heat of battle, men forgot to take the ramrod out before firing.

3. **Where do I obtain black powder?**
    Black powder can be purchased from any reputable gun dealer. It comes in different grades, and you should ask the dealer which kind you need for your specific firearm. Grades AAA and AAAA are the most commonly used.

4. **Are there special cleaning requirements for black-powder firearms?**
    Yes! Black powder is extraordinarily corrosive, and weapons MUST be cleaned daily, after use, or they will pit and corrode from the effects of the black powder left unburned in the barrel. Black powder contains a great deal of sulphur, which is toxic, and reacts quickly with metal parts. Obtain a cleaning kit from a gun dealer and use it religiously. Clean and lightly oil the outside of the firearm as well to keep it rust free.

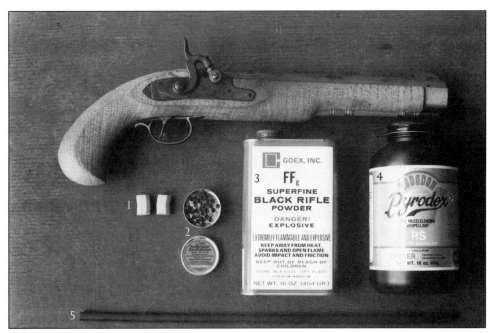

Figure 6-17. *A reproduction percussion cap pistol showing: (1) ear plugs for ear protection; (2) a tin of percussion caps; (3) a one-pound can of black powder; (4) a one-pound container of Pyrodex powder; and (5) the ramrod.*

5.   **How should I teach the performers black-powder safety?**
Organize a gun safety day or rehearsal. Explain to the cast the dangers of firearms in general. Explain that there should be no fooling around with the weapons, on- or offstage. Demonstrate loading and firing techniques. Answer questions that the cast may have. Supervise the prop personnel or performers who must perform this task. Explain where the weapons will be kept and where the black powder will be stored (separately, of course!).

When the performers are familiar and comfortable with the functions of the firearms, slowly and carefully position the firearms on the stage where they will be when the performers shoot. Allow the performers to rehearse the action "dry"—that is, without powder. Make sure that no one is pointing the firearms at anyone else, either on- or offstage. When everyone is comfortable with the staging, load the weapons and rehearse the action in *slow motion*. Keep an eye out for dangerous moments. *Never* point the weapon at another person but rather up- or downstage of that person or over that person's head by several feet. *Never* point the gun at the audience. *Never* run with a cocked, loaded gun. *Never* struggle with a loaded gun.

Avoid "dry firing" during rehearsals, which means to pull the trigger and allow the hammer to fall on an unloaded nipple or frizzen, as this weakens the weapon.

Tip!

All of this presumes that a firearms expert or a qualified fight director has previously tested the firearms and determined the exact amount of powder needed for a production. *Always test the weapons many times in a safe area before giving them to the performers!*

Black-powder firearms must *always* be loaded with as little powder as possible and must *never* be loaded with a solid wad or projectile. *Never* use an antique gun for it may explode in your face. Find a reputable dealer in modern replicas of antiques, and purchase or rent through that dealer. Obtain safety manuals and be thoroughly familiar with the loading and handling of these replicas. Black powder is a volatile explosive and must be treated with care and respect.

Remember that percussion cap guns are more reliable onstage than flintlocks or matchlocks are.

Using black-powder weapons can be very satisfying theatrically! They are, however, temperamental, balky, and smokey and require a lot of hands-on maintenance by a trained individual.

When one decides to use black-powder firearms, one should consult an expert and allow lots of extra rehearsal time to get used to them.

Staging a Gunshot!

Once one has decided to use a live gunshot in a stage production, and has arranged to rent or purchase an appropriate firearm, one must now solve the problem of safely staging the gunshot itself.

A bit of preparation is in order before, say, a fight director gives a gun to the performers and positions them onstage. Here are a few questions that should be answered first:

1. Who might be in the way of the shot itself? other actors onstage? extras? offstage personnel?

2. Are there any flammables nearby that might catch fire from the flash and from the burning powder exiting the muzzle?

3. Will the staging threaten the audience at all? Audience members must not feel threatened, for example, by excessive waving of the gun in their direction before or after the shot.

4. Can the scene be staged in such a way that, from the audience's perspective, the gun looks as if it were pointing at the victim, though it is actually pointing up- or downstage?

5. Is there a way to aim or draw the gun so that the motion does not cross the line of the face of the victim? A rising motion of the arm is usually safer than a descending one.

Proscenium Theaters

The most common type of staging is the proscenium style, wherein the victim is downstage of the person shooting and the shot is aimed several feet upstage of the victim (Figure 6-18). Five to six feet (approximately two meters)

Figure 6-18. Note that although the pistol appears to be aimed at the victim, it is aimed several feet upstage.

Figure 6-19. Here, the pistol is aimed several feet downstage from the victim.

off-line of the victim is a reasonable distance away. The larger the theater, the farther off-line the gun may be pointed, while still maintaining the illusion. Be sure that the person firing is at least twenty feet away from the victim, *and* aiming off-line.

The reverse of this staging also works but is not used as often. Here, the victim stands upstage of the person shooting, and the shot is also aimed upstage of the attacker (Figure 6-19). Notice how hard it is to tell exactly where the pistol is aimed. (The pistol is aimed toward the attacker's left.)

If the victim is upstage center, and the person shooting is either downstage right or downstage left, the angle of fire can be safely turned away by firing downstage of the victim. Always check the angle of fire to see that no offstage personnel are threatened. (In Figure 6-20 the pistol is aimed toward the attacker's right in the first photo and to his left in the second photo.)

Thrust Stage

It is more difficult to stage an off-target gunshot in a thrust stage environment. If the victim is downstage, a shot fired off-line in any direction is aimed directly at the audience! This arrangement is highly unacceptable (see Figure 6-21).

The only possible way to effect a live gunshot on a thrust stage is to have the victim upstage of the person shooting. In this way the weapon may be safely misdirected away from the body of the victim by several feet in either direction, left or right. If the gun is raised and fired quickly (not to mention accurately!) the illusion of firing toward the victim is maintained.

Another solution is the offstage gunshot, or the use of a blowback, starter pistol, or cap pistol, wherein the discharge is either minimal or nil.

Theater-in-the-Round, or Arena Staging

The most difficult type of theater in which to stage a safe, live, blank gunshot is the arena style, or theater-in-the-round. The safety problem here is obvious: nowhere onstage can a performer aim a weapon off-line of a victim without aiming directly at the audience! However, there are a few ways to possibly save the day with some creative staging.

1. Use an offstage shot, coming from a vomitory entrance close to the action.

Figure 6-20. These two photos show a situation where the victim is upstage center and the attacker is downstage right, then downstage left, aiming downstage of the victim each time. In the first photo, the attacker aims to his own right and in the second photo he aims to his own left.

Figure 6-21. *Here, in an effort to protect the performer, the audience is threatened. Never threaten the audience by pointing a firearm in its direction! In this case, the scene would have to be restaged so that the gunshot poses no danger to the performer or the audience.*

2. If the entrances/exits into the space are particularly wide, whether ramps, stairs, or vomitories, position the victim nearby, so that the weapon may be aimed toward this open area. The person shooting must be very accurate, so as not to aim at any audience member. This trick requires lots of rehearsal to be safe and look real.

3. Position the victim on the floor, so that the gun may be discharged into the floor, several feet away from the body of the performer (Figure 6-22). This prevents the weapon from being pointed toward the audience or the victim.

4. Stage a struggle over the gun (completely *unloaded*) in which the gun will disappear between the combatants, hidden from the audience. An offstage gunshot may then be fired, as if the weapon had discharged during the struggle.

Figure 6-22. Here the victim has fallen downstage center. The safest way to fire here is to aim the pistol at the floor at least six feet upstage. Be careful not to threaten the audience by waving the weapon toward them.

The Offstage Shot

An offstage shot that simulates a live onstage shot is a common device in the theater. It is used when the age or inexperience of the performers is such that using a firearm loaded with a blank is too dangerous. It is also used when the performers are too close together to make the discharging of a gun safe. For example, in *Sleuth, Hedda Gabler,* and modern dress productions of *Julius Caesar,* stage directions require the performers to be quite close to "discharging" guns, thereby creating a dangerous situation. The offstage shot can solve this problem and should never be avoided because of the assumption that it is a "fake" shot. When correctly timed, it is very effective and, furthermore, absolutely safe for the performers.

The offstage shot is usually fired by someone in stage management, though sometimes a prop person will fill in for this job. Care must be taken to use a metal can to absorb the sound and any projectile material that may exit the gun. Eye and ear protection are a must.

It is important to know what kind of firearm to choose to simulate the noise. It is comical to fire a .22-caliber starter pistol loaded with a crimp blank off-stage to simulate the firing of a shotgun onstage!

Rehearsals of the gunshot must be arranged so that the performer who is holding the weapon and the person who is shooting offstage can coordinate the shot. Occasionally a third party such as a stage manager will cue the shot over a headset, since the offstage shooter isn't always able to see the stage. One should experiment with placing the offstage shooter in various positions back-stage. Off-left, off-right, up-center behind a curtain, or even sometimes underneath the stage will sound best. The director or fight director should sit in the audience and listen to the different sounds that the firing placement has.

Timing the offstage shot is crucial! When badly timed, the performers will be nervous, and the audience will be aware of the trick to the detriment of the play in general. It is especially embarrassing to pull the trigger of an unloaded pistol and for the audience to hear a click of the hammer fall, followed by an awkward pause, a tardy feigned death from the victim, while offstage a shot is heard! One timing trick is to agree on a word cue, as from the assassination scene in *Julius Caesar*. In this scene, Casca says "Speak hands for me!" and delivers the first blow to Caesar. In a modern dress production, the usual dagger could be replaced by a pistol and an offstage shot could happen one beat after the word "me" or directly on the word "me" or "speak" or any other word. An offstage shot would allow Casca to put his gun (unloaded) directly on the body of Caesar.

This trick works best when the person who is shooting the pistol, rifle, or other firearm does not pull the trigger at all. Pulling the trigger and allowing the hammer to fall "dry" confuses the audience with an extra sound that calls attention to itself. The only sound that the audience should hear is the report of the offstage firing. The "victim" must also wait until the offstage report to react to the shot.

This three-way timing should be rehearsed many times before opening night, and one should have a satisfactory (and safe!) illusion.

Finally, it is important to rehearse the "kick" of the gun in the hands of the shooter, who should react a split second after hearing the offstage report of the gun. This helps to simulate an onstage firing, gives energy to the move, and greatly improves the illusion of firing.

Figure 6-23. *This shows how far "off-line" the pistol may be aimed for safety. This is a minimum of three feet (one meter) measured at the victim's position. Note as well that the pistol is not aimed at the performer's face, but below his shoulders.*

Firearm Purchase or Rental

After reading and becoming familiar with the information on the previous pages, one's options should be somewhat clearer. It is important to understand and appreciate one's limits, and the limits of performers, before purchasing or renting a firearm. I wish to repeat several points that I have made in the body of the preceding material.

Firearms are potentially *deadly!*

Always treat a firearm as if it were loaded!

Always train theater staff and performers in firearm safety.

Use the smallest load blank available to minimize danger.

Never struggle over a gun.

Use eye and ear protection when possible.

Don't leave firearms laying around where they may be played with.

Consult with an expert when staging or acquiring a firearm.

Check local laws concerning firearm permits.

Second in importance to safety is reliable information when purchasing or renting a firearm. I recommend the suppliers listed in the appendix at the end of this book. These individuals are trained professionals familiar with theatrical needs. They can talk to you in person or over the phone and can supply the safest type of firearm for a theatrical production.

Remember that the most reliable type of firearm to use onstage is a revolver-style pistol or a bolt-action, single-shot rifle. It is usually unnecessary to use a firearm larger than a .22-caliber one. Also remember that with larger weapons (.38 caliber, 9 millimeter), you can vary the sound of the "bang" by ordering smaller blank "loads." Usually these run in one-quarter-, one-half-, three-quarter-, and full-load types.

If a theater regularly produces modern plays that use firearms, it should consider purchasing its own. In the long run, this will be much more cost effective than renting weapons. Secure storage is necessary, as is a regular cleaning program, but creating one's own stock of firearms is not a bad idea. A simple stock of firearms should include the following:

.22-caliber revolver-style pistol

.38-caliber "police special" style

.32-caliber snub-nosed revolver

several plastic pistols

.22-caliber bolt-action, single-shot rifle

percussion-cap, black-powder pistol

cleaning materials

trigger guards (locks) for each firearm

shoulder holster

belt holster

clip-on holster

Most theaters do not have the capability of owning and storing firearms, so renting weapons is the easiest answer. A theater that rents firearms should expect to pay a deposit, usually the value of the firearm(s) if purchased new, as well as a weekly or monthly fee. The cost of blank ammunition and of shipping and handling should be factored into the theater's budget. The theater should find out if someone on its staff needs a firearms license. The theater should contact the local police department to check on local gun laws and to see if it needs any special permits.

One should always use reliable firearms with an eye out for the safety of all involved in a theatrical production.

The Brady Bill Waiting Period

Effective March 1, 1994, theatrical handgun props shipped to production companies located in the following states are subject to a five-day waiting period before the local firearms dealer who receives the shipment may release the props to production personnel:

Alabama	Minnesota	Rhode Island
Alaska	Mississippi	South Carolina
Arizona	Montana	South Dakota
Arkansas	Nevada	Tennessee
Colorado	New Hampshire	Texas
Georgia	New Mexico	Utah
Idaho	North Carolina	Vermont
Kansas	North Dakota	Washington State
Kentucky	Ohio	West Virginia
Louisiana	Oklahoma	Wyoming
Maine	Pennsylvania	

Remember that the law requires a waiting period of *five business days* before a dealer in these states may release any handgun from the time that the dealer notifies the chief law-enforcement officer in his area of the impending transfer.

Productions renting handguns from out of state must factor in the extra time it will take to actually clear the five-day waiting period. A theater should make sure that it doesn't get caught on opening night with its handgun sitting on a shelf at the local gun store.

That's a Wrap!

Nothing is as satisfying as seeing an exciting, rip-roaring sword fight. Nothing is as heartbreaking as seeing a dramatic moment of contemporary violence. However, nothing is as awful as a bad stage fight.

When the audience is aware of the choreographer's hand or of the performer's technique, the audience is transported out of the theatrical experience and will laugh at the fight.

As a young fight director, I was often crushed to hear the audience tittering at fights that I had staged. However, on reflection, this reaction is sometimes merely a release of emotion. There is a difference between that reaction and an audience's becoming uncomfortable about watching actors who are struggling with difficult choreography.

When all the elements pull together—and the production team, the performers, the text, and the fight choreography blend seamlessly—the effect is magical! Disbelief is willingly suspended, and the audience is transported into the physical lives of the characters. Applause often follows a well-conceived fight!

If there is a goal to this book, it is to enable a fight director to stage a fight scene safely, creatively, and with technical perfection and to share it with an audience. My message to the performer is to involve yourself emotionally in the fight and to train throughout your career. Create for us an event worth watching—that tells the story and that is technically brilliant.

If you wish to be a fight director, train! You must spend thousands of hours in a studio learning all you can about period weaponry, firearm safety, tumbling, and contemporary violence. Study theater history, directing principals, and stage effects. Take classes in vocal production and movement. Acquire books on combat, warfare, and weapons, and collect theatrical arms to start your own armory. Analyze your communication skills and work hard to improve them. And finally, don't get in over your head. Never accept work that is beyond your skills or that may endanger the actors.

Stage combat is a wonderful part of theater. It has kept me active and fit for more than twenty years and, I hope, for twenty more. You too may find your place in this business. I encourage you to do so. It may just happen that you get to create or perform many thrilling fights in your career. Maybe you wish to direct fights professionally. Either way, there is a place for you. As long as playwrights write plays, there will be scenes of violence.

But the beginning of all these journeys is the classroom. I'll even open the door for you and turn on the lights. The swords are ready, gleaming on their racks, and the mats are laid out. First, a salute, and . . . Allez!

Appendices

Theatrical Arms Suppliers

This is a list of current suppliers. Check them all for price and availability. The individuals that hand make weapons need a lot of lead time, from one to six months for custom equipment.

Swords

Vulcan's Forge
3013 Shannon Drive
Baltimore, MD 21213
(410) 325-2046
Lewis Shaw

Custom-made swords, daggers, blades. Steel and bronze guards of good quality and value. Sales and rental. Custom orders. Catalog and price list.

Dennis Graves
255 S. 41st Street
Boulder, CO 80303
(303) 494-4685

Handmade swords of all types. Custom- and museum-quality work. Sales and rental. Catalog and price list.

Arms and Armour
Christopher Poor
1101 Stinson Boulevard NE
Minneapolis, MN 55413
(612) 331-6473

Supplier of custom-made armor and armor pieces. Also shields weapons, helmets, daggers, maces, and pole arms. Catalog and price list.

Steve Vaughan
800 Vernal Road
Attica, NY 14011
(716) 591-3673

Custom-made swords, knives, broadswords, natural quarter-staves, hardwood sword handles. Rental and sales.

American Fencer's Supply
"The Armoury"
1180 Folsom Street
San Francisco, CA 94103
(415) 863-7911

Inexpensive rapiers, smallswords, broadswords. Lots of basic weapons. Imported and assembled. Big inventory. Catalog sales only.

Alan Meek
180 Frog Grove Lane
Wood St. Village
Guildford, Surrey
England GU3-3HD
(4448) 323-4084

Largest supplier of theatrical
weapons in England. Large
quantities of weapons of all
periods. Will ship Federal Express
to America or anywhere.
No catalog. No price list.

Lundegarde Inc.
P.O. Box 287
Crompond, NY 10517
(914) 271-9798

Private maker of edged weapons.
Lost wax brass parts with fantasy
motifs. Will custom design.
Catalog and price list.

Museum Replica
2143 Gees Mill Road
Box 840
Conyers, GA 30207
(800) 241-3664

Mainly costume weapons.
Costumes, jewelry, shields,
fantasy weapons, helmets, books.
Sales only. Few practical items.
Catalog and price list.

Blade Inc.
212 West 15th Street
New York, NY 10011
(212) 620-0114

Sport-fencing equipment of
all types. Some period arms.
Small salle for classes.
Price list available.

Santelli, Inc.
465 S. Dean Street
Englewood, NJ 07631
(201) 871-3105

Sport-fencing equipment of all
types. Large salle for classes. Price
list available. Some period arms.

Triplette Competition Arms
162 West Pine Street
Mt. Airy, NC 27030
(919) 786-5294

Sport-fencing equipment of all
types. Épée and broadsword blades.
Large catalog and price list.

Firearms

Center Firearms
10 W. 37th Street
New York, NY 10018
(212) 244-4040

Sales and rentals of all types
of guns for theater and film.
They have it *all*. Will ship
anywhere in USA.

Golden Age Arms
115 E. High St.
Ashley, OH 43003
(614) 747-2488

Huge inventory of parts and assembled black-powder firearms. Clothing, accessories, blank hardwood stocks, barrels, etc.

Dixie Gunworks Inc.
Gunpowder Lane
Union City, TN 38261
(800) 238-6785

Black-powder kits and antique reproductions. Large selection of weapons. Large illustrated catalog.

Collector's Armoury
800 Slaters Lane, Dept. CA-8
P.O. Box 59
Alexandria, VA 22313-0059
(703) 549-2509

Weapon replicas, noncombat swords, knives, interesting guns. Books, military memorabilia. Catalog.

Weapons Specialists Ltd.
33 Greene St. #1W
New York, NY 10013
(212) 941-7696
(212) 941-7654 Fax

Rental, consultation, training and safety supervision. Film, television, theater. See Rick Washburn.

ACE PROPS
1 West 19th Street
New York, NY 10011
(212) 206-1475
(212) 929-9082 Fax

Rental of nonworking replicas of famous guns. No license required.

SFX Design, Inc.
6099 Godown Road
Columbus, OH 43220
(614) 459-3222
(614) 459-5087 Fax

Decorative and firing handguns, rifles, machine guns. Any period; able to fire blanks. Also special effects to order.

Other Suppliers

AAI American Athletic Inc.
200 American Avenue
Jefferson, IA 50129
(800) 247-3978

Gymnastic equipment, mats, harness, climbing ropes, flooring. Large catalog.

Alcone Co. Inc.
5–49 49th Avenue
Long Island City, NY 11101
(718) 361-8373

Big theatrical supply house.
Breakaway bottles, blood, novelty
items. Large illustrated catalog.

Bamboo and Ratan Works
470 Oberlin Avenue South
Lakewood, NJ 08701-6997
(908) 370-0220

Quality source for ratan poles
for quarterstaffs. (Get them
"sanded" without fail!)
Price list.

Gordons Novelty
933 Broadway
New York, NY
(212) 254-8616

Large novelty supplier in New York.
Rubber items: swords, knives,
tricks. Costumes, makeup, gags.
Extensive catalog.

F & J Police Equipment
378 East 161st Street
Melrose, Bronx, NY 10451
(212) 665-4535

Uniforms, guns, shoes, bullet-
proof vests—everything.
Hours: 9–6, Mon.–Fri.; 9–5, Sat.

Reef Industries
P.O. Box 750245
Houston, TX 77275
(713) 484-6892

Yellow barricade ribbon
("Crime Scene" "Do Not Cross",
etc.). Brochure available.

Sullivan Glove Co.
100 S.E. Miller Avenue
Bend, OR 97702
(541) 382-3092

Supplier of high quality leather
gloves for horseback riding, which
are superior to fencing gloves.
Sized in men's and women's.

The Society of American
   Fight Directors
1834 Camp Avenue
Rockford, IL 61103
(800) 659-6579

Information on equipment,
fight directors, training.

U.S. Cavalry
2855 Centennial Avenue
Radcliff, KY 40160-9000
(800) 777-7732
(502) 352-0266 Fax

Military memorabilia, clothes,
weapons, uniforms, books.
Knives, police equipment.
Large illustrated catalog.

National Rifle Association
P.O. Box 37484, Dept. EF-15
Washington, DC 20013

General information on firearms
and firearms safety.

Gratzner Period Accoutrements
P.O. Box 12023
Marina Del Rey, CA 90295
(310) 823-2050

Handmade leather sword belts,
frogs, hangers. Custom work
available. Catalog.

Costume Armour Inc.
2 Mill Street
P.O. Box 85
Cornwall, NY 12518
(914) 534-9120
(914) 534-8602 Fax

Sale and rental of stock and custom
armor, accessories. (Armor is
vacuformed and can be pre-
assembled, or you can assemble
and paint it.) Catalog.

Bok Lei Tat Inc.
213 Canal Street
New York, NY 10013
(212) 226-1703

Samurai swords, karate and kung-
fu equipment, books, clothing.

EFEX
35–39 37th Street
Long Island City, NY 11101
(718) 937-2417

Blood effects, rigging and wire
flying, fire and smoke effects.
Breakaway glass. Sales and rentals.
Catalog.

Zeller International Ltd.
Main Street, Box Z-2
Downsville, NY 13755
(212) 627-7676 or
(607) 363-7792

Fire, steam, fog, wind, rain.
Z-Blood (nonstaining), special
effects designed and created.
Catalog.

Foy Inventerprises Inc.
32–75 E. Patrick Lane
Las Vegas, NV 89120
(702) 454-3500
(702) 454-7369 Fax

Riggers for flying (*Peter Pan*).
Also custom flying and special
effects. Contact Peter or Garry Foy.

Fight Directors Canada
39 Wheatsheaf Crescent
North York, Ontario
Canada M3N 1P7
416-667-1346
Robert Seale

In 1996, The Society of British Fight Directors (SBFD), changed their name, and split into two independent groups.

The British Academy of
    Stage and Screen Combat
10 Cranbrook Park
Wood Green, London
England N22 5NA
(0144) 181 881 1536
Richard Ryan

The British Academy of
    Dramatic Combat
20 Lincoln St.
Canton, Cardiff
United Kingdom CF5 1JX
(0122) 223 8428
Steven Wilsher

Both groups will supply information on equipment, training, and fight directors in England and in Europe.

The Stage Manager's Checklist

During the rehearsal process and the run of the show, the stage manager is responsible for the quality and safety of the fight scenes. Most professional stage managers have had some experience in dealing with fights and fighters, props, swords, and guns. They have had to deal with "fight calls" and actors' changing the choreography. The best stage managers that I have worked with know how to anticipate problems and how to not let anything or anyone get out of hand. Once the play has opened and the director and the fight director have left town, the stage manager (with help from the fight captain) is the boss.

For those individuals who haven't ever dealt with a "fight show," here are some ideas to keep in mind.

The Rehearsal Process

During the rehearsal process, the stage manager should be responsible for the setup of the rehearsal room and should make sure that all the props are in place for rehearsal. Here is a rehearsal process checklist:

    1.   Is the rehearsal room floor clean, taped out, and free of excess furniture?

    2.   Is there a well-stocked first-aid kit handy?

    3.   Are there knee/elbow pads available for use in rehearsal?

    4.   Is the room lighting bright and even?

    5.   Are all the fight props available at the start of the rehearsal?

    6.   Are all the fight props accounted for at the end of the rehearsal and stored securely?

    7.   Is an emergency phone number at your fingertips in case of an accident?

    8.   Have an adequate number of fight rehearsals been called each week?

    9.   Have the other departments (lighting, props, costumes, set) been consulted about any changes in the fight?

315

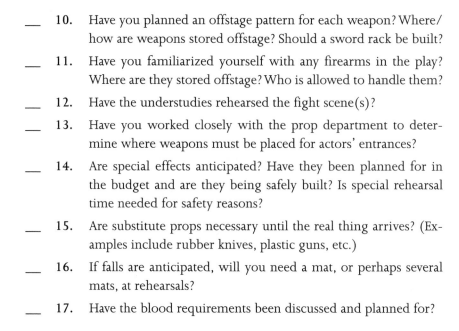

___ 10. Have you planned an offstage pattern for each weapon? Where/how are weapons stored offstage? Should a sword rack be built?

___ 11. Have you familiarized yourself with any firearms in the play? Where are they stored offstage? Who is allowed to handle them?

___ 12. Have the understudies rehearsed the fight scene(s)?

___ 13. Have you worked closely with the prop department to determine where weapons must be placed for actors' entrances?

___ 14. Are special effects anticipated? Have they been planned for in the budget and are they being safely built? Is special rehearsal time needed for safety reasons?

___ 15. Are substitute props necessary until the real thing arrives? (Examples include rubber knives, plastic guns, etc.)

___ 16. If falls are anticipated, will you need a mat, or perhaps several mats, at rehearsals?

___ 17. Have the blood requirements been discussed and planned for?

During the rehearsal process, an alert stage manager is an enormous lift to the performers and fight director, as well as another eye toward safety! The fight scene(s) in a play is not the only important item on the stage manager's plate, but one that requires concentrated attention since the potential for accident is very high. Pay attention to such details as how each performer works into the fight, cuing the performers (if necessary) from offstage, and how the special effects (such as music, fog, explosions, etc.) work into the scene.

During the Run of the Show

After tech-week madness and opening night fury, the run of the show is where breakdown in equipment and performers is likely to happen. Special problems occur during a long run of several weeks or more, during a tour, or during a play performed in rotating repertory with several other plays. Keeping the fight scenes fresh and safe over a period of weeks is partly the stage manager's responsibility.

An important ally in this responsibility is the fight captain, an individual chosen by the fight director, in consultation with the director, and picked for his or her expertise in keeping up with fight calls and equipment and in maintaining the fight choreography. (Read the section on the fight captain.)

The most important aspect of keeping fights "up to par" during the run of a show is the fight call. A half hour before "half-hour call" is the normal time for a fight call. Usually, the larger the fight scene, the later the call. Therefore, if there is a large battle scene to rehearse, the majority of the cast is called closer to normal "half hour" and not at the beginning of the fight call. An example would be running the fights in *Romeo and Juliet* in reverse order, keeping the act 1 brawl for last, and starting with the fight between Romeo and Paris.

Pre-performance fight call must be rehearsed on the set, under adequate work light and with all necessary props. Always check the integrity of weapons and fight props, and allow company members to warm up, especially those with complicated sequences. Fight call must be mandatory, especially in rotating repertory and touring situations where the performers must get used to different theater spaces quickly. Fight call is never a time to rehearse understudies or replacements, though they should watch. A separate call must be arranged for this to occur. The following is a checklist for stage management during the run of a show:

___ 1. Have a first-aid box offstage where it is easily found.

___ 2. Have emergency phone numbers posted in obvious places in the booth, offstage, and in the dressing areas.

___ 3. Supervise fight call before every performance.

___ 4. Make sure that the stage is clear and swept and that all work is finished before fight call starts.

___ 5. Arrange for all props to be in place at the start of fight call.

___ 6. Arrange for blood effects to be built and maintained. Have blood props cleaned and blood sponges onstage refilled before each performance.

___ 7. Arrange for understudies to observe fight call. (This must be a separate rehearsal call.)

___ 8. Have a notated version of each fight in the prompt book, to refer to in case of changes.

—   9. Be alert to "actor's improvements" in the fight scenes, and fix them, or bring them to the attention of the fight captain.

—   10. Be alert to drug or drinking problems affecting the performance of any cast members.

—   11. Arrange with the fight captain and prop personnel for the maintenance of the weapons (i.e., gun cleaning, sword maintenance, etc.).

—   12. For touring situations, or long runs, always have replacement sword blades among the props for quick replacement of accidentally broken props. For a long run in the same theater, have an "emergency sword" offstage left *and* right in case one breaks onstage. In this way, any actor can simply walk offstage to get a new one and carry on!

You will find, almost immediately, that performers who are required to attend a fight call will stall, grumble, disappear, and even lash out at you on occasion! This is normal behavior. It is up to you to keep your head and to firmly stick to your guns. A union production (AEA) requires that performers rehearse the fights. If your attitude is to "blow it off," then the performers will pick up on it and view the fight call as a chore rather than a necessity.

The idea of keeping an extra weapon offstage in case of breakage is an old fight director's trick. When there is an especially long run of a show, the chance of a thin rapier blade's breaking increases. During a performance of the 1990 production of *Hamlet* at the North Carolina Shakespeare Festival, a blade broke during the second bout between Hamlet and Laertes. I had arranged that a spare weapon be left offstage, on the outside chance that this might happen. After a pause, the character of Osric left the stage and came back immediately with a "new" weapon and the performers could pick up where they had left off. The alternative would have been that they would have had to improvise the rest of the fight with a "real" broken sword—a very dangerous proposition! Whenever possible, a sword should be kept in reserve just offstage left or right—one that is as close as possible to the style of sword that the performers are using. This will ensure that the performers aren't "thrown" by the new weapon and that it can stay in the show until a new blade can be ordered, mailed, received, and remounted, often a period of several days.

A stage manager should always try to have a written version of each fight in the official prompt book. This is a check against "actor's improvements" since the notation can always be referenced. An experienced fight director will be happy to supply this.

Emergency phone numbers should be *prominently* posted in the booth and in areas backstage. Precious minutes have been lost, when an accident happens, looking for the phone number of the ambulance crew. Hand make a sign, if necessary, in big letters, and post it around the theater, just in case!

There should also be a discussion about "what to do" if, God forbid, a weapon accidentally breaks and sails off into the audience, frightening—or worse, hitting—an audience member. Should the show be stopped, the house lights lit, and management called to look at the gravity of the incident? Should the audience member be checked over by a doctor, just in case? Laurence Olivier, in his foreword to William Hobbs's book *Techniques of the Stage Fight*, speaks of blades, "zinging out into the auditorium to be greeted by a female shriek, an outraged masculine snort of 'look here, I say,' and a sobbing exit through one of the swing doors." This is a potentially explosive situation—one that should be discussed by management with the theater owner, producer, and director.

Finally, I would suggest that anyone who wishes to make their career in stage management take some classes in first aid and cardiopulmonary resuscitation (CPR). You MUST know what to do in a situation in which a performer, staff member, or audience member is hurt. The American Red Cross holds classes of very high quality, as does the YMCA/YWCA organization. Attending classes in armed and unarmed stage fighting are also a good idea, because you will quickly learn what the performers experience.

I have a great deal of respect for stage managers. They are the linchpin of a production, and they have their finger on the pulse of each department as they work toward a common goal. Beyond the advice mentioned above, I would only add that a stage manager must always keep an eagle eye out for safety problems and anticipate them whenever possible.

Basic Safety Checklist

Rehearsal Space or Stage

___ 1. Sweep and mop the floor. Check for wet spots.

___ 2. Fix any nails and splinters and remove any excess furniture, props, or storage cabinets from the rehearasl room.

___ 3. Make sure the lighting is bright and even throughout the room.

___ 4. During "tech" rehearsal, help actors get accustomed to low light for performance.

___ 5. Check platforms for shifting, holes, and splinters.

___ 6. Have a first-aid kit available, and have hospital or emergency squad numbers posted backstage and in the booth.

___ 7. Check that the rehearsal room has enough height.

___ 8. Round sharp corners of the set or furniture.

Weapons

___ 1. Check for burrs, pits, and splinters; if necessary, repair.

___ 2. Check that each performer uses his assigned weapon.

___ 3. Count weapons before and after rehearsal or performance.

___ 4. Check for loose pommels, handles, and guards.

___ 5. Have a separate table or a sword rack backstage to organize the weapons.

___ 6. Clean and oil weapons at least once a week.

___ 7. Clean and oil guns every time they are used.

___ 8. Lock away guns and ammunition separately. Use trigger locks.

___ 9. Create a fail-safe loading and cleaning procedure for modern and black-powder firearms.

___ 10. Track all weapons through the production.

___ 11. Check shields for cracks, splinters, and loose handles.

___ 12. Preset an "emergency" weapon offstage in case of breakage.

Performers

___ 1. Check for old injuries.

___ 2. Organize warm-ups, and walk through rehearsals.

___ 3. Arrange for braces, ace bandages, and padding to be available during rehearsals and performances.

___ 4. Watch for signs of tension, exhaustion, drug or alcohol abuse, or "red-light fever."

___ 5. Make sure that performers wear adequate rehearsal shoes and clothes.

___ 6. Arrange a safety routine in case of injury or memory loss during performances or rehearsals.

Staff

___ 1. Have first-aid equipment nearby and stocked regularly. Have emergency room and ambulance phone numbers posted.

___ 2. Discuss and create a theater policy for injury onstage to performers and injury to audience members.

___ 3. Someone on the staff should have the equivalent of Red Cross first-aid training, as well as CPR.

A Costumer's Safety Checklist

A key player on the production team is the costume designer. While working toward a strong visual statement and historical accuracy, sometimes a costume or costume piece can endanger a performer by interfering with safe movement or vision. The following checklist is a reminder for those costumers who have faced these problems and is a guide for those who have not.

___ 1. All the footwear have nonslip tread.

___ 2. All underarm and crotch seams are reinforced or double stitched for strength.

___ 3. Helmets, hats, cowels, turbans, wigs, or other headgear are not limiting the performer's eyesight.

___ 4. Knee and elbow pads are available to performers.

___ 5. Custom-fitted padding is secured and invisible to the audience.

___ 6. Blood effects are accounted for in cleaning.

___ 7. Armor is padded and custom fitted to each combatant.

___ 8. Leather straps and buckles are maintained, or replaced if worn.

___ 9. Lace, ribbons, or cuffs aren't restrictive to hand movement when sword fighting.

___ 10. Leather gloves are provided for all performers who fight with swords.

___ 11. Belts, hangers, and scabbards are provided for all characters who carry or fight with swords.

Glossary of Terms

The Society of American Fight Directors

Advance	Sometimes referred to as "the fencing step." The leading foot steps forward, followed by the trailing foot.
Avoidance	A movement intended to "dodge" an attack.
Balestra	A combination of a jump forward and a lunge. There are two counts in this action: one-jump, two-lunge.
Beat attack	A sharp "tap" against the middle, or the foible, of the opponent's blade, with the object of opening a line, or provoking an attack.
Beat parry	A parry that clears the line by striking an attacking blade, as opposed to blocking or redirecting the attacking blade.
Bind	A blade-taking action that carries the opposing weapon diagonally from high line to low line or vice versa, across the body. The bind is a prise de fer.
Blocked punch	A move that deliberately stops an incoming punch, usually with the forearm or hand.
Break fall	Any maneuver that dissipates the energy or force from a fall or roll and gives the illusion of impact.
Butt end	The trailing end of the staff in the en garde position.
Change beat	A change of engagement immediately followed by a beat attack.
Change of engagement	To release contact of the blades, and reestablish contact in a new line.
Contact strike	A blow delivered to a major muscle group. The energy of the strike is pulled, but contact is made.
Corps à corps	Means "body to body." Describes the moment when the combatants come in close contact and the weapons are immobilized.

323

Counterparry	A parry that begins in one line and travels a full circle to meet the attacking blade in the original line. Counterparry two is sometimes called the "actor's parry" because of the flashy appearance.
Coupé	A change of engagement that takes the blade around the opposing blade's point. Sometimes called a cutover.
Covered or closed	Said of a line of engagement, when the defender's weapon prevents an attack to that line of engagement.
Croisé	A blade-taking action that carries the opposing weapon from a high line to a low line or vice versa, but on the same side as the engagement, not diagonally across like a bind. The croisé is a prise de fer.
Cross parry	A parry using both rapier and dagger held forte to forte so that the blades cross, forming an open V to catch the attacking blade.
Cut	An attack made with the edge of the blade.
Cut across the head	A horizontal cut designed to look as if it would strike the head if it landed. It may travel right to left or vice versa, and is avoided usually by ducking.
Cut across the stomach	A horizontal cut designed to look as if it would cut the stomach open if it landed. It may travel right to left or vice versa. The wrist is often held to present the true edge. It is avoided usually by jumping back.
Deception of parry	The evasion of the partner's attempt to make contact with the attacker's blade as the partners try to parry.
Demivolte	A method of effacing the target by swinging the rear leg backward and sideways, so that the trunk is brought 90° in relation to the attack.
Diagonal cut with avoidance	An off-line cut to either the inside or outside line. It may be a rising or falling cut. It is usually avoided by leaning to the side away from the cut.
Disarm	The act of removing a combatant's weapon from his hand by threat, force, or leverage.

Disengage	1. The act of removing the blade from contact with the partner's blade.
	2. Passing the blade under that of the opponent in the high line, or over it in the low line, and terminating on the side opposite to the original engagement.
Doublé	An attack in any line that deceives a direct parry and a counterparry.
Elbow attack	Any attack giving the illusion of contact with the elbow.
Engagement	When the blades are in contact with each other, they are said to be engaged.
En garde	The basic "ready" position of sword fighters.
Envelopment	An attack on the blade that, by describing a circle, picks up the opposing blade and brings it back to the original line of engagement. An envelopment is a prise de fer.
Eye contact	The technique of frequently cueing your partner by looking in their eyes during the course of a fight, in order to assure continued connection between partners.
Fencing measure	The correct distance between combatants when engaged in stage combat. Six to ten inches out of distance when one combatant is in a lunge.
Feint attack	Any attacking action deliberately intended not to land on a target. The aim is to draw a reaction or a parry.
Flip/Throw	An offensive movement that controls or appears to control the victim's center, giving the illusion of lifting the victim off his feet and returning him to the ground.
Fore end	The leading end of the staff in the en garde position.
Glissade	An offensive action against an opponent's blade that applies lateral pressure while moving forward. Sometimes referred to as a pressure glide, or coulé.
Hand parry	A defensive move in which the hand (usually gloved) is used to deflect, block, or seize an attack.
Hanging parry	A parry protecting the high lines with the hilt high and the point down, such as a high parry of prime.

Invitation	Any movement of the weapon or body intended to tempt the opponent into an attack.
Kick	An attack made with the foot.
Knap	The sound created by one of the combatants, which mimics the contact of the blow. Used for noncontact blows, i.e., clap knap, body knap, slip hand knap, or shared knap.

•**Body knap** The sound made by striking a major muscle group on the body. Either partner can make this knap.

•**Clap knap** The sound made when both hands clap together, usually made by the victim.

•**Slip hand knap** The attacker claps hands and follows through during the act of delivering the strike.

•**Shared knap** The sound made when the attacker's open hand meets his partner's open hand or major muscle group.

Knee attack	Any attack giving the illusion of contact with the knee.
Lines of Attack or defense	*(for right-handed combatant)*

•**Outside line** The lines or parry positions protecting the combatant's right side.

•**Inside line** The lines or parry positions protecting the combatant's left side.

•**High line** The lines or parry positions protecting the combatant from the waist up.

•**Low line** The lines or parry positions protecting the combatant from the waist down.

•**On-line** 1. Any attack that is aimed directly at the combatant's body.

2. The orientation of combatants' bodies when both partners' vertical center lines are lined up, either face to face, back to back, or front to back.

326

•Off-line	**1.** Any attack that is directed toward a target away from the body.
	2. The orientation of combatants' bodies when the center lines of the combatants are offset to the left or to the right.
Long form	Sliding hand positions for quarterstaff utilizing the full length of the staff for attack or defense.
Lunge	The "extended" leg position used as a method of reaching the opponent on an attack. To lunge, the leading leg extends forward in a long step, while the trailing leg stays in place.
Moulinet/ Molinello	Means "little windmill" and describes the action of pivoting the blade in circles in a diagonal, vertical, or horizontal plane.
Noncontact strike	A blow delivered with the illusion of contact, properly masked from the audience, with a well-timed knap. A noncontact strike always misses the target.
Parry	The defensive action of deflecting or blocking an attacking weapon.

The following are the parries most commonly used in stage combat in this country (for right-handed combatants).

•Parry prime, or Parry 1	The hand is in half pronation with the point down. Although this parry is intended to protect the left, or inside, line of the body anywhere from the shoulders to the ankle, it is usually used against attacks from the waist down. When used to protect the low line it is sometimes referred to as the "watch parry" because the wrist position is similar to looking at a wrist watch.
•Parry seconde, or Parry 2	The hand is in pronation with the point down protecting the low line of the right, or outside, line.
•Parry tierce, or Parry 3	The hand is in pronation with the point up protecting the right, or outside, high line (waist to head).

•Parry quarte, or Parry 4	The hand is in supination with the point up protecting the left, or inside, high line.
•Parry quinte, or Parry 5	The hand is in pronation protecting the head from a downward vertical or diagonal cut. The hilt is on the right side of the body; point extends to the left.
•Parry sixte, or Parry 6	1. Protecting the same area as a parry tierce or 3, except that the hand is held in supination. Usually used against a thrust. 2. Protecting against a vertical or diagonal cut to the head. The hilt is on the left side of the head, and the point extends to the right. Sometimes called a "5A."
•Parry septime, or Parry 7	Protecting the low inside line with the hand in supination.
•Parry octave, or Parry 8	Protecting the low outside line with the hand in supination.
Pass forward	The placing of the rear foot in front of the leading foot (a walking step).
Pass backward	The placing of the front foot in back of the rear foot.
Pommel attack	An attack made, usually in close distance, with the pommel of the weapon instead of the blade.
Prise de fer	Means "taking of the blade (or iron)." Refers to any controlling attack on the blade that takes an opponent's blade from an existing line to a new one. Examples are a bind, envelopment, or croisé.
Pronation	The position of the sword hand with the palm down.
Punch	An attack made with the fist.
Punto reverso	A point attack delivered from the attacker's inside line to the partner's outside line with the hand often in supination.
Recovery forward	To arrive at an en garde position from a lunge by bringing the rear foot forward.

Recovery backward	To arrive at an en garde position from a lunge by bringing the forward foot backward.
Retreat	The rear foot steps backward, followed by the front foot.
Riposte	An attack immediately following a successful parry.
Short form	A hand position for quarterstaff that divides the staff into three equal sections.
Slap	A blow usually delivered to the face with an open hand.
Supination	The position of the sword hand with the palm up. The opposite of pronation.
Thrust	An attack made with the point of the weapon.
Traverse	Any foot movement that takes the combatant off-line.
Volte	A method of effacing the target by swinging the rear leg backward and sideways, so that the trunk is brought 180° in relation to the attack ("bum in the face").
Yield parry	A defensive movement immediately following a parried attack, whereby the initial attacker gives way to a counter-attack while the blades remain engaged. Also called a ceding parry.

Bibliography

Angelo, D. A. 1971. *The School of Fencing.* 1787. Reprint, New York: Lands End Press.

Aylward, J. D. 1945. *The Small Sword in England.* London: Hutchinson.

Aylward, J. D. 1953. *The House of Angelo.* London: Batchworth Press.

Baldick, R. 1965. *The Duel.* London: Chapman and Hall.

Burton, R. F. 1987. *The Book of the Sword.* New York: Dover.

Castle, E. 1969. *Schools and Masters of Fence.* London: Arms and Armour Press.

Davis, D. 1988. *Muzzle Loading.* Friendship, Indiana: Friendship.

Diagram Group. 1980. *The Complete Encyclopedia of Weapons.* England: Galley Press.

Dufty, A. R. 1974. *European Swords and Daggers in the Tower of London.* London: Her Majesty's Stationery Office.

Eggenberger, D. 1985. *An Encyclopedia of Battles.* New York: Dover.

Funcken, L., and Funcken, F. 1977. *Le costume, l'armure et les armes au temps de la chevalerie.* 2 vols. Belgium: Casterman.

Hart Picture Archives. 1978. *Weapons and Armour.* New York: Hart.

Hope, W. 1687. *The Scots Fencing Master; Or, Compleat Small Sword Man.* Edinburgh: John Reid.

Hobbs, W. 1967. *Techniques of the Stage Fight.* London: Studio Vista, Limited.

Hutton, A. 1973. *The Sword and the Centuries; Or, Old Sword Days and Old Sword Ways.* Vermont: Charles E. Tuttle.

Hutton, A. 1889. *Cold Steel.* London: Clowes and Son.

Hutton, A. 1892. *Old Swordplay.* London: Greval and Co.

Keegan, J. 1988. *The Face of Battle.* London: Penguin.

Kübler-Ross, E. 1969. *On Death and Dying.* New York: Macmillan Publishing Co.

Laban, R. 1975. *Laban's Principles of Dance and Movement Notation.*

Marshall, H. 1977. *Stage Swordplay; Or, "So You Want To Be Errol Flynn?"* New York: Marymount College.

Martinez, J. D. 1982. *Combat Mime.* Chicago: Nelson-Hall.

Bibliography

Morton, E. D. 1988. *A–Z of Fencing*. London: Queen Anne Press.

Musashi, M. 1974. *A Book of Five Rings*. New York: Overlook Press.

Newlove, J. 1993. *Laban for Actors and Dancers. Laban's Movement Theory into Practice: A Step-by-Step Guide*. New York: Rutledge Theater Arts Books.

Oakeshott, R. E. 1960. *The Archeology of Weapons*. London: Lutterworth.

Oakeshott, R. E. 1961. *A Knight and His Armour*. London: Lutterworth.

Oakeshott, R. E. 1964. *The Sword in the Age of Chivalry*. London: Lutterworth.

Silver, G. 1599. *The Paradoxes of Defence*. London.

Sweatnam, W. 1616. *Schole of the Noble and Worthy Science of Defence*. London.

Turner, C., and Soper, T. 1990. *Methods and Practices of Elizabethan Swordplay*. Southern Illinois University Press.

Talhoffer. 1467. *Das Fechtbuch*.

Wilkenson-Latham, R. 1981. *Phaidon Guide to Antique Weapons and Armour*. Oxford, England: Phaidon Press.

Wise, A. 1971. *The Art and History of Personal Combat*. Connecticut: ARMA Press; New York: New York Graphic Society.

Wise, A. 1968. *Weapons in the Theater*. New York: Barnes and Noble.

Yakim, M. 1990. *Creating a Character: A Physical Approach to Acting*. New York: Back Stage Books.

Index